Forty Years Among the Indians

Forty Years Among the Indians

Experiences of a Mormon Pioneer on the
South-West Frontier

Daniel W. Jones

LEONAUR

Forty Years Among the Indians
Experiences of a Mormon Pioneer on the South-West Frontier
by Daniel W. Jones

`

First published under the title
Forty Years Among the Indians

Leonaur is an imprint of Oakpast Ltd

ISBN: 978-1-78282-481-7 (hardcover)
ISBN: 978-1-78282-482-4 (softcover)

http://www.leonaur.com

Publisher's Notes

The views expressed in this book are not necessarily
those of the publisher.

Contents

Preface

The Scriptures tell us that the truth should not be spoken at all times. Does this imply that a falsehood should ever be told? I think not, but simply means that silence is often profitable.

In answer to the solicitation of many friends, I have concluded to write something of my personal history and experience in frontier life, especially relating to that portion spent among the Indians and Mexicans. In doing this I shall aim to write the plain, simple truth. I have to trust mainly to my memory, never having kept a journal. I have preserved a few letters that will aid me, but the greater part of this history will be given as it comes to my mind, just as it occurred to me at the time, modified or strengthened, as the case may be, by after circumstances.

One rule I shall endeavour to follow—to speak the truth without malice toward anyone. This will doubtless be hard for me to carry through, but I make a record of the desire, that it may be continually before me.

If the educated reader should find any mistakes in this book, please do not spend much time or money in pointing them out, as they may be too common. No one has been paid for a literary revision. The Author has used his own language and style. The unlearned will be able to understand the language without the use of a dictionary.

The Author.

CHAPTER 1

Attacked by Mounted Comanches

In the year 1847, I crossed the plains with the volunteers from St. Louis, Missouri, going out to take part in the war with Mexico. At that time the Comanche Indians were a power on the plains. The battalion I belonged to was attacked while in camp on the Arkansas River. On the opposite side of the river were sand hills. Wood was very scarce in the region and on arriving in camp, it was customary for a number of the most active young men to go out in search of fuel, generally "buffalo chips."

On looking across the river there was seen a few small piles of what looked like driftwood. This had been placed there by the Indians as a decoy; but no suspicion was felt at the time, as we had heretofore seen no Indians, neither was there anyone along who understood the Indians' "tricks."

Some thirty men started in haste for this wood. Only one man taking his gun, one other had a small pocket pistol. A few of the most active men secured the wood piled up, whilst the others remained gathering the scattered sticks and picking berries that grew among the sand-hills. Suddenly there charged upon them about twenty-five mounted Comanches. Using their long, sharp spears they would ride a man down, spear him through, catch him by the hair, and scalp him without dismounting. They killed and scalped eight men, wounding and scalping another that recovered. Although there was a battalion of infantry and a company of cavalry in camp, this was done before help could reach the men. The men in camp rushed across the river, firing at the Indians, who retreated as soon as they were in danger. The cavalry company mounted and pursued for some time but could not overtake the Indians. This was my first introduction to Indians.

After this we were more watchful. Many attacks were made and men killed in those days in open daylight in what might be termed a fair field fight, while others were surprised, and sometimes whole parties murdered, as was the mail company at Wagon Mound in 1849. Some of them were personal friends of mine.

At that time, in common with white men generally, I looked upon all Indians as fit only to be killed.

After the war was over, I remained in Mexico until July, 1850. Of my stay in that country for some three years, I will give only a brief sketch and write that which has a bearing on my future life and actions, as will be given in this work. There are many things that have occurred in my experience which might be interesting to some but not to the general reader.

I will say this, and say it truly, I took part in many ways in the wild, reckless life that was common in that land, so much so that I often felt condemned, and longed for something to call me away from where I was, and lead me from the evils I was surrounded by. I had much pride, always believing myself better than many others. This caused me to preserve myself from degradation. There was a feeling continually with me, that if I would keep my body pure and healthy, I would yet find a condition in life that would be satisfactory to me.

This spirit enabled me to abstain from strong drink and other worse vices that I could see were destroying the lives of my associates. Notwithstanding this, I found enough to practice in the way of gambling, swearing, fighting, and other rough conduct to feel heartily condemned in my own conscience.

While in Mexico I formed a kindly feeling toward many of the Mexican people, studied the Spanish language, so as to read and write it and act as interpreter.

My mind often reverts to those days. I had been left an orphan at eleven years of age. I then left all my friends and relatives and went out into the world alone, probably as wilful a boy as ever lived. No one could control me by any other means than kindness, and this I did not often meet with. The result was, I found myself among rough people in a wild country among those who knew no law but the knife and pistol. The old Texas Rangers and many of the Missouri planters being the leading characters.

I often wonder how I got through, and I can only account for it in one way: I did not like this way of living. I felt condemned, and often asked God in all earnestness to help me to see what was right, and how to serve Him; telling Him I wanted to know positively, and not be deceived. I felt that the people of this age ought to have prophets to guide them, the same as of old, and that it was not a "square thing" to leave them without anything but the Bible, for that could not be sufficient or the people would not dispute so much over it. These feelings grew upon me, and I began to be more careful of my conduct, and felt a greater desire to leave the country.

CHAPTER 2

Surrounded and Threatened by Indians Many Times on the Road

In the summer of 1850, quite a large company fitted up at Santa Fe, New Mexico, to go to California by the old Spanish trail, leading to Salt Lake; thence by the northern route to Upper California. I had heard some strange stories about the Mormons, such as were common at that time. I heard of the Mormon Battalion and Pioneer move to Great Salt Lake, a country then only known as the "Great Desert of America," that the Mormons had moved into the desert away from everyone, etc. My sympathy was drawn toward them, for I had often felt as though I wanted to find something different from anything yet seen. So when I heard of this company being made up to go through the Salt Lake country, I determined to make the trip with them.

At that time the Ute nation was very powerful, possessing the country from near the settlements of New Mexico clear to Utah Valley. They were known as a proud, haughty people, demanding tribute from all who passed through their country, even in times of peace. The party fitting up were taking through some eight thousand head of sheep. The old mountaineers prophesied that we would never get through the Ute country with so much to tempt the Indians.

However the owners concluded to risk the venture, as mutton was very high at the mines in California.

We left the settlements of New Mexico at Abiquin, the trail soon entering the wild mountain country, which was at that time only known to a few venturesome traders, and to Mexicans. Very few white men had ever been through the country. At the time of our trip the Utes were supposed to be at peace; but peace in those days meant that if they could rob without killing you, all well; but if necessary to do a little killing without scalping they considered themselves quite friendly. Scalping means hating. Often, when remonstrating with Indians for killing people, they would say they did not scalp them. On enquiring what this meant, I finally learned that the Indians believed that in the spirit world friends recognised each other by the hair, and when they were scalped did not know one another. This accounts for the great risk they will run to remove those killed in battle to prevent their falling into the hands of the enemy.

Nothing exciting occurred for several days after leaving the settlements.

Our first meeting with Indians was on the Rio Piedras, a day's travel beyond the crossing of the Rio San Juan. Here I got my first scare.

The river bottom was spotted with cottonwood trees and willow groves. On arriving in camp, a small party of us unsaddled and started to the river to take a bath, passing through several yards of willows before getting to the river, While enjoying ourselves bathing, we heard a volley of rifle shots from the direction of camp. The shots continued to rattle for some time; then a stray shot occasionally finishing off just as a battle with Indians naturally would. We were out of the water and dressed in short order, fully believing that our camp had been attacked and probably all killed. We rushed for the brush to hide. I got separated from the rest, hid myself and laid quiet reflecting upon my situation. My only chance for life seemed to be to keep hid until night, then try and get on the trail and travel back to the settlements, over one hundred miles distant. This I fully expected to try and hoped to accomplish.

Finally I gained courage enough to creep to the edge of the willows toward camp to see if I could discover what had become of the camp. In and around where we had unsaddled, I saw a great lot of savage looking Indians on horseback; some were still, others moving about. I dodged down now fully convinced that all our company was killed. I lay for a few moments in terrible fear. When I looked out again, taking a careful survey of camp I discerned one of our company hanging a camp-kettle over a fire. Soon I saw some others engaged in camp work. I now concluded that the Indians had spared a few and put them to cooking, so I decided to surrender as a prisoner. When I approached near camp I saw most of the company attending to their own affairs as usual.

I concluded to say nothing about my scare and walked in quite un-

13

concernedly; asked what they had been firing at, when I was told that just as the Indians came into camp a band of deer had run by. Both Indians and whites had been firing at, and had killed several deer. The Indians were perfectly friendly, and all hands were making ready to enjoy a feast of fat venison. I kept silent; no one but myself knew how I suffered during my first "big scare."

I never questioned my companions about our mutual fright neither did they ever make any reference to the affair, why I do not know unless they, like myself, were afraid of being laughed at.

We were surrounded and threatened by the Indians many times on the road; but through the influence of our guide and interpreter, we were allowed to pass along on easy terms. We had for guide Thomas Chacon, a Mexican Indian, the same who will be remembered by many of the Mormon Battalion, as he travelled in company with them as assistant guide, and returned and wintered at the old fort in Salt Lake in 1847-48.

Once at the bend of the Dolores River our chances for life seemed very slim. We were surrounded by over five hundred warriors, well armed. We numbered about fifty men, mostly Americans. The chief had sent a deputation to our camp on the Mancos river, the day before, stating that his son had died, and that either an American or Mexican would be demanded from our camp for a sacrifice, and if not given up peaceably, war would be opened upon us, and all would be killed. This demand was made by the old Elk Mountain chief. Our interpreter, who had lived many years among these Indians, felt quite uneasy, telling us of the power of this chief and his tribe. He did not advise us to give up a man, but probably would not have objected, as he knew we could not spare hint, he being the only one who knew the trail. Captain Angley, who had charge of this company, looked upon the threat as an insult, and told the Indians to say to their chief that he had no men to voluntarily give up, but plenty to fight; if he wanted any to kill he would have to fight for them.

We were a half day's march from the great chief's camp, and I will admit that I was frightened, for I was much under the influence of the old guide, being conversant with his language. I was in the habit of riding along with him and listening to his talk about the Indians; he often told me how he succeeded in making peace with them.

Previous to this time we had had several "close calls," but Old Thomas seemed to always have some way to talk the Indians into peace. This time he appeared uneasy and fearful. On arriving at the Big Bend of the Dolores, we took the best position possible for defence, where there was some fallen timber. Soon the Indians commenced crossing the river above us on horseback and fully prepared for battle. There were about fifty of them, all well armed and mounted. They took position some two hundred yards from camp in a line facing us, and there stood. I was keen to commence firing upon them, thinking if we got in the first shot we would be more likely to conquer and several of the company felt the same; but when we tried to urge this upon the captain and Old Thomas—for nothing was done without the guide's consent when Indians were in the question—the old man smiled and said, "Wait, friend, there ain't enough yet to shoot at; you might miss 'em." By this time we had learned that the old guide's wisdom and policy had saved us, when if a shot had been fired we would doubtless have been destroyed.

It was not long until we understood his meaning; we saw others coming in tens and twenties and doing as the first had done till they formed a half-circle around us. We were near the bank of the river, our rear being somewhat protected by the bank and width of the stream. (In those days nothing but old fashioned Kentucky rifles were in use.) Others followed till they were several files deep. There were not less than five hundred, and all had their arms ready in a threatening attitude. After approaching to within some fifty yards of camp, where we had got behind logs and piled up our packs in the best way possible for defence. The chief, with a few others, rode a little forward and in a loud voice made known his wants, showing us his warriors with arms ready, demanding that we at once should submit. This was interpreted to the captain by the guide. The captain and most of the company understood Spanish. I thought surely our day had come, and so did many others, but all felt they would rather die fighting than to cowardly submit to such an arrogant and unreasonable demand.

The captain requested the chief to approach nearer, saying that he did not wish any trouble and desired to pass through the country in peace, and was willing to respect all his rights. At this the chief approached and finally, by much persuasion, he got off his horse, followed by a few others, the main body keeping their places in stolid silence. The captain carefully passed the word so that it went through camp, that if shooting had to be done, he would "open the ball." He did not expect them to attack us in our present position, but if peace could not be made he intended to shoot the chief down. It was about two o'clock when this commenced. The parley continued until near

15

sundown before peace was decided upon, but it was finally concluded after agreeing to let the chief have some beads, paints, tobacco, etc., articles we had for the purpose of making treaties. In those days, before the white men taught them to lie and betray, the word of an Indian was sacred. Not so now.

The moment the captain spoke telling us all was right, there was a general hand-shaking, and what time was left before night was spent in trading and no uneasiness was felt by any of the company, for all had perfect confidence in the word of the Indians; neither were we deceived.

During the parley, when the Indians found they could not obtain a man, the next thing they wanted was flour. They were told we had none to spare, but would give them such presents as have already been mentioned. They persisted in wanting flour. We were getting short and so could not spare any. While the debate was going on an Indian went and got his blanket full of good dried meat, rode up near the captain, who was sitting down, and threw the meat on to him, saying, "You poor, hungry dog, if you have nothing for us we can give you something." The captain took it coolly and thanked him for it. When they found they could get nothing more they accepted the presents offered.

Some may ask, "What of all this? There was no one killed; nothing of a blood and thunder character to admire." I will say to such: Just stop reading this book, for it is not of the blood and thunder style, such are written by authors who have never seen what they write about. I am simply telling that which I have seen, known of and taken part in. I cannot help whether it pleases or not. I can only tell it as it occurred, or appeared to me at the time; neither do I make any allowance for lack of memory. Anything that was not impressed sufficiently upon my mind at the time of its occurrence so as to remember the same, I consider not worth relating.

I have had some close calls in my life; but those just related occupied my attention about as closely for a short time as anything that ever occurred.

A few days after this, just before reaching Grand River, we came very near opening fire on another party of Indians. About half of the company went ahead daily as a front guard, and just as we were emerging from a cedar grove the guide cried out: "Now we have to fight, sure; there comes a war party full drive for fight." Sure enough. There they came, some five or six hundred yards away, out of a ravine

16

on to a rise of ground some three hundred yards distant. We dodged back into the cedars, every man taking his tree. The Indians cautiously approached to within one hundred yards, there being a few scattering cedars in their direction. The guide took them for Navajoes; he was afraid of them, but friendly with the Utes. As the Indians were fully in earnest and seeking to get an advantage, we were about to commence firing to try and pick some of them off or keep them back until the rest of our company could come up. Just at this critical moment one of our men said, "If there is one who will follow me I will go out and make friendly signs. May be they are friends." I felt afraid, but being a boy I wanted to appear brave, so I told him I would go; we went out to an opening with our guns ready for use. As soon as the Indians saw us they called out "Friends?" and came toward us making friendly signs.

We told them if they were friends to stop until Thomas could come. The old fellow was so sure they were hostile Navajoes that he had got as far away as convenient, but seeing they had not fired on us he picked up courage and came to where we stood facing the Indians with our guns aimed at them. Mine was cocked, and I can well remember placing my finger on the trigger several times with dead aim at the one I supposed to be the chief. As soon as Old Thomas showed himself there was a big laugh all around at the mistake, they having mistaken us for Navajoes the same as we did them. They were on the war path hunting Navajoes who had just made a heavy raid upon them. Soon all was well, as these Indians were Utes and friendly with the guide, he having lived with this same band several years. These were the same Indians who afterwards broke up the Grand Valley or Elk Mountain settlement. During the excitement, after the Indians were recognised, an accidental shot was fired, wounding a man by the name of Tattersall severely in the leg. This came near starting a fight, as many thought it came from the Indians. I am satisfied that much blood has been shed, and many cruel wars brought on by some little act that might have been avoided. Here are two cases within a few days that seemed certain fight, and to fight meant certain death; for in those days the Indians were ten to one of us on the ground, and plenty more to come.

I now come to the place where my whole feelings changed toward the Indians, and as the accident that I am about to mention seemingly had an effect on my future life, I will beg leave to write freely. From this time dates my friendship for the red man, which many think so

17

strange. Until this time I had felt about the same as my associates did toward the natives, possibly I was not so bitter as many. There seems to be something providential in my experience so far in never having had to fight with them. I had never been required to shed their blood, and I now made up my mind I never would, if it could possibly be avoided.

About the middle of August, 1850, we were camped on Green river, not far from where the Denver & Rio Grand Railway now crosses it. I shot myself accidentally; the wound was one of the most dangerous possible, not to prove fatal. When I found where the ball had entered my clothing, I took out the other pistol from the holster with the intention of "finishing the job." The ball had struck the waist button of my pants as I was standing by the side of my mule. I was placing the pistol in the holster, after saddling up, when the hammer caught on the edge of the holster, pulling it back slightly, when it slipped and went off. The ball ranged downward, entering the groin and thigh, passing through some fourteen inches of flesh. Some good spirit told me to hold on, that I would live. Almost everyone in the company expressed the belief that I would die.

We were about to cross the river, which was up to its highest mark. We had to cross on rafts made of half decayed cottonwood logs which made it very dangerous. I suffered terribly during the day, once having the lockjaw. I could hear remarks being made that I was dying. When I rallied enough to speak, the first use I made of my tongue was to give all a good cursing, telling them I would live longer than any such a set who were so willing to give me up. I felt at the time that I would try and live just for spite, for I fully realised I was looked upon as an encumbrance. They could not see how they were to take care of me, as we were travelling with pack animals. I was left most of the day entirely alone, all hands being occupied in rafting over the provisions and baggage. I lay in the shade of a cottonwood tree, thinking that my companions wanted me to die, so as to get rid of bothering with me. I was some distance from them, and every half-hour I would give a yell just to let them know that I was not dead. Before night I was placed on a raft and floated over to camp. There had been much delay in crossing, and it was found that at this rate it would take three days to get over. This gave some hope that I would have time to die decently, and the company would have no further trouble with me only to care for me while I remained. Old Thomas was kind to me and felt as though I might live if I had a little attention.

There was a camp of Indians of Tabby's band not far from us. My old friend, the guide, went and told the Indians about me, saying I was his boy, an expression that means a great deal among the Indians, meaning that I was the same as a son to him in friendship. The Indians came, both men and women, and I can never forget their expression of sympathy, or their looks of kindness. They offered to take me and try to cure me. This seemed to stir up the feelings of some of my companions, and they began to discuss the possibility of taking me along. Finally, a few of the kindest hearted determined to try it; so a rig was gotten up, and Old Thomas advised me to endeavour to get to the Mormon settlements, telling me about their goodness, and that if I could reach them, they would care for me. I felt almost disappointed not to go with the Indians, for my heart was melted toward them, and I felt as though I could always be their friend and trust them, and I can truly say that this feeling has ever remained with me. I felt to be guided by the old man, for his judgment was generally good, and I knew him to be a true friend. His description of the Mormons seemed strange to me, and I told him they were a bad people, who had been driven out from the States because they were thieves and murderers, and that for their bad conduct they were banished from decent people. His reply astonished me. He asked, "How can you say that? There is not one word true. I travelled with the Mormon soldiers from Santa Fe to California; they never stole anything from the settlements like the other soldiers did. The Mormons are honest and have no bad habits like other people. I came back with some of them to Salt Lake and remained there last winter. I traded with the Indians and Mormons, and lived with them. The Mormons have no harlots or bad people among them, and all those stories are lies; why do you speak so about them?" The old fellow seemed terribly offended at my words. I felt there was something wrong. I told him I knew nothing about the Mormons, that I had only told him what others said. He replied, "Then wait and see for yourself; they are the best people you ever saw." This caused me to reflect and wonder why such stories were told of the Mormons, for I not only had confidence in the old guide's truthfulness, but I believed he had been with the people enough to know them.

A frame was made and placed upon the back of a good stout mule, the foundation being a Mexican *Apparejo*. I had to sit entirely above the mule, as the wound would not allow to sit in a saddle. This made the load top-heavy. The trail from Green River down Spanish Fork canyon, was quite rough and steep in many places. Guy ropes were rigged, and three men took care of me, and I must say that after taking the labour in hand to bring me in, all hands became interested and I was treated with great kindness.

I suffered a great deal during the fifteen days I thus journeyed, but I never lost courage. Our drives were short; sometimes being two days in a camp engaged in cutting roads through the brush for the sheep to pass. This gave me a chance to rest. I attended to my wound myself, as I could not bear anyone else to touch it; neither would I take anyone's advice about dressing it. I felt like being my own doctor. I have always believed that if I had been, in a good hospital, I would have been "done for," as the wound was terrible. I starved myself almost to death—an idea obtained from two men's experience in southern Arizona. These two men, Green Marshall and Robert Ward, left Santa Fe with a party going to California by the Southern Trail. Close by where Silver City now is, the party was attacked, as supposed, by Apache Indians; all were left for dead. The surprise occurred early in the morning. About noon Marshall and Ward recovered consciousness. They were stripped and both wounded in several places and almost perishing for water, they being in a dry camp. They started for water and after going a short distance they separated, each in time finding water, but they never met until reaching settlements.

According to the account given by each of them, on arriving at the Mexican settlements, they were out some twelve days with scarcely anything to eat, each one supposing the other dead; and it was several days before they heard of each other, having come into settlements that were some distance apart. The wounds of each had seemingly dried up and healed for the want of something to feed on.

I was well acquainted with both men, one being a relative. I took much interest in their case, as it was one of the worst on record. I felt like trying as much as possible the same regime, and believe to this day, in case of severe wounds, that the system should be reduced by abstinence to the lowest possible living condition. Nature so directs many of the lower animal creation. I have known some domestic animals, as well as wild ones, that on being dangerously wounded would hide up for days without food or drink and come out well in time.

Finally on the 6th of September, 1850, we came in sight of a settlement, then a fort on the Provo River. This surprised us considerably for we had not expected to meet anyone before reaching Salt Lake City.

I shall never forget the peculiar feelings that came over me when we arrived at the fort. The little party with me had become separated from the main company while coming down Spanish Fork Canyon, and we were considerably behind when we saw signs of settlements. We felt somewhat uneasy for fear "the bad Mormons" would take advantage of us and rob us, as we had some money. When the company of fifty were all together we felt as though we could stand the Mormons off, but the four of us counting myself, I wounded and weak, feared we might be taken in. I had my pistols by me and told the boys I would do my best, if molested. When we got to the fort instead of trouble we found the people with about the same kindly look of the eye and expression of sympathy as was manifested by the Indians on Green river. There are many now living in Provo who remember the circumstance, and how I looked, a mere skeleton sitting on the top of a mule. The Indians also remember me to this day from these circumstances, and call me "Chacon's boy." I now felt conquered as far as Mormon goodness was concerned for many offered me help if needed.

I was at first tempted to accept their kind offers, but a spirit of pride came over me. It seemed humiliating to receive a favour under any circumstances, so I went into camp with the rest. I was now out of danger; my wound having done well, but the position in which I had to ride had set the muscles so that crawling on hands and knees was my only means of moving about; still I had not lost my spirits. I had started to California to get rich and did not want to fail.

The Mormons often visited our camp, selling us butter, vegetables, and such supplies as they had to spare. Owing to the conflicting stories I had heard about them, I watched them very closely. Some of our company were Missouri mobocrats, who told hard stories about the Mormons. These they related to me as though they were their own personal experiences with them. Some of these men I had known for years and looked upon them as men of truth and honour. How then could I help believing their stories? And yet, how could I believe people to be such monsters of iniquity as the Mormons must have been if these stories were true? When looking at their friendly eyes and hearing their voices of sympathy, I could see nothing that indicated depravity, but on the contrary, all seemed industrious, kind, honest and peaceable, ever ready to do us a favour or give any wanted information frankly, without any show of craftiness whatever. To this day it is a mystery to me how anyone can call the Mormon people crafty and dishonest. That individuals among us may be, is too true; but as a people we have a right to be judged collectively, let each person answer for himself I was sorely perplexed, but each day induced a more friendly feeling toward the Mormons. As yet I had never heard a word of their doctrine, or history, not even having heard of Joseph Smith's martyrdom. In fact, I knew nothing about them.

One of our company, who boasted of his cruel exploits in Missouri, went up to the fort and under the guise of friendship procured a book of Doctrine and Covenants from a Sister Higbee, to read and make sport of. There were a number listening and ridiculing the book. I was some distance away, lying alone in the shade. I though I might enjoy the fun with the rest and crawled up nearer. When I got within hearing distance something was being read about God revealing Himself, telling certain ones what to do. This had a peculiar effect on my mind. My oft-repeated prayer asking for this very thing came to my mind.

I had heard but very little of their reading, for just as I came within hearing distance someone took the book from the mobocrat and read the account of Joseph and Hyrum's martyrdom. On hearing this I believe I felt just as the Saints did when they first heard of the murder of the prophets at Carthage. The feeling that came upon me at that time was that they were men of God and were murdered by wicked men just as it was there recorded. At once the desire came over me to get away from those who were exulting over their death, and deriding the revelations that I thought might be true. So I determined to stop and see who the Mormons were. I asked the first teamster that passed to take me to the fort, about two miles distant, as I wished to see if I could find someone to take care of me.

After being helped on the wagon, the owner, Thomas Ross, asked me a few questions then remarked, "You had better remain in Utah, my son, and you will soon be a Mormon."

This seemed strange to me, for according to my idea he might as well have said, "You will be a Chinaman." I asked how that could possibly be?

He replied, "By obedience to the gospel and baptism."

I asked if the Mormons had a religion.

He said, "Yes, the same that Christ taught; we believe in the New Testament."

I replied, "That is what I believe; but I believe it as it reads."

"Well," said he, "that is what we think; I guess you'll be a Mormon yet."

This was something new to me and I was continually asking myself: How can I be a Mormon? On arriving at the fort, I went to Bishop Isaac Higbee's house where I was kindly received, his wife agreeing to care for me on reasonable terms. She is now, (1890), living in Salt Lake City and has ever been a friend to me. I went back to camp and bade goodbye to my old friends and associates, determined that I would stay and see for myself, and if Mormonism was what they said it was, I would go no further for all the gold in California. Since I was ten years old I had believed there was something before me worth living for and that God would eventually answer my prayers and let me know how to serve Him. I often wonder why I am not more faithful, and if I will ever learn to do as I should. Much of my life seems to have been governed by circumstances over which I have had but little control. That is, I have been impelled by influences that urged me on to certain labours, especially among the Indians, which I have felt compelled to answer.

CHAPTER 3

My Scrutiny of the Mormons

After settling myself with the Bishop's family, I soon got so that I could hobble around a little. Everyone was kind and treated me with great confidence. I listened to the elders preaching and soon concluded they were honest and knew it, or were wilful liars and deceivers. I was determined, if possible, not to be fooled, therefore I commenced to watch very closely. I soon found that the people took an interest in the Indians, and although they had been at war and the Bishop's son had been killed by them, there was no general feeling of bitterness. The Indians were around the fort more or less, and the people were desirous of friendship.

After I had been there a few weeks recruiting, Messrs. Patrick and Glenn came to Provo; they were traders on their way south to barter with the Indians and whites. They knew nothing about trading with the Indians, something I had learned considerable about from Old Thomas, who had traded with them during our trip. I had also dealt with them while in New Mexico. This firm offered me employment for the winter, to go to Sanpete Valley, then the head quarters for trading with the Ute Indians. This suited me, for I wished to become better acquainted with the Indians and gain their friendship, also to learn their language. Some of them could speak more or less Spanish, but not enough to converse satisfactorily. While in Manti, during the winter, I boarded with Father Isaac Morley. During the winter I made the acquaintance of Dimick B. Huntington. He told me about the *Book of Mormon*, its relationship to the Indians, etc. It seemed natural to me to believe it. I cannot remember ever questioning in my mind the truthfulness of the *Book of Mormon*, or that Joseph Smith was a prophet. The question was: Are the Mormons sincere, and can I be one? I heard a great many hard remarks about the Missourians, and being one myself,

I felt to resent the wholesale accusations made against them.

About that time a great many "dead beats" and "winter Mormons" joined the Church, emigrants who stopped over simply for convenience. Quite a number came to Manti, led by one Loomas. They all joined the Church. They tried to induce me to be baptised when they were. I gave them a good cursing for being miserable hypocrites, at which they only laughed, saying they would have the advantage of me among the girls, at least. Sometime near spring this gang arranged to make a general raid upon the settlements, and steal all the horses upon the range from Draperville going south through Utah Valley. In those days numerous herds of horses ran loose, as the range was good. The gang of outlaws had confederates in Salt Lake City where some of them robbed a jeweller's store. They sent for me one night and laid their plans before me. They proposed that I would be their guide and meet them at the head of Spanish Fork Canyon, conduct them through to New Mexico and have one-fourth of all the horses. I declined the offer, telling them it was a good speculation, assigning as my reason for not going that I had not sufficiently recovered from my wounds to risk the trip. This they seemed to believe, as I was yet somewhat lame. They made me promise not to betray them, and I soon satisfied them on that point.

I realised my awkward situation, but was determined to warn the people, thus putting them on their guard. Accordingly on going to Provo, I informed the Bishop of their plans; he warned the different settlements and without any fuss the people were put on their guard. These men were closely watched until spring, when they all left for Lower California, most of them going about the time of the move to San Bernardino. In a fit of anger a friend of Loomas told me I would get killed some day, that Loomas was on my track.

It is true I had in a measure betrayed him and his companions, still I had felt it my duty to do as I had done; and to prevent myself being killed I resolved to kill him on sight. So intent was I on this, that I came near shooting another party, that I mistook for Loomas. At this time I was camped at Spanish Fork. As I was returning from a hunt, I saw a person sitting with his back toward me, that in every way resembled Loomas in point of size and peculiarity of dress. Loomas was expected to visit us. I approached with my gun ready, greatly tempted to shoot without speaking, as he was also armed, but thinking this cowardly I spoke in order to draw his attention when, on his turning round, another face presented itself.

As it turned out, no one knew of my intentions but myself. It makes me shudder even now when I think of my intentions and feelings at that time. I never saw any of the gang afterwards, but read an account of Loomas and others being lynched for robbery in California.

My feelings at this time were very conflicting. I became fully convinced of the truth of Mormonism, and that it was my duty to obey, but I tried to excuse myself in many ways. I said nothing to anyone, but kept up a "terrible thinking." Being a Missourian it seemed, from the remarks made even in public, that salvation could never reach me. I remembered that my father always opposed mobocracy, so much so that he was called by some of our neighbours a Mormon. I was too proud to mention this to anyone; I knew I was honest and was not to blame for being born in Missouri.

CHAPTER 4

Walker, the "Napoleon of the Desert"

During the winter I made several trips to Salt Lake City in company with Patrick, one of the firm in whose employ I was. The winter was very cold, we were glad to get under shelter, no matter how poor it was. At that time, there were few settlements from Salt Lake City to Manti. The first was at Willow Creek, Ebenezer Brown's farm, then Provo. The first house in American Fork was built in mid-winter, 1850-51, by Matt Caldwell. A bitter cold night brought four of us to this humble abode, made of unhewn cottonwood logs, where we were kindly greeted and housed for the night. Beyond Provo A. J. Stewart erected the first cabin at Peteteneet creek, which place is now known as Payson. From there on there were no settlements until Manti was reached.

About this time, mid-winter, I commenced to consider whether it would not be best for me to go on to California, make a lot of money, then return and join the Latter-day Saints. Arguing that they would have more confidence in me then than if I should join now. As I knew that "winter Mormons" were looked upon with suspicion, my mind was much occupied in trying to determine what was best. After considering well the prejudices I would have to meet, I finally spoke to Father Morley, who baptised me January 27th, 1851. There was over a foot of ice on the water at the time.

When I spoke to Brother Morley about baptising me, he was just starting out after a load of wood with his axe under his arm. He replied, "I am ready; here is my ax to cut the ice. I have been expecting this for some time." I wondered why he expected it, as I had said nothing about my intentions.

After baptism I felt more at ease, although I knew many doubted my sincerity. This made no difference as long as I knew I was sincere. I made quite an acquaintance with the Indians during the winter. Walker and portions of his band came around occasionally to trade. They were a fine race of people. Walker's life and exploits with his band would fill a volume; he was sometimes called the "Napoleon of the desert," being a great strategist, often out-generaling those he had to meet in war or whom he designed to plunder. He often made raids into lower California, robbing the people and bringing away large herds of their best horses, always laying his plans with great skill so as to not lose his men.

One of these trips made by him in 1852, I think, shows his ability. With about twenty-five of his most venturesome braves he went down. As usual, the Mexicans were expecting them and their best horses were corralled nightly, their picked saddle horses, valued so highly by every Mexican gentleman, were kept in stables under guard. Walker and party succeeded in cutting an opening in the rear of the corral, turning out the stock and getting away with them. This time the Mexicans were determined to follow them into the desert, make a good killing and recover their stock. They had not expected such a bold move as cutting into the corral, but as soon as it was discovered the Mexicans started in hot pursuit. Walker pushed on with all speed, passing a spring where he calculated the Mexicans would make a short halt. Here he left fifteen of his men afoot secreted near the spring. Soon the Mexicans arrived, having ridden hard for some distance. As Walker expected, they were soon unsaddled, their horses tied out to grass and all hands asleep, expecting to take an hour's rest and then go on.

The Indians waited till all were settled, then quietly loosened the horses, each one mounted, some taking the lead while others drove the loose animals. After reaching a safe distance from gunshot they gave a loud whoop and started to run. I have seen them in mimicry go through the whole performance, showing how the Mexicans looked when they realised the situation.

The Indians always claimed that there was nothing hostile in this, as they killed no one. At the present time I do not know of one representative of this once powerful band. Walker could meet and out-general his Indian foes and outwit the Mexicans; in fact, hold his own with almost anyone whom he met; but neither he nor his band could stand fine flour and good living. This finally, more than anything else, conquered them. I sometimes wonder if the Latter-day Saints have done their duty toward these Indians, professing, as we do, that they are of the seed of Israel.

Chapter 5

Patrick and Glenn fail

I remained in Manti until April, 1851, when I, still in the employ of Patrick and Glenn, came down to Spanish Fork and helped to open the first farm on that stream; it was known as the Reece Farm. Here we had many Utes about us. I often traded with them and they were always friendly remarking that I had a different expression in my eyes, a more kindly look than the people in general had for them. The fact is, I felt from the depths of my heart sincere friendship for them, and no doubt manifested it in my looks. My employers had failed in business, having no capital to commence with, and turned over their property to the Reece Brothers of Salt Lake City.

Patrick proved to be a rascal. When I called on him for a settlement he denied the most he was owing me. He was then in Provo, in charge of several thousand dollars worth of stock belonging to Enoch Reece, who was sending him out to meet his train of merchandise coming in. He was to meet it at Green River. I was determined to make him pay me before he went on. Finally, he offered to settle by arbitration, naming a person.

I felt safe with this proposal and asked him if he would abide the decision if I would. He answered yes. I felt sure of the money, for I had great confidence in the person chosen. He seemed a just and good man and in my simplicity I supposed he would be able to judge correctly in the case. I was careful not to make any demand excepting what I knew to be perfectly just. Mr. Patrick denied *in tot*o my account, and the arbitrator decided that I was attempting to wrong Mr. Patrick. This was a "stumper" for me, but I said I would stand it, and inasmuch as I had to pay for the privilege, I intended to tell all hands what I thought of them. I then told the arbitrator that he had believed a lie and condemned the truth, that some day he would know it, and that Mr. Patrick would get away with Brother Reece's property, for he had proven himself a thief. Enoch Reece was present and resented what I said, telling me to stop talking, but I made my little speech all the same.

About six weeks afterwards I met Brother Reece in Provo and the first words he said to me were: "Well, Brother Jones, what do you think has occurred?" I replied, "Patrick has got away with your stock." "Yes," said he, "he has sold the whole of it and 'sloped' for Oregon." I told him I was glad of it, for he might have listened to me. I also learned afterwards what had blinded the arbitrator. He was owing Mr. Patrick some five hundred dollars, and the latter had told him he could wait six months for all except what was owing Jones; so all that was decided in my favour he had to look up. Consequently it was easy to understand why Patrick did not owe me much!!! I had not belonged to the Church long, but if any one had hinted to me that my faith was shaken in Mormonism by this unjust decision, I should have resented it as an insult. To me it was simply a human weakness which Mormonism had nothing to do with.

CHAPTER 6

My Visit to Salt Lake City

My health became entirely restored. After coming to Provo I worked wherever there was a demand for help, and after harvest was over I concluded to go to Salt Lake City to have a rest and play the gentleman for awhile. This did not last long. I arrived one Saturday, spent Sunday in the city and on Monday morning started for a stroll through town, met an acquaintance, Lyman Woods from Provo, and stood talking to him in the street, when we were approached by a man who enquired of my friend, if he knew of anyone he could get to help harvest twenty acres of late wheat. He seemed anxious, saying he could find no one, and that his wheat was going to waste. I told him I would help him. He looked at me a moment, then said he wanted a man who could follow him, and rake and bind what he cut. I replied that I could do it. Still looking at me he commenced laughing and said, "Well, you will have to change your clothing anyway." My friend then introduced me to Mr. Edmund Ellsworth, President Young's son-in-law, and told him I was a good worker. Brother Ellsworth told me to get ready and come on. I soon changed to buckskin pants and hickory shirt and returned. He remarked, "You will do now." I had never till this time thought dress made any difference in a man's looks in regard to work. We finished up the wheat and returned to town. On Saturday after supper. Brother Ellsworth said, "We will now go and see Brother Brigham, who lives opposite, in the white house." I asked him to wait until I changed my clothes. This he would not allow, but insisted I should go as I was, adding that Brother Brigham did not judge a man by his dress. I went and can say I was completely won by President Young's manner. He asked me a great many questions, and I was satisfied that he did not doubt my sincerity. He gave me a note to Brother Joseph Young, directing him to ordain me a Seventy, saying that he wanted me to preach the gospel wherever I had an opportunity, especially to the people speaking the Spanish language. I went and was ordained September 8th, 1851, by Joseph Young.

I remained in the city some time boarding with Brother Ellsworth. I was present at the meeting where Judge Brochus delivered his famous speech, in which he applied to the women of Utah for a block for the Washington monument, telling them that before they contributed to so glorious a work they must become virtuous, and teach their daughters to become so. I sat and listened, looking at Brother Brigham who sat perfectly still with his mouth twisted a little to one side. Beginning to lose my respect for him and Mormons generally, I spoke to a man sitting next to me. Brother Everett, telling him I would not allow such talk, if I had a wife or mother there; that I would kick Brochus out of the stand. Brother Everett, being more patient, told me to wait. When Brother Brigham arose and answered Brochus, I understood why nothing had been said to interfere with his speech. Brochus was given full liberty to "empty himself." Then he got his dose, which so frightened him that he and his companions left for the States in a few days. No one threatened him or his associates, but he was simply told what he was and who the people were that listened to his abuse. This did him up entirely.

CHAPTER 7

My Desires to Travel

I returned to Provo after the October conference. Soon after my return a large party of Mexican traders from New Mexico arrived in Utah and camped near by. They came in on their usual trading business, the main object being to buy Indian children for slaves.

That the reader may more fully understand the situation, I will give a little of the history and customs of New Mexico. Santa Fe is one of the oldest cities in the United States. The correct history is not perfectly known, but the one told by the natives, and generally accepted, is that soon after the conquest of Mexico by Cortez, an expedition went out to explore the northern country. Nothing was heard from them, and all trace was lost, until a number of years afterwards, when another party went north. On arriving at Santa Fe they found a people among whom many of the younger ones spoke the Spanish language. They found, after much trouble and enquiry, that these were children of the former explorers, who, on arriving in that country, had found rich mines of gold and silver. They concluded to keep silent and work these mines for themselves.

They also found the natives peaceable and in every way well disposed toward them. These natives lived in towns and cultivated the soil. The Spaniards took wives from among the natives; and all went well, until the Spaniards had accumulated many millions of dollars, when they began to tire of their friends and families, and longed for the more congenial society of the people they had left, believing that with their great, wealth they would be received with honour, consequently they determined to abandon all their new made friends and return to Old Mexico. The natives remonstrated, for they now looked upon them as a part of their tribe, inasmuch as they had given them wives and homes, and had assisted and protected them in every way.

The Spaniards had made them believe that they were directed by the Great Spirit to come among them and be united with them.

So when they proposed leaving, the natives looked upon them as deceivers and forbade their departure. The Spaniards heeded not their warnings and felt no apprehensions, for the natives were not a warlike people. So, with their treasure, they started south, but were attacked and all killed. Tradition says that their treasure is buried in a plain near a salt lake, south of Santa Fe. That there is more or less truth in all this, can not be doubted, for history tells us that the second party found descendants of these former explorers in Santa Fe where they had built quite a village and worked mines.

In fact, much evidence was found to corroborate the statement of the natives, although no records were found, and not one of the original Spaniards was living. The second party remained and reported themselves to the government of Mexico. Others came and strengthened the colony; the mines were worked, yielding immense wealth; the Catholic Church was established among the natives, the Spaniards taking Indian women for wives; the natives became converted and adopted Spanish civilization, mixed with their own traditions; a new class of people, commonly called Spanish Mexicans, was the result. A few of the natives retained their ancient customs, remaining apart and never mixing with others. Many of these can still be found living in towns and villages along the Rio Grande. They are known as Pueblos, and are much more honest and moral than the mixed race.

New Mexico was almost an unknown country to the people of the United States until the last half century. Many of the pioneer traders to that land were from Howard County, Missouri, where I was born, and I remember when a child hearing numbers of them on their return recount their exploits and strange experiences. I felt as if I could not wait to be a man before going to see these strange countries and peoples. Well do I remember when studying geography at school and seeing "unexplored region" marked on the map, feeling a contempt for the author and thinking if I were a man I would go and see what there was in that land and not mark it unexplored.

These New Mexicans were a venturesome people. They penetrated through to California; trails were opened that were a marvel of pioneering. They were doubtless assisted by the natives. The Jesuits were leaders in most of these moves. There is hardly a tribe of Indians in the Rocky Mountains but what has a tradition of the priests having been among them. Sometimes these priests gained quite an influence with the wild tribes. At one time the Uintahs were their friends, but a break occurred and the priests were killed. Thus we find that the people of New Mexico at the time I am writing of them, in 1851, were making annual trips, commencing with a few goods, trading on their way with either Navajoes or Utes (generally with the Navajoes) for horses, which they sold very cheap, always retaining their best ones. These used-up horses were brought through and traded to the poorer Indians for children. The horses were often used for food. This trading was continued into Lower California, where the children bought on the down trip would be traded to the Mexican-Californians for other horses, goods or cash. Many times a small outfit on the start would return with large herds of California stock.

All children bought on the return trip would be taken back to New Mexico and then sold, boys fetching on an average $100, girls from $150 to $200. The girls were in demand to bring up for house servants, having the reputation of making better servants than any others. This slave trade gave rise to the cruel wars between the native tribes of this country, from Salt Lake down to the tribes in southern Utah. Walker and his band raided on the weak tribes, taking their children prisoners and selling them to the Mexicans. Many of the lower classes, inhabiting the southern deserts, would sell their own children for a horse and kill and eat the horse. The Mexicans were as fully established and systematic in this trade as ever were the slavers on the seas and to them it was a very lucrative business.

CHAPTER 8

A Noted Trial

At this time Brigham Young was governor of Utah and had the oversight of Indian affairs. Some little business in the slave trade had been done on the trip the summer before by our old guide, who was a regular trader. Governor Young asked me something about this business, telling me to look out, and if any of these traders came in, to let him know, as the laws of the United States, which then extended over this Territory, prohibited this business, and that it would be his duty to put a stop to the same. He hoped to do this by advising these traders in regard to the present conditions. When this party of traders spoken of arrived. Governor Young was notified and came to Provo. The leaders of this company came to see the governor, I acting as interpreter. Mr. Young had the law read and explained to them, showing them that from this on they were under obligations to observe the laws of the United States instead of Mexico; that the treaty of Guadalupe de Hidalgo, had changed the conditions, and that from this on they were under the control of the United States. He further showed that it was a cruel practice to enslave human beings, and explained that the results of such a business caused war and bloodshed among the Indian tribes.

The Mexicans listened with respect, admitting that the traffic would have to cease. It was plainly shown to them that it was a cruel business which could not be tolerated any longer; but as it had been an old established practice, they were not so much to blame for following the traffic heretofore. Now it was expected that this business would be discontinued.

All seemed satisfied and pledged their words that they would return to their homes without trading for children. Most of them kept their promise, but one small party, under Pedro Lion, violated their obligations and were arrested and brought before the United States court. Judge Snow presiding.

This was quite a noted case. I was employed as interpreter. George A. Smith defended the prisoners, and Colonel Blair prosecuted with great wisdom and tact, he knowing all about the Mexican character, having been in the Texan war. A great deal of prejudice and bitter feeling was manifested toward the Mexicans. Governor Young seeing this, used all his influence that they might have a fair and impartial trial, and the law be vindicated in a spirit of justice and not in the spirit of persecution. The defence made by the Mexicans was that the Indians had stolen a lot of horses from them and that they had followed and overtaken them. On coming to their camp they found the Indians had killed and eaten the horses. The only remuneration they could get was to take some children which the Indians offered in payment, saying they did not mean to break their promise. This defence had some weight, whether true or not. Still they were found guilty and fined. The trial lasted several days; the fines were afterwards remitted, and the Mexicans allowed to return home. They had been delayed some time, and made nothing on their trip. No doubt they felt sour, but considering the law, they were dealt leniently with. This broke up the Indian slave trade.

Stopping this slave business helped to sour some of Walker's band. They were in the habit of raiding on the Pahutes and low tribes, taking their children prisoners and selling them. Next year when they came up and camped on the Provo bench, they had some Indian children for sale. They offered them to the Mormons who declined buying. Arapine, Walkers brother, became enraged saying that the Mormons had stopped the Mexicans from buying these children; that they had no right to do so, unless they bought them themselves. Several of us were present when he took one of these children by the heels and dashed its brains out on the hard ground, after which he threw the body towards us, telling us we had no hearts, or we would have bought it and saved its life. This was a strange argument, but it was the argument of an enraged savage. I never heard of any successful attempts to buy children afterwards by the Mexicans. If done at all it was secretly.

CHAPTER 9

Peaceful Life Among the Savages

On the 29th of January, 1852, Miss Harriet Emily Colton was united to me in marriage. All I will say at present is, that her life and labours are as much a part of mine as is possible for a wife's to be. She was my heart's choice from first sight, and so continued till the day of her death. We lived on a farm quite a distance from the settlement for some time after our marriage. My wife's father, Philander Colton, went to California the spring we were married, leaving me in charge of his farm and affairs. The farm was near the Indian camping ground; hundreds of them were often around us. Sometimes they were more or less saucy, but we treated them kindly. My wife seemed to have the same spirit as myself in regard to the Indians, feeling friendly towards them and wishing to see them taught and helped out of their degraded condition.

Nothing occurred in my experience during the remainder of the year worth recording. All of the Indians around were friendly toward us, but frequently spoke of being dissatisfied with the treatment received from some others. Many will say, and with some truthfulness, that Indians visit their revenge upon whites indiscriminately. Yet if one treats them so as to get their real friendship, they are not apt to harm him.

I went as interpreter for President Young in the spring of 1853, to Sanpete county, where some disturbance was threatened by Mexicans under the leadership of a certain Dr. Bowman from New Mexico who seemed inclined to make himself a name by committing some violent act in defiance of law. There seemed to be a determination on his part and those with him to revive the slave trade. He threatened anyone that might interfere with him, saying he could bring all the Indians in the mountains to help him. I was acquainted with this man while in New Mexico. I met him while on a trip to Sanpete Valley a few days before I went with President Young's party. The moment Bowman saw me he began to curse me for being a Mormon, saying he had power at his back to use all the Mormons up. I felt some little friendship for him as is natural for me to feel for anyone I have formerly known, and advised him to act more careful, or he would get into trouble. I tried to reason with him, but to no purpose, he went on down to Utah valley and there acted in an insulting and threatening manner. Bowman's Mexicans were encamped on the west side of the Sanpete valley. It was deemed prudent to bring them in and keep an eye on them, until it could be decided what their intentions were, for at this time it was seen that a growing spirit of war was upon the Indians, and almost anything would stir them up.

Several little fusses of a private nature had lately occurred.

At this time many of the settlers, contrary to the counsel of President Young, had settled on farms and were much exposed. This had a tendency to make the Indians aggressive. Many times the settlers were sorely annoyed by the Indians' horses getting into the fields. When remonstrated with they would ask, "Whose lands are these you are on." The continual advice of President Young was to build in towns, fence their lands and be kind to the Indians; that it was cheaper to feed than to fight them, etc. Some heeded this counsel, while many did not.

I was one of a party of four or five who went out and brought in the Mexicans. They were a little suspicious, asking a great many questions about Bowman, where he was, etc. But I finally persuaded them to go with us. We had no authority to arrest them, neither was it the intention to do so, if it could be avoided. In the meantime Bowman got into some trouble with the Indians by deceiving them in some of their promised trades, and he was ambushed and killed by some of them. Owing to his manner and threats, it was rumoured the Mormons had killed him. I was actively engaged as interpreter and was continually around during this time. I never had the least suspicion or proof that Bowman was killed by any Mormon agency, and I believe I would have heard something of it, if such had been the case. I know in those days it was no uncommon thing for a man to be killed whether a Mormon or not by the Indians, either for revenge or plunder. The Mexicans soon left in peace.

In the summer of 1853, about harvest time, the war broke out. The immediate cause of the Indian war was the striking of an Indian with a gun by a white man at Springville. This Indian was whipping his squaw, when the party interfered to stop him. The Indian drew his gun to shoot, it was wrenched from him. The man using the gun as a club, broke both stock and Indian's head. I believe the Indian died from the effects of the blow; he was one of Walker's band, and the latter at once painted for war.

The same day A. J. Stewart and I were returning from Payson. When about a mile from there some twenty-five warriors painted black, came from a ravine, approaching us in flank with guns and bows ready. Mr. Stewart remarked, "We are in for it; that means war." We had no time to turn and run as they were within one hundred yards of us. I knew I had never wronged them, but had always been a friend, and I believed if we went straight along they would not hurt us. Brother Stewart agreed with me. We never halted or gave the road, but drove along as though nothing was in the way.

As we went they parted and allowed us the road, never speaking or making any sign of recognition. This same party went on up to the Payson mill and in less than an hour commenced killing our people.

This was the commencement of what is known as the Walker War. It caused a general moving in of those who had settled out on farms, making towns and villages spring up like magic. I remember President Young remarking in public that the people seemed readier to obey Brother Walker's invitation to live together in towns, than they did his counsel. Brother Brigham always gave Walker great credit for helping to build up Utah. There was plenty to do as soon as the war commenced. An attempt was made to follow and chastise the Indians, but nothing that resulted in much good was ever done by fighting them. The counsel was for all to move in, gather the stock together, and in every way possible guard against attacks or surprises. There was a general move in this direction; cattle were gathered and herded under strong guards. Guards were also placed at the different trails leadings into the valley. This had a much better effect than following the Indians, getting shot at and having to retreat in good order.

There was quite a band of Provo Indians who took no part in the fight; they were camped on the bench near the river bottom. I had not yet moved into town; the Indians were around me daily and I believed them to be friendly. An order was issued by someone in Provo to have them taken prisoners and brought in. Accordingly a company of militia was called out for the purpose. Happening along just as they were starting on the expedition, I was asked to go and help take the Indians, but declined, and protested against the move, well knowing that they would not be taken, as they had done nothing to justify any harsh measures against them. My remonstrance was in vain, the Indians had to be taken, and I was ordered to go as interpreter. So we marched over in good militia style, every man keeping step with himself. I felt much amused at our turnout going to war. The flower of our army was then out after Walker. As we neared the camp of Indians I asked permission to go ahead and tell them what was wanted. I was on horseback and unarmed; the Indians were up at once and ready for fight. They said that taking them prisoners meant to kill them, and they would not go. The company numbering some twenty-five men—about the same number as the Indians—had now come up and stood about fifty yards off, facing the camp. I went and told the captain what the Indians said. He replied, "Then we have got to take them by force." At the same time ordering his company to load their guns. I now became frightened, for I knew if they commenced loading, the Indians having their guns ready, would fire the minute they saw the whites making such a movement; but as long as they did not know that the guns were not loaded we were safe. I asked the captain to hold a minute and let me ask a few questions. He agreed.

"How many of you have loads in your guns?" I asked.

No one had. Several spoke and said they had nothing to load with, while some of the guns were out of repair. I never before or since saw anything so ridiculous. Some of the members of the company are still living in Provo, and will remember the incident. I asked the captain what he thought best to do; he said he would take my advice under the circumstances. I told him I would say to the Indians that it was all right; that they were friends; and we did not think it right to take them but would go back.

This made them suspicious. They moved off up Provo Canyon and committed various petty thefts from time to time, annoying the people for several months.

CHAPTER 10

Peace with the Indians

When the troubles began Brother George A. Smith, who was presiding in Utah county was in Salt Lake City. There was much confusion in the county. All the cattle belonging to Provo, twelve hundred head, were got together on the lake bottom. Barney Ward and I were placed as guard over them, with orders not to let them get away. We stayed with them until we were about worn out. No one would come to our relief till Brother Smith came to give directions. On the third day we heard he had arrived. I went in early to see him. I had not slept for three nights and had been in the saddle most of the time, consequently I did not feel very good-natured. As I was going up to Brother Smith's house I met three of the principal brethren on the street. They asked where I was going. I told them to see Brother Smith. They replied that he was not up and I could not see him. I answered, "I will go and see."

Sure enough they were right and somewhat sarcastically said, "You will learn some day to not be in such a hurry." I was very angry and made an ill-natured remark.

After going and getting my breakfast I went back to G. A. Smith's house. He was sitting by the door in company with the men I had met before.

Brother Smith shook hands with me saying, "I understand you called me a big lazy lout. What do you mean by such talk? Did you say it?"

I replied "Yes sir. I have been up with Brother Ward three nights herding cattle; he is with the cattle now, we are worn out and cannot stand it any longer; I thought when you only rode from Salt Lake City in a carriage, and have slept all night, you could just as well get up and attend to business as for us to be up three nights. That is why

43

I said it."

Brother Smith turned to one of these men, saying, "Go get some men and relieve Brother Barney immediately. Bro. Jones go home and go to sleep; when you wake up you will feel better." I felt ashamed for Bro. Smith manifested no anger.

When I awoke in the afternoon I went to see Bro. Smith intending to ask his pardon. On seeing me he took me by the hand, laughing heartily, asking me if I felt any better, and talking in a very pleasant manner, giving me no chance to apologize. Many years afterwards he spoke of it, and laughed about it as a good joke. I relate this to show the nobility of his character, being above small prejudice. I have met others who ought to be as good as Brother Smith, who would never have forgiven me if I had made such a remark about them.

How long the war continued is a question. Active hostilities were kept up more or less according to opportunities during the summer of '53. When the Indians had a good chance they would steal or kill. Some were more or less peaceable when it suited them. I never went out to fight as I made no pretensions whatever of being an Indian fighter. I did my portion of military duty. I assisted in various ways in helping to protect ourselves against the natives, but I always made it a rule to cultivate a friendly feeling whenever opportunity presented; so much so that the Indians always recognised me as a friend to their race.

I had learned some little about military affairs while in Mexico. I assisted in organising and drilling the militia from time to time. I also acted as adjutant under Col. P. W. Conover as early as '51, afterwards filled the same position under Col. Pace in '53. I did not like the office and resigned, but was induced to accept the office again for the purpose of making out returns to the government for services rendered by some of the Utah militia. These returns were accepted, the men paid, and land warrants issued. I was assisted by L. J. Nuttall and G. W. Hickman as clerks. After this Brother Nuttall was appointed in my place and continued to act under Col. Pace to my knowledge, as late as the Echo Canyon War.

President Young advised the people to wall in their towns. This puzzled the Indians. We told them it was our intention to shut them out and have no more to do with them. This they did not like for there was no great length of time, but what some of the different bands were on friendly terms with the settlers. Walker finally said if we would quit building walls, they would quit fighting. But the good peace was broken, and there was always some of the whites holding grudges against the Indians. Still we called it peace. The local troubles are matters of general history. I aim to deal more with that which is not written.

I always considered the natives entitled to a hearing as well as the whites. Both were often in the wrong. The white men should be patient and just with the Indians and not demand of them in their untutored condition the same responsibility they would of the more intelligent class. Further along in this history we will see the Indians' defence.

CHAPTER 11

One party of Emigrants found in a Starving Condition

I attended the October conference of 1856. When conference was opened President Young arose and said:

> There are a number of our people on the plains who have started to come with hand-carts; they will need help and I want twenty teams to be ready by morning with two men to each team to go out and meet them. If the teams are not voluntarily furnished, there are plenty of good ones in the street and I shall call upon Brother J. C. Little, the marshal, to furnish them. Now we will adjourn this conference until tomorrow.

Brother Young was in earnest; he seemed moved by a spirit that would admit of no delay.

A few days before this a number of elders had arrived from the old country reporting that the hand-cart people were on the road, but they did not know how far they had advanced. In those days there was no telegraph, and mails from the east only reached Utah monthly, they being many times delayed by high water, Indians or other causes.

Brother Young called upon every one present to lend a hand in fitting up these teams. As I was going out with the crowd. Brother Wells spoke to me saying: "You are a good hand for the trip; get ready."

Soon after Bishop Hunter said the same thing to me.

Also Brother Grant met me and said: "I want you on this trip."

I began to think it time to decide, so I answered, "all right."

I had a saddle horse. We were instructed to get everything we could ready and rendezvous between the Big and Little Mountains, a short day's drive out from Salt Lake. Next day teams and volunteer men were ready. A better outfit and one more adapted to the work before us I do not think could have possibly been selected if a week had been spent in fitting up. Besides the wagons and teams, several men went horseback. We had good teams and provisions in great abundance. But best of all, those going were alive to the work and were of the best material possible for the occasion.

As soon as all were together we organised and moved on. George D. Grant was selected captain, with Robert Burton and William Kimball as assistants; Cyrus Wheelock, chaplain; Charles Decker, guide. I was given the important position of chief cook for the head mess. I was quite proud of my office, for it made me the most sought after and popular man in the camp. The rest of the company was made up of the following persons: Joseph A. Young, Chauncey Webb, H. H. Cluff, D. P. Kimball, George W. Grant, Ed. Peck, Joel Parrish, Henry Goldsbrough, Thomas Alexander, Benjamin Hampton, Thomas Ricks, Abe Garr, Charles Grey, Al Huntington, "Handsome Cupid," Stephen Taylor, William K. Broomhead, Ira Nebeker, Redick Allred, Amos Fairbanks and Tom Bankhead, a coloured man. These are all the names that I remember, if there were any more I have been unable to find them.

The weather soon became cold and stormy. We travelled hard, never taking time to stop for dinner. On getting into camp all were hungry and willing to help. No doubt many of the boys remember the hearty suppers eaten on this expedition. There was some expectation of meeting the first train. Brother Willie's, on or about Green River. We began to feel great anxiety about the emigrants as the weather was now cold and stormy, and we, strong men with good outfits, found the nights severe. What must be the condition of those we were to meet. Many old men and women, little children, mothers with nursing babes, crossing the plains pulling hand-carts. Our hearts began to ache when we reached Green River and yet no word of them. Here an express was sent on ahead with a light wagon to meet and cheer the people up. Cyrus Wheelock and Stephen Taylor went with this express.

At the South Pass, we encountered a severe snowstorm. After crossing the divide we turned down into a sheltered place on the Sweetwater. While in camp and during the snow-storm two men were seen on horseback going west. They were hailed. On reaching us they proved to be Brothers Willie and J. B. Elder. They reported their company in a starving condition at their camp then east of Rocky Ridge and said our express had gone on to meet the other companies still in the rear.

We started immediately through the storm to reach Brother Willie's camp. On arriving we found them in a condition that would stir the feelings of the hardest heart. They were in a poor place, the storm having caught them where fuel was scarce. They were out of provisions and really freezing and starving to death.

The morning after our arrival nine were buried in one grave. We did all we could to relieve them. The boys struck out on horseback and dragged up a lot of wood; provisions were distributed and all went to work to cheer the sufferers. Soon there was an improvement in camp, but many poor, faithful people had gone too far—had passed beyond the power to recruit. Our help came too late for some and many died after our arrival.

William Kimball with a few men and wagons turned back, taking the oversight of this company to help them in. Capt. Grant left a wagon load of flour near the Pass with Redick Allred to guard it. There were several hundred people with Brother Willie. They had a few teams, but most of them had become too weak to be of much service. When we left Salt Lake it was understood that other teams would follow until all the help needed would be on the road.

The greater portion of our company now continued on towards Devil's Gate, travelling through snow all the way. When we arrived at Devil's Gate we found our express there awaiting us. No tidings as yet were received of the other companies.

CHAPTER 12

Terrible Sufferings

Having seen the sufferings of Brother Willie's company, we more fully realised the danger the others were in. The Elders who had just returned from England having many dear friends with these companies, suffered great anxiety, some of them feeling more or less the responsibility resting upon them for allowing these people to start so late in the season across the plains. At first we were at a loss what to do for we did not expect to have to go further than Devil's Gate. We decided to make camp and send on an express to find where the people were and not to return until they were found.

Joseph A. Young, Abe Garr and I were selected. (Some histories give other names, but I was there myself and am not mistaken). With picked saddle horses and a pack mule we started out.

The first night we camped, our horses followed a band of buffaloes several miles; it was near noon the next day when we returned with them. We determined to get even with them so rode at full gallop wherever the road would permit. After riding about twelve miles we saw a white man's shoe track in the road. Bro. Young called out, "Here they are." We put our animals to their utmost speed and soon came in sight of the camp at Red Bluff. This was Brother Edward Martin's hand-cart company and Ben Horgett's wagon company. There was still another wagon company down near the Platte crossing.

This company was in almost as bad a condition as the first one. They had nearly given up hope. Their provisions were about exhausted and many of them worn out and sick. When we rode in, there was a general rush to shake hands. I took no part in the ceremony. Many declared we were angels from heaven. I told them I thought we were better than angels for this occasion, as we were good strong men come to help them into the valley, and that our company, and wagons loaded with provisions, were not far away. I thought this the best consolation under the circumstances. Brother Young told the people to gather "up" and move on at once as the only salvation was to travel a little every day. This was right and no doubt saved many lives for we, among so many, (some twelve hundred) could do but little, and there was danger of starvation before help could arrive unless the people made some head-way toward the valley.

After talking to and encouraging the people, they agreed to start on the next morning. We then started full gallop for John Hunt's camp fifteen miles further. On arriving no one noticed us or appeared to care who we were. Their tents were pitched in good shape, wood was plentiful, and no one seemed concerned. Joseph A. Young became offended, not expecting such a cool reception and remarked, "Well it appears we are not needed here." So we went down into the bottom and made camp for ourselves. After a while someone sauntered down our way, thinking probably we were mountaineers. These recognised Brother Young and made a rush for camp, giving the word; soon we were literally carried in and a special tent was pitched for our use. Everything was done to make "amends" for the previous neglect. I never could see where the amends came in, for no one happened to know us when we first arrived, and strangers were often passing, this being near where several camps of old traders were located.

About the time we were settled in our tent, Captain Hunt and Gilbert Van Schoonhoven, his assistant, arrived from the Platte bridge, also Captain Ben Horgett. They were rejoiced to meet us. Here I first met "Gib Spencer" and formed a friendly acquaintance with him which continues to this day, (1890).

These people were just on the eve of suffering, but as yet had not. Quite a number of their cattle had died during the snow storm which had now been on them for nine days.

Next morning Brother Young and others went to Platte bridge, leaving Brother Garr and I to get the company started according to agreement made the evening before. There was a spirit of apathy among the people, instead of going for their teams at once, several began to quarrel about who should go. This made us feel like leaving them to take care of themselves. We saddled up to do so. The clouds were gathering thickly for storm, and just as we were about to start it commenced snowing very hard. The heavens were obscured by clouds, excepting a small place about the shape of the gable end of a house. This opening was in the direction of the valley and the sun seemed to shine through with great brightness. We mounted our mules; Brother Garr, pointing to the bright spot in the heavens, said, "Do you see that hole? You had better all get out of here before that closes up, for it is your opening to the valley. We are going." The people, I believe, took this for a warning and soon started for their cattle.

Next morning they moved on. Brother Garr and I went back to where E. Martin's camp had been. They had rolled out and Captain Horgett's wagon company were just starting.

We continued on, overtaking the hand-cart company ascending a long muddy hill. A condition of distress here met my eyes that I never saw before or since. The train was strung out for three or four miles. There were old men pulling and tugging their carts, sometimes loaded with a sick wife or children—women pulling along sick husbands— little children six to eight years old struggling through the mud and snow. As night came on the mud would freeze on their clothes and feet. There were two of us and hundreds needing help. What could we do? We gathered on to some of the most helpless with our *riatas* tied to the carts, and helped as many as we could into camp on Avenue hill.

This was a bitter, cold night and we had no fuel except very small sage brush. Several died that night.

Next morning, Brother Young having come up, we three started for our camp near Devil's Gate. All were rejoiced to get the news that we had found the emigrants. The following morning most of the company moved down, meeting the hand-cart company at Grease-wood creek. Such assistance as we could give was rendered to all until they finally arrived at Devil's Gate Fort about the 1st of November. There were some twelve hundred in all, about one-half with hand-carts and the other half with teams.

CHAPTER 13

Myself and Company Left to Guard the Goods

The winter storms had now set in, in all their severity. The provisions we took amounted to almost nothing among so many people, many of them now on very short rations, some almost starving. Many were dying daily from exposure and want of food. We were at a loss to know why others had not come on to our assistance.

The company was composed of average emigrants: old, middle-aged and young; women and children. The men seemed to be failing and dying faster than the women and children.

The hand-cart company was moved over to a cove in the mountains for shelter and fuel; a distance of two miles from the fort. The wagons were banked near the fort. It became impossible to travel further without reconstruction or help. We did all we possibly could to help and cheer the people. Some writers have endeavoured to make individual heroes of some of our company. I have no remembrance of any one shirking his duty. Each and everyone did all they possibly could and justice would give to each his due credit.

All the people who could, crowded into the houses of the fort out of the cold and storm. One crowd cut away the walls of the house they were in for fuel, until half of the roof fell in; fortunately they were all on the protected side and no one was hurt.

Many suggestions were offered as to what should be done, some efforts being made to cache the imperishable goods and go on with the rest. Accordingly pits were dug, boxes opened and the hardware, etc., put in one, while clothing, etc., were put in another.

Often these boxes belonged to different persons. An attempt was made by Brother Cantwell, to keep an account of these changes.

This *caching* soon proved to be a failure for the pits would fill up with drifting snow as fast as the dirt was thrown out, so no *caches* were made. The goods were never replaced.

Each evening the Elders would meet in council. I remember hearing Charles Decker remark that he had crossed the plains over fifty times (carrying the mail) and this was the darkest hour he had ever seen. Cattle and horses were dying every day. What to do was all that could be talked about. Five or six days had passed and nothing determined upon.

Steve Taylor, Al. Huntington and I were together when the question, "Why doesn't Captain Grant leave all the goods here with someone to watch them, and move on?" was asked. We agreed to make this proposal to him. It was near the time appointed for the meeting. As soon as we were together, Capt. Grant asked if anyone had thought of a plan. We presented ours.

Capt. Grant replied, "I have thought of this, but there are no provisions to leave and it would be asking too much of anyone to stay here and starve for the sake of these goods; besides, where is there a man who would stay if called upon."

I answered, "Any of us would." I had no idea I would be selected, as it was acknowledged I was the best cook in camp and Capt. Grant had often spoken as though he could not spare me.

That a proper understanding may be had, I will say that these goods were the luggage of a season's emigration that these two wagon trains had contracted to freight, and it was being taken through as well as the luggage of the people present. Leading these goods meant to abandon all that many poor families had upon earth. So it was different from common merchandise.

There was a move made at once to adopt this suggestion. Accordingly, next morning store rooms in the fort were cleared and some two hundred wagons run in and unloaded. No one was allowed to keep out anything but a change of clothing, some bedding and light cooking utensils. Hauling provisions was not a weighty question.

This unloading occupied three days. The handcart people were notified to abandon most of their carts. Teams were hitched up and the sick and feeble loaded in with such light weight as was allowed. All became common property.

When everything was ready Brother Burton said to me, "Now Brother Jones we want you to pick two men from the valley to stay with you. We have notified Captains Hunt and Horgett to detail seventeen men from their companies to stay with you. We will move on in the morning. Get your company together and such provisions as you can find in the hands of those who may have anything to spare. You know ours is about out. Will you do it?"

I said, "Yes."

"Well take your choice from our company. You are acquainted with the boys and whoever you want will stay."

I had a great mind to tell him I wanted Captains Grant and Burton.

There was not money enough on earth to have hired me to stay. I had left home for only a few days and was not prepared to remain so long away; but I remembered my assertion that any of us would stay if called upon. I could not back out, so I selected Thomas Alexander and Ben Hampton. I am satisfied that two more faithful men to stand under all hardships could not have been found.

That night we were called together and organised as a branch. Dan W. Jones, Thomas Alexander and Ben Hampton were chosen to preside, with J. Laty as clerk. The rest of the company was composed of the following names: John Cooper, John Hardcastle, John Shorton, John Chapel, John Galbraith, John Ellis, John Whitaker, William Handy, William Laty, Edwin Summers, Rossiter Jenkins, Elisha Manning, Henry Jakeman George Watt, George Watts and —— ——

Captain Grant asked about our provisions. I told him they were scant, but as many were suffering and some dying, all we asked was an equal chance with the rest. He told us there would be a lot of worn out cattle left; to gather them up and try to save them.

They consisted mostly of yearlings and two-year-old heifers, some-one was taking through. The storm had now ceased to rage and great hopes were felt for a successful move. We were daily expecting more help and often wondered why it did not come. Next day all hands pulled out, most of them on foot.

After getting my camp regulated a little and giving some instructions, I got on my horse and rode on to see how the train was moving along. All were out of sight when I started. After travelling a few miles, I came upon a lady sitting alone on the side of the road, weeping bitterly. I noticed she was elegantly dressed and appeared strong and well. I asked her what was the matter. She sobbingly replied, "This is too much for me. I have always had plenty, and have never known hardships; we had a good team and wagon; my husband, if let alone, could have taken me on in comfort. Now I am turned out to walk in this wind and snow. I am determined not to go on but will stay here and die. My husband has gone on and left me, but I will not go another step."

The train was two or three miles ahead and moving on. I persuaded her after a while to go on with me.

This lady, Mrs. Linforth, and her husband now live in San Francisco, California. They could not stand the hardships of Zion; but I believe they are friendly to our people.

After overtaking the train and seeing them on the move. Captain Grant asked me to go back with instructions for the brethren left with me; then to come on next day and camp with them over night.

On calling the company together at the fort that night, I told them in plain words that if there was a man in camp who could not help eat the last poor animal left with us, hides and all, suffer all manner of privations, almost starve to death, that he could go on with me the next day and overtake the trains. No one wanted to go. All voted to take their chances.

On taking stock of provisions, we found about twenty day's rations. No salt or bread excepting a few crackers. There was at least five months of winter before us and nothing much to eat but a few perishing cattle and what game we might chance to kill. The game was not very certain, as the severe storms had driven everything away. The first move was to fix up the fort. Accordingly Brother Alexander, being a practical man, was appointed to manage the business; Brother Hampton was to see about the cattle.

I followed the train this day to their second encampment and the next day travelled with them. There was much suffering, deaths occurring often. Eph Hanks arrived in camp from the valley and brought word that some of the teams that had reached South Pass and should have met us here, had turned back towards home and tried to persuade Redick Allred, who was left there with a load of flour, to go back with them. The men who did this might have felt justified; they said it was no use going farther, that we had doubtless all perished. I will not mention their names for it was always looked upon by the company as cowardly in the extreme.

If this had not occurred it was the intention of Captain Grant to have sent someone down to us with a load of flour. As it was, by the time any was received, the people were in a starving condition, and could not spare it.

From the third camp, where I saw the last of the brethren, an express was sent on to catch the returning supplies and continue on to the valley, giving word that the train was coming. I know nothing more of them except from reports. As I am writing mainly from my own observations, I will simply state that after great suffering and much assistance (hundreds turning out to help) the emigrants were finally landed in the valley.

Chapter 14

A Mail Company Nearly Perishes

I left the company feeling a little downcast, to return to Devil's Gate. It was pretty well understood that there would be no relief sent us. My hopes were that we could kill game. We had accepted the situation, and as far as Capt. Grant was concerned he had done as much as he could for us. There was more risk for those who went on than for us remaining.

On returning to camp, I found that the cattle left were very poor. The weather had moderated and we hoped to get them on good feed and recruit them a little. Over two hundred head of cattle had died in the vicinity of the fort. Along the road each way for a day's travel were carcasses. This led droves of prairie wolves into our camp, it was almost impossible to keep them off from the cattle in the day time. We were obliged to corral them at night. Once in the day time a small bunch was taken and run off in spite of the efforts of the herders to stop them. In fact, it became dangerous to face these wolves, they were at times almost ready to attack men.

We soon found it would be impossible to save the cattle. Already some twenty-five had died or been killed by the wolves within a week. It was decided to kill the rest, some fifty head. A few were in living order, but many would have died within twenty-four hours. In fact we killed them to keep them from dying. We had a first-class butcher from London, who dressed everything in the best style. Everything was saved that we thought might be eaten. We hung the meat up. The poorest of it we did not expect to eat, but intended to use it for wolf bait further along when the carcasses were all devoured, provided we could get traps from the Platte bridge, which we afterwards did. We never used our poor beef for wolf bait as we had to eat the whole of it ourselves, and finally the hides were all consumed for food.

After killing the cattle we had nothing much to do but fix up the fort and look after four ponies we had left. Brother Hampton and myself had our saddle horses yet in good order.

There were plenty of guns and ammunition left with us, also dishes and cooking utensils. After thoroughly repairing the houses, chinking and daubing them, we overhauled the goods stored away.

While storing the bales and boxes the snow had drifted in among them. There was nothing but dirt floors and the goods had been tumbled in without any regard to order. Having cleaned out everything, we took ox yokes, of which there were a great many, and made floors of them and then piled the goods on them. While handling the goods we found some coffee, sugar and fruit, also a roll of leather. These we kept out and put in our store room for use. We also found a box of soap and candles. These goods were marked F. D. Richards, Daniel Spencer, John Van Cott, James Furgeson, William Dunbar, Cyrus Wheelock and Chauncy Webb; most of them John Van Cott. We were told by Captain Grant to use anything we could find to make us comfortable.

During the time we were at a loss what to do, men's minds did not run much upon property, the main interest was to save life. One prominent Elder became very liberal. He had several large trunks filled with valuable stuff. He opened his heart and trunks, making presents to several of the boys from the valley of socks, shirts and such things as would help to make them comfortable. He left his trunks in my rooms, giving me the keys and telling me to use anything there was, not to suffer for anything that could be found, and asked God to bless me.

I told the boys who remained with me that we had better not open this man's trunks, that when he got to the valley and had time to think, he would change his mind and would doubtless be thinking we were using his goods, and if we touched anything belonging to him we would be accused of taking more than we had. Later occurrences proved this to be a good suggestion.

With the cattle killed that were fit to eat, and what provisions we had on hand, we managed to live for a while without suffering, except for salt. Bread soon gave out and we lived on meat alone. Some of us went out hunting daily but with poor success.

A day or two before Christmas, Ephraim Hanks and Feramorz Little arrived at the fort, bringing the mail from the valley with the following letter of instructions from President Young:

President's Office, Great Salt Lake City,
Dec. 7th, 1856.

Brothers Jones, Alexander and Hampton, in charge at Devil's Gate, and the rest of the brethren at that place:

Dear Brethren: Quite unexpectedly to us we have the opportunity of sending you a few suggestions, as Judge Smith, the post master here, has concluded to forward the eastern mail by Brothers Feramorz Little and Ephraim Hanks.

Being somewhat aware of a natural disposition in many to relax their vigilance after a temporary and unaccustomed watchfulness, more especially in case no particular cause of alarm is of frequent occurrence, I feel impressed to write a few suggestions and words of counsel to you all. You are in an Indian country, few in number, blockaded by the snows, and far from assistance at this season of the year. Under such circumstances you can but realise the necessity of all of you being constantly on the alert, to be firm, steady, sober-minded and sober-bodied, united, faithful and watchful, living your religion.

Do not go from your fort in small parties of one, two or three at a time. But when game is to be sought, wood got up, or any other operation to be performed requiring you to travel from under the protection of the fort guns, go in bands of some ten or twelve together, and let them be well armed; and let those who stay by the stuff be watchful while their comrades are out. And at all times and under all circumstances let every person have his arms and ammunitions ready for active service at a moment's warning, so you cannot be surprised by your foes nor in any way be taken advantage of, whether in or out of the fort. Always have plenty of water about the buildings, and be very careful about fires, and the preservation from damp, fire or other damage of the goods in your care.

Unless buffaloes and other game come within a reasonable distance, you had better kill some of the cattle than run much risk in quest of game. Use all due diligence for the preservation of your stock, and try to so ration out your flour as to have it last until we can send you relief, which, as before stated, will be forwarded as early as possible in the spring, but may not reach you until May, depending somewhat on the winter snows and spring weather, of which you will be able to form an estimate as the season advances.

We will send teams to your relief as early as possible in the spring, and trust to learn that all has been well with you and the property in your care. Brothers Little and Hanks will furnish you with items of news from the valley, and I will forward you some packages of our papers by them.

Praying you may be united, faithful and protected,

I remain, Your brother in the gospel,

Brigham Young.

From this letter it is plain to see that Brother Brigham was not apprised of our condition. He afterwards said if he had known our situation he would have relieved us if it had taken half the men in the valley. I never felt to complain. The brethren who left us knew but little about what was left to provision us. The supposition was that the cattle would have furnished us in case game could not be killed.

Brother Alexander and I were out for several days, killing some game on this trip. We were much disappointed on our return to find that Brothers Hanks and Little had gone on east without us seeing them. Brother Little looked around at our supplies, telling the boys to take care of the hides, that they were better than nothing to eat. This proved good advice.

Soon after, the Magraw mail company came along under the charge of Jesse Jones. They left their coaches, fitted up with packs and started for the valley. Brother Joseph L. Heywood, United States Marshal for Utah, was a passenger. They went as far as the South Pass. The storm setting in so severely they could not face it, they came near freezing to death; it was with great difficulty that Brother Heywood was kept alive. The day they returned to our camp we had killed a buffalo some twelve miles distant, it took all hands three days to get it into camp. This buffalo I shot at the risk of my life. He was coming toward me in a snow trail. I lay on the trail with nothing to protect me.

If I had not killed him he would doubtless have run on to me; but he dropped at the first shot. We were about out of anything fit to eat and it did not require much bravery to take the risk, for almost anyone will take desperate chances when hungry. We wounded two others, that we expected to get, but about the time we commenced dressing the one killed, there came on a regular blizzard that lasted several days. We had hard work to save the lives of the men getting the meat into camp.

CHAPTER 15

An Unexpected Supper

The mail company went down fifty miles to Platte bridge to winter. Marshal Heywood decided to remain with us and live or die, as the case might be, preferring to be with his brethren. There were no provisions to be had at the bridge, for three of us had been down to see if we could get supplies. We barely got enough to last us back. The mountaineers there had some cattle but no bread, they lived by hunting.

Game soon became so scarce that we could kill nothing. We ate all the poor meat; one would get hungry eating it. Finally that was all gone, nothing now but hides, were left. We made a trial of them. A lot was cooked and eaten without any seasoning and it made the whole company sick. Many were so turned against the stuff that it made them sick to think of it.

We had coffee and some sugar, but drinking coffee seemed to only destroy the appetite, and stimulate for only a little while. One man became delirious from drinking so much of it.

Things looked dark, for nothing remained but the poor raw hides taken from starved cattle. We asked the Lord to direct us what to do. The brethren did not murmur, but felt to trust in God. We had cooked the hide, after soaking and scraping the hair off until it was soft and then ate it, glue and all. This made it rather inclined to stay with us longer than we desired. Finally I was impressed how to fix the stuff and gave the company advice, telling them how to cook it; for them to scorch and scrape the hair off; this had a tendency to kill and purify the bad taste that scalding gave it. After scraping, boil one hour in plenty of water, throwing the water away which had extracted all the glue, then wash and scrape the hide thoroughly, washing in cold water, then boil to a jelly and let it get cold, and then eat with a little sugar sprinkled on it. This was considerable trouble, but we had little else to do and it was better than starving.

We asked the Lord to bless our stomachs and adapt them to this food. We hadn't the faith to ask him to bless the raw-hide for it was "hard stock." On eating now all seemed to relish the feast. We were three days without eating before this second attempt was made. We enjoyed this sumptuous fare for about six weeks, and never had the gout.

In February the first Indian came to our camp. He was of the Snake tribe, his people were located a day's travel up the river. At the time of his arrival we were out of everything, having not only eaten the hides taken from cattle killed, but had eaten the wrappings from the wagon-tongues, old *moccasin*-soles were eaten also, and a piece of buffalo hide that had been used for a foot mat for two months.

The day the Indian came was fast-day, and for us fast-day in very truth. We met as usual for we kept our monthly fast-day. During meeting we became impressed that there were some wrongs existing among the brethren in camp that should be corrected, and that if we would make a general cleaning up, and present our case before the Lord, He would take care of us, for we were there on His business. On questioning some of the company privately, we found that several had goods in their possession not belonging to them. When we felt satisfied all goods were replaced we went *en masse* and cut a hole in the ice on the river. There were several carcasses of cattle that had died lying near the fort, that the wolves had not devoured. Some of the boys, contrary to counsel, had cut steaks from them during the time we were eating the hides; it made them quite sick.

There was a pile of offal in the butcher shop from the poor cattle killed. But what looked more tempting than all to starving men was a pile of more than one hundred fat wolf carcasses, skinned, piled up and frozen near the fort. They looked very much like nice fat mutton. Many of the company asked my opinion about eating them. I told them if they would all do as I advised we would have a good clean supper of healthy food; that these carcasses were unclean; that we were on the Lord's service, and did not believe He wanted us to suffer so much, if we only had faith to trust Him and ask for better.

We all became united in this feeling. Accordingly we hauled all these carcasses of cattle, the wolves, also the offal from the store-house and shoved them into the hole cut in the ice, where they floated off out of our reach. We then went and washed out our store-house and presented it before the Lord empty, but clean.

Near sundown the Indian spoken of came to our quarters. Some of the boys hunted up a small piece of rawhide and gave it to him. He said he had eaten it before. None of us were able to talk much with him; we invited him to remain with us over night. Evening came on and no supper; eight o'clock, no word from anyone. And the word had been positively given that we should have supper. Between eight and nine o'clock all were sitting waiting, now and then good-naturedly saying it was most suppertime. No one seemed disheartened.

Bro. Heywood was still with us. All at once we heard a strange noise resembling human voices down the road. Bro. Heywood rushed out exclaiming, "Here comes our supper." The voices were loud and in an unknown tongue. Bro. H. came back a little frightened saying there was something strange going on down the road. Several of us, taking our arms, started in the direction of the noise. On getting nearer we recognised the voices. The Magraw party under Jesse Jones was making another effort to get through with their coaches; they had got stuck in a snow drift and the noise we heard was Canadian Frenchmen swearing at their mules. We helped them out and guided them into the fort. It was a bitter cold night but we had good houses with rousing fires.

After unhitching and turning out Jesse said, "I am glad to get here."

I replied, "I am as glad to see you."

"Why are you so glad to see us?" he asked.

I told him we had not a mouthful of anything to eat, nor had we tasted food that day.

"Then what are you stopping here for?"

I replied, "We were waiting for you to bring our supper."

He laughed and said, "Well you shall have it if it takes the last bite we have got."

He gave to our cook all of his provisions. About ten o'clock twenty-six hungry men sat down to about as thankfully a received supper as was ever partaken of by mortal man.

In January when this party passed through to Platte bridge, I sent word by them to the mountaineers there that we would pay a good price for meat brought to us. Two of the best hunters, Messrs. Maxim and Plant, made the attempt to get us meat, but failed, almost starving themselves on the hunt. They never reached our fort but returned to their homes on the Platte.

When Jesse Jones left us going down we had but little provisions on hand. Maxim and Plant's failure to reach us with food caused the people at Platte bridge to suppose we had all perished. Jesse told me he fully expected to find our skeletons.

Some may ask why we did not leave. There was no time during the winter but what the attempt would have been certain death to some of us. The company at no time was strong enough to make the trip to Platte bridge, neither did we wish to abandon our trust that we had accepted with our eyes wide open to the perils around us.

After supper we found there was scarcely enough left for break-fast. Jesse asked what we proposed doing. One of the mail company, a Frenchman, commenced talking with the Indian explaining our situation to him. He said their camp was also out of meat; that they were hungry, and that he was out prospecting for game, as there was none in the neighbourhood of their camp; but he thought he could find game next day if someone would go with him to protect him from the Crow Indians, who were supposed to be in the direction of the game. This seemed the only show, so Jesse decided to "lay over" and send out his hunter with some pack animals; also ten of our company, the stoutest and most willing. They, no doubt, would have fought the whole Crow nation to have protected our Indian friend.

Late that evening the Frenchman and Indian came into the fort with their animals loaded with good buffalo meat. I asked about the boys of our company who went out on foot. The Frenchman answered, "I left them about twenty-five miles from here roasting and eating bones and entrails; they are all right." They got in next day, each man loaded with meat. They were all delighted with the Indian, telling how he killed the buffalo with his arrows, the Frenchman shooting first and wounding the animal and the Indian doing the rest.

These Indians of the plains years back killed a great many buffalo with arrows. They would stick two arrows into a buffalo's heart, crossing their direction so that as the buffalo ran these arrows would work and cut his heart almost in two. This would soon bring the poor brute down; whereas with a single arrow in the heart they would run a long distance.

CHAPTER 16

Visit from an Indian Chief

The mail company again fitted up with packs, leaving their coaches. They took Brother Heywood with them. This time making the trip successfully. They left all the meat they could spare, taking only scant rations with them.

Brother Heywood, although very weak in body, manifested the spirit of a hero during the whole time of our suffering. I have always remembered him with the kindest of feelings. As he sometimes remarks, "rawhide makes a strong tie."

The Indian went away saying he would tell his people about us, and if they could find any meat they would divide.

It did not take long for twenty hungry men to eat up our supplies. About the 4th of March the last morsel had been eaten for breakfast. We went hunting daily, sometimes killing a little small game, but nothing of account.

Our provisions were exhausted and we had cleaned up everything before Jesse Jones came to our relief. We were now in a tight place. There was a set of harness and an old pack saddle covered with rawhide still on hand, that some of the boys considered safe to depend upon for a few days, still we had great hopes of getting something better. Our faith had been much strengthened by receiving the supplies mentioned.

As usual we went out to see what we could find in the way of game. After travelling through the snow for several miles at the foot of the mountains, we saw a drove of mountain sheep. They were standing, seemingly entirely off their guard. I was in front and saw the sheep, as I supposed before they did me. We dodged down out of sight. I crept to a large rock, fully expecting to get meat. When I looked to get a shot the game was gone, I could see it making for the top of the mountain. We watched them for a minute or two and they were soon too far for us to follow. My heart almost failed me, and I could have cried like a child, for I knew that nothing was in camp when we left and our comrades expected us to bring something for supper.

We were convinced that nothing could be obtained this day by hunting, so we started for home. After travelling a few miles we struck the road below Devil's Gate and here we stopped to hold a council.

As will be remembered, our instructions from Brother Brigham were never to leave the fort with less than ten men. There never had been a time when we had that many men able to stand very hard service. Sometimes I felt like disregarding counsel and going out to try to get food, or perish in the attempt. But up to this time we had all followed instructions as nearly as possible. Now here was a trial for me. I firmly believed I could go on foot to Platte bridge and get something to save the lives of my comrades.

Very few of the others were able, but all were willing to go with me. I told them if counsel had to be broken I would risk no one but myself, and would go alone. The boys thought they could live five days before starving. So it was arranged that I should start alone next morning for the Platte bridge. I had now been one day without food, it would take two more to reach the bridge, where there were traders, as the snow was from eighteen inches to three feet deep. This looked a little hard, but I had fully made up my mind to try it.

On arriving in sight of camp we saw a number of horses; we knew someone had arrived but had no idea who it was. A shout of joy rang out from our crowd that made the hills ring. All mankind were friends to us then. I often wonder why people are enemies. My experience in life, with a few exceptions, has been more of the friendly than warlike nature. I have been fed and helped by all classes of people, and mankind in general are not so bad when properly approached.

The new arrivals proved to be the first company of the Y. X. Express, with William Hickman in charge. This was the first effort of this firm to send the mail through. Several old acquaintances were along, and of course we were rejoiced to see them, especially so when we learned they had a good supper for us. Among the party were George Boyd of Salt Lake City and Joshua Terry of Draperville.

A day or two before their arrival Brother Terry had killed a large buffalo and they packed the whole of it into our camp.

I remember about the first thing I did after shaking hands, was to drink a pint of strong salty broth, where some salt pork had been boiled.

When Hickman's company arrived, some of our boys were getting the pack saddle soaked up ready for cooking the hide covering. Boyd always calls me the man that ate the pack saddle. But this is slander. The kindness of him and others prevented me from eating my part of it. I think if they had not arrived, probably I would have taken a *wing* or *leg*, but don't think I would have eaten the whole of it. As it was, the saddle was allowed to dry up again, and may be in existence yet and doing well so far as I know.

In Hickman's book he says he found us starving with plenty of provisions in store houses, but did not dare to take them; that on his arrival he burst open the store houses and told us to help ourselves. Can anyone believe such stuff? If all his book is like this for truth, one would do well to believe the reverse. Hickman left about the 6th of March, going on east.

Ben Hampton and myself started to go on to Platte bridge with this party, intending to get some supplies if possible. Hickman left us two animals and with one of ours (the other three had long since been eaten by the wolves) found nearby we felt ourselves rich.

We had gone but a few miles when we met some men from the Platte bringing us some beef. They had heard in some way that we were still alive. I think the Indians must have passed the word. They could not get buffalo meat, so had killed some cattle and were bringing them to us. They had been four days on the road, tramping snow and working through drifts, expecting to find us starving. I often think of these old pioneers, who were always so ready to help a fellowman in need.

We bade goodbye to Hickman and party and returned to the fort with the meat. We paid for it in goods from Brother Van Cott's boxes, paying mostly calico and domestic. They charged us ten cents per pound, which was very cheap considering.

With our animals and meat we felt quite well fitted out; for we had now become so used to taking what we could get thankfully, that we looked upon these two mules left us as sure food when all else failed.

While Jesse Jones was in camp, one of his men gave me a small book of words in the Snake language. I expected the Indians around and studied hard every day. Soon they commenced coming in to see us. There were over one hundred lodges of Snakes and Bannocks came in from the Wind river country and camped about fifteen miles from us. Small bands camped around us in different directions. They soon learned we were short of provisions.

The first party that brought meat to us wanted to charge an un-reasonable price for it. I talked with them quite a while before they would consent to sell it cheaper. They said that they themselves were hungry, showing us their bare arms, how lean they were. But I told them it was not just to take advantage of our circumstances. I weighed up a dollar's worth of meat on a pair of spring balances, marked the scales plainly and told them I would give no more. They consented, and we bought hundreds of pounds afterwards without more trouble. In buying we had to weigh one dollar's worth at a time, no matter how much they sold us.

We exchanged various articles with them, many of the company trading shirts, handkerchiefs and such things as they could spare. We had some coffee, for which the Indians traded readily. This helped us out for a short season; but game became so scarce that this camp of natives (several hundred) had to move out or starve. They came up the first day and pitched their lodges near us. We had but little provisions on hand, some meat and a few pounds of flour that we used to thicken our broth was all. We had about lost our appetite for bread. We were a little uneasy to have all these hungry Indians come upon us at once; the greatest care had to be taken to avoid trouble.

They were not of the best class, being a party made up of Snakes and Bannocks, who had left their regular tribes and chiefs and joined together under an ambitious young fellow named Tabawantooa. Washakie, the old Snake chief, called them bad men.

There was one little party under an old petty chief, Toquatah, who kept apart from the main band. From them we had procured most of our meat. Toquatah had informed us that the main band and his were not on the best of terms, and that Tabawantooa was "no good." This naturally made us feel a little uneasy. We had some two hundred wagon loads of valuable goods under our charge, and only twenty men, the greater portion of them with no frontier experience.

The store rooms were blocked up with logs, and had been all win-ter.

By this time I could talk considerable Snake and many of these Indians understood Ute.

Tabawantooa and his band came in sight of our quarters about noon. They were all mounted and well armed. The chief with many others rode up in quite a pompous style, no doubt expecting to be looked upon with awe and treated with great deference.

I had time to get my wits together before they got to our gate where an armed guard was stationed. Brother Alexander was to be chief cook. Knowing that from such as we had we would have to make a great showing of hospitality, we concluded to make up in ceremony what was lacking in food. So all the camp-kettles and coffee-pots were filled and put on. The one for weak soup the other for strong coffee. We had plenty of the latter on hand.

The company were instructed to go into their rooms, shut the doors, keep quiet, and not to show themselves unless ordered to do so. Brother Hampton was to be general roust-a-bout, ready for any emergency; I was to meet these Indians outside and invite them in the gate, as we knew the chief and *grandees* of the band would expect to be entertained.

Soon the chief with some fifty others rode up to the fort, while hundreds more passed on a short distance and commenced to put up their lodges. I met the chief, shook hands, and asked him to get down and come in. He wanted to know if they could not ride inside. I told him no, and explained to him that we had a lot of men in the fort who were afraid of Indians; that they had gone into their houses and shut the doors; but the door of my house was open for them, but that these men, who were afraid, should not be frightened; they must leave their horses and arms outside the fort.

This the chief agreed to do and appointed a man to see that no one came in with arms. Soon my room was full. I explained to the chief that we had but little to eat and could not entertain many; but half we had they were welcome to. I talked and acted as though we were glad to see them, still I, with all my friendship for Indians, would have been willing for *this* band to have taken another road.

Brother Alexander soon had plenty of weak soup and strong coffee ready; cups were filled and the feast commenced. The chief sent word for those outside to go on to camp, probably seeing his rations would be short if many more came in.

Brother Hampton kept his eye on things in general and would come in and report from time to time. All except one respected our arrangements. Indians, like white men, have their bullies. One fellow in spite of the guards rode into fort armed. Brother Hampton took his horse by the bit, and guided him back out of the gate. He was quite saucy but went out all right.

We were asked how many men were in the houses. I told them *shouts* (great many). They then wanted to know if the men had guns.

We told them "lots," which was a fact as there were more guns than men.

Indians, when hungry relish anything that tightens their belts, so our friends filled and emptied their cups many times. Soon all who had remained were satisfied, bade us goodbye, mounted their horses and started to their camp, the chief inviting us to go up and take supper with him. Went up late in the day. Some coffee had been given the chief and at supper we feasted on poor antelope meat and coffee. We were told that but one antelope had been killed that day and the chief had been presented with it.

The whole camp were about out of food except thistle roots. These were not very plentiful, as we had already dug and eaten the most that could be found for miles around our quarters.

These natives moved on next morning. Toquatah's band being still in the rear. In a day or two the last band came along and camped near us. We were glad to see them and wanted them to remain near us, but they were afraid of the Crow Indians and desired to keep in the vicinity of the larger band for protection against their common enemy.

We explained to them our destitute condition, telling them that we were again about out of provisions, and would be sorry to have them leave, for while they were near they had never let us suffer for meat.

Next morning the old chief said he would go out twelve miles to a gap in the mountains and camp, and if he could find any game he would let us have some dried meat he had reserved.

We waited a day and then went to see if our friends were prospered. Nothing had been found. Ten of us stayed all night with the Indians and we barely got enough for supper and breakfast. The chief told us to go back home; he would move on a little farther; if he found anything he would send it to us. His spirit towards us was something like a mother's with a lot of hungry children.

Now some might ask why we did not do our own hunting and not depend on the Indians. An Indian will manage to kill game where it is so scarce and wild that but few white men would even see it. We were much safer to depend upon the Indians as long as they were around in the country. Again, they considered it their business to hunt, and if we had made the attempt it would have been resented by them.

We went home feeling a little sad. We had our animals, but did not wish to kill them; still we felt safe as long as mule flesh was on hand. To our joy, next day some Indians came from their camp, bringing us some three hundred pounds of buffalo meat and informing us that they had seen signs of game; and if we would come to them the next morning, they might let us have some more.

Brother Hampton and I saddled up taking our extra animal, a large mule, and started for our friends. The weather was still cold, but the snow was mostly gone from the lowlands, it being now near the first of April. When we arrived at their camp the Indians were just starting out to move a few miles further towards where the signs of buffalo had been seen. Brother H. and I rode along with them, chatting with the old chief. We had taken a few things with us to trade for the meat. We camped in the afternoon some thirty miles from home. The old chief called out and soon the squaws commenced bringing in a few pounds each of good dried meat. We traded for about three hundred pounds—all our mule could pack and about all the Indians could spare. This, of course, was all we could expect, but the old chief said maybe they could do more for us in the morning.

I think Brother Hampton and I really enjoyed ourselves that night. We slept in a lodge, ate meat, and drank coffee. The squaws' dirt, or dogs sticking their noses into the meat dishes, made no difference to us; or if it did we ate all the same.

Next morning after breakfast, we saddled up, packing our dried meat on the mule. As we were about ready to start there was quite a commotion in camp. We thought at first the Crow Indians were upon us, but the old chief, looking in an easterly direction said, "It is some of the young men driving a buffalo. Now goodbye. You go on your road (our track was to the north) and you wilt find some more meat ready for you soon."

We started and had gone but a short distance, probably three miles, when we found the buffalo that was being chased had been run into our trail, killed and made ready to deliver to us. We gave them some few things we had left and they loaded both of our saddle animals. This left us nearly thirty miles to go afoot. We did not mind this on the start, but did before we got home.

CHAPTER 17

Our Safe Return to Camp

I had been wearing *moccasins* all winter, had done a great deal of walking and had felt well and strong; but the winter had commenced to break and there was mud and wet snow to encounter on our trip. Someone had induced me to put on a pair of heavy, stiff-soled English shoes. About sundown I gave out; got so lame that it was impossible for me to wear the shoes and travel. We had about ten miles to go yet, and no trail, as the Indian trail was much longer than to cross directly over the country, and we wished to take the shortest cut. Moreover there was still a few inches of snow on the ground part of the way on the most direct route.

We were bent on getting to camp that night, if possible, so determined to keep going. I was compelled to pull off my "stoggas" and go in my stocking feet. This did very well till the snow gave out, which it did as we got on to lower country. My socks soon failed then, and the ground commenced to freeze hard. Travelling became slightly unpleasant to me. I put on the shoes again, but could not possibly walk; it was as though my shin bones were being broken at every step. (Some may wonder why my companion did not change his foot gear with me. The reason was he wore a number six shoe, and I could squeeze on a number ten. Will that do?)

So I determined to go bare-footed. It now became really unpleasant, for the country was spotted with prickly pears (thorny cactus). When I placed my number ten foot, pressed down by my 175-pound body, on these desert ornaments, they had a piercing effect, often causing me to halt. Several times it hurt so badly that I dropped, desiring to take a seat so that I could pull the thorns out of my feet, but on striking the ground I had a sudden desire to rise, as the cactus formed the only place to sit. This was really amusing. Still, I soon had enough of this fun and commenced to figure how to avoid having any more of it. The horses dreaded the cactus, and if left to pick the road would avoid them; so we allowed them to go ahead. I carefully watched their tracks and followed them, getting along much better after this.

About midnight we got in, my feet a little the worse for wear; but so happy were we with our success that my feet soon got well.

Another blessing had befallen the company while we were gone. Three large work oxen, one wearing a big bell, had come into camp. These cattle had travelled nearly one hundred miles from where they had been lost; they were in fair order. We supposed the reason why the wolves had not killed them was that the noise of the bell scared them away.

With the meat on hand and these cattle we felt pretty safe for the balance of the season. We had hopes of keeping a yoke of the cattle to haul wood with, this having been done all winter with a light wagon, ten men for team, or in hand-carts. The ice was melted on the river and in going for wood it had to be waded. This was hard on the boys, and we were very grateful for the cattle.

About this time the second company of the Y. X. Express, under Jet Stoddard, passed down. They had but little to spare us, but we were now out of danger. We got a little flour, salt and bacon.

The word was that the next company would bring us flour. The most of us had got so we cared but little for bread if we could have plenty of meat. Our cattle were our pets now. We hauled up a lot of wood. The grass being quite good off toward the east, the cattle were taken out every day. At night someone went and brought them in and corralled them. Our horses were hoppled in sight of camp, where they ran day and night.

One evening the boys who went for the oxen came in rather late without them, saying that they could not hear the bell. We supposed they had laid down for the night; still, we were anxious, as our meat was about out and we expected to soon butcher the fattest of them.

Early next morning Brother Hampton and I saddled up and started out before breakfast to hunt the cattle, not expecting to be gone more than an hour. We soon struck their trail going east, most of the time showing they were on the move, not often feeding. At sundown we were about thirty miles from camp, still trailing and tolerably hungry; but that trail *could not be left.* We followed on, the tracks running almost parallel with the road but gradually nearing it. It now became too dark to see the trail.

We were continually expecting to hear the bell, but no bell sounded. We continued in the same direction until we reached the main road. After following it a short distance Brother Hampton dismounted and felt for tracks. He soon decided that the cattle were now on the road as he could feel the tracks where the ground had been lately disturbed, the road being dry and soft in places. Thus we continued to travel for some four or five miles feeling for tracks.

At length we came to a gulch crossing the road, several feet deep and full of snow. We could see where the cattle had crossed as the moon was now up and we could trail quite well; but on attempting to cross the drift, we sank down. At this season of the year these snow-drifts freeze in the night time, thawing out in the afternoon and gradually melting away so that from noon until after midnight it is impossible for a horse to cross them; men often crossing on hands and knees, or if the snow is quite soft lying down and rolling across. This we could have done but our horses did not feel as anxious as we did to go on; so when we proposed to them to roll across the drift, they pretended not to understand us.

We followed up the drift for quite a distance, but it remained the same white streak of snow as far as we could see by moonlight, so we concluded to turn in until morning when the snow would be hardened. It was now getting quite chilly, we had eaten nothing all day, all the bedding we had was a couple of small saddle blankets, and there was nothing to make a fire with but a little green sagebrush. But if there had been fuel we would have been afraid to light a fire as the Crow Indians were in the country and might steal our horses.

We went to "ground" but did not sleep much. It soon became so cold that we almost froze to death. When we thought the snow was hard enough we got up, but were so chilled we could not saddle our horses. We were almost lifeless, and commenced stirring about to bring life back. We commenced bumping against each other, sometimes knocking one another down. We got to laughing at the ridiculousness of our actions, more life returned, our teeth began chattering and our bodies shaking, but we kept up this jostling each other until we started circulation and were able to saddle up and go on. It was daylight before we got thawed out. We walked until we got well warmed up the trail following right on the road.

About ten o'clock a. m. we found the cattle. They had finally turned off the road to feed. We were now about forty-five miles from home. The first thing I proposed after finding the cattle was to cut their tails off, tie a string around the stubs to keep them from bleeding, roast the tails and eat them, for I felt wolfish. Ben objected, saying it might weaken the cattle and that he believed we could stand it back home; that the cattle were good travellers and may be we could reach the fort by midnight. Our horses (or rather, horse and mule. As I will soon have to deal a little with a mule it will not do to call him a horse now) were all right, having been on good feed the night before. The cattle, on being turned back, took the road in good shape, starting on a trot.

We were anxious to get back and cross the snowdrift before it softened up. This we succeeded in doing, and continued travelling until after noon before "bating." We had more sympathy for ourselves than for our animals, for we were getting a little hungry and dreaded the thought of having to "go to ground" again. So we kept up our speed. Finally Ben's mule began to weaken. We had considerable trouble to get it along, but by one leading and the other walking and whipping we got to Independence Rock, where there were three or four men camped in some old houses. This was about six miles from our fort. Here we had a trial I think few men would have stood. As we rode up they had a good fire burning, a nice supper cooked and were just ready to commence eating.

They had stayed the night before at our camp where they had arrived destitute and out of provisions. Brother Alexander had told them about us. Our company was very anxious about us. They had given these poor fellows what provisions they could spare, enough to last them to Platte bridge provided they made the trip in reasonable time. One of the party had frozen his feet and was suffering terribly. We soon learned their condition, but they insisted on us eating supper. We thought of the poor lame fellow getting out of food; we were within six miles of home so we pretended that we were not very hungry, and advised them to be careful of what they had and we would go on home. The smell of the food to us was like piercing our stomachs with a dagger. It was really hard to refuse taking a few bites, but we did.

When we had got about halfway home I went ahead with the cattle, Ben driving the tired mule. I wished to get in and have supper ready by the time my comrade arrived, which I did not suppose would be over one half hour. On arriving at the fort, most of the company were up waiting in suspense our arrival.

Brother Alexander had a camp kettle full of meat and soup with dumplings ready. It was rations for seven men. He had kept it warm all day, and commenced to dish some up for me, but I told him that I would not eat a bite until Ben came. It was more than an hour before he arrived, the give-out mule having broken loose and ran away from him and he had been following it. Finally he arrived, bringing the mule and feeling very much like beefing it when he got home.

All now was ready for our supper. We sat down on some wolf skins before the fire, the camp-kettle in reach, and commenced to eat, but not hurriedly. Before daylight we had emptied the kettle. We relished this feast fully and did not suffer any inconvenience. Both of us were well and feeling first rate next day after having a good sleep. As the cattle were so much bother we concluded to kill them.

CHAPTER 18

A Relief Party Arrives

About this time another Y. X. company, under Porter Rockwell and John Murdock, arrived going east. They gave us a little flour and other provisions; they also brought us letters telling us when the relief train would arrive. With the three head of cattle and what this company furnished us, we felt safe for supplies until time for the relief trains.

Here I will give an account of a little personal matter that may seem like boasting, but I do not intend it so. This company stayed with us two nights. They were picked men, thirty in number, able-bodied, tough boys. On hearing of our sufferings many remarks were made showing deep sympathy for us.

At this time we were well recruited, having had plenty of meat for some time but scarcely any flour for some five months. Bread we had hardly tasted. In fact, the first biscuit I got almost choked me, I had entirely lost my appetite for it.

The morning the Y. X. company were getting ready to start on, a young man, Mr. Eldredge, who was going down as a passenger, expressed much indignation, saying that there could be no excuse for leaving men to suffer as we had. I did not like to hear this said, for I knew there were justifiable reasons for leaving us to take care of the goods. I also knew Brothers Grant and Burton would have sent us help if they could. It was expected that the cattle left would have been better beef than they turned out to be.

I had neither time nor disposition to explain all these things, so to stop the talk that I had got a little tired of hearing, I said to Mr. Eldredge, "We do not need your sympathy; we are all right now; none of us have died, and I am a better man than any of your company, picked men as you are."

"How do you propose to prove this, Mr. Jones? Will you pull sticks with our best man? I will not allow you rawhide-fed fellows to banter the corn-fed boys that way."

I was a little fearful that I was "sold," for I knew there were some stout men in their company; but as the banter was made, to back out would be worse than to get beat, so I said, "Bring him on; I will hoist him."

Mr. Eldredge came back with John Murdock, who was smiling. Now I really wished I had not made the banter, for John was an old friend who was hard to pull up.

A ring was formed, both companies helping to form a circle. "Rawhide against corn" was the cry. We sat down and got an even start. It was a hard pull, but "Rawhide" won, and we got no more pity from that company.

Making a close estimate of the food we now had, we found it would last us till the promised provisions could arrive, which would be about the 1st of May.

There were twenty of us now. We quit rationing and ate all we wanted. As may be imagined, some big eating was done. Now the food soon began to diminish very fast. At this time we could go to the Platte bridge and get provisions, but on calling the company together all hands agreed to make the meat last by again rationing. We could do this quite easily, allowing one and a half pounds per day. We lived a few days on these rations and all seemed content.

One day Brother Hampton and I were out and on returning to the fort we learned that a small herd of buffalo had been seen passing within three miles of the fort. All hands were excited, as they were the first seen for a long time. The boys were all sure that Ben and I could get meat and we could again go to feasting. We started out and soon came in sight of the buffalo feeding. We dismounted and crept close to them, but just as we got in shooting distance it commenced to snow so hard that we could not see to shoot with any certainty. We sat there trying to get sight of a buffalo until our fingers were too much benumbed to hold our guns. I had brought an extra gun in anticipation of having to chase the buffalo on horseback. We concluded to blaze away, hit or miss, and then take to our horses and have a running shot. At the crack of our guns all the herd ran away. We mounted and started in pursuit.

The horse I was riding could easily outrun the buffalo, but for the life of me I could not get him up along side of one. When I would follow straight behind he would get within about twenty-five yards, but when I would try to get him up nearer he would bolt and run off to one side. This game we kept up for some time. Occasionally the buffalo would get two or three hundred yards away from me, when the horse would start in after them and soon run up to about the same distance, then he would bolt again. I felt almost like blowing his brains out. I finally commenced shooting at the buffalo, but to no purpose. As none were killed we had to give up the chase and go home without meat, feeling quite chagrined.

We had not been in camp long until I was informed that there was a great dissatisfaction being manifested by some of the company about the rations. I immediately called the company together to see what was the trouble. Several expressed themselves quite freely, finding fault for being rationed when provisions could now be had, and saying that they thought I ought to go and get something to eat and not have them suffer any more. This grieved me very much as I had a kindly feeling towards all the company. We had suffered everything that men could suffer and live. We had often been on the point of starvation. Sometimes becoming so weak that we could scarcely get our firewood, having to go some distance to the mountain for it.

We were now all in good health and had, as I understood, willingly agreed to be rationed for a few days, until relief came from Salt Lake City. I did not care so much for the trouble of going for provisions, but I felt a great deal of pride in the grit of the company and this was a sore disappointment for me, for no one had just reason to find fault. All I said was, "Well, brethren, I will go and get you all you want. Now pitch in and eat your fill. I will have more by the time you eat up what is on hand."

Brother Hampton felt very indignant at the faultfinders. He told them that they would soon be ashamed of themselves; spoke of the hardships we had endured uncomplainingly, and of the hard labours in hunting, and many efforts made to keep alive. Now when we were about through and no one suffering, some had shown their true colours, and marred their credit for being true men. Ben got warm and finally said, "You will regret this. Instead of having to wait twelve days there will be plenty of provisions here inside of twelve hours, and then you will wish you had kept still." At this he ceased talking, sat down and turned to me saying a little excitedly, "What do think? Will it come?"

I said "Yes," for I felt the prophecy would be fulfilled. Sure enough that same evening twenty men arrived at our camp bringing nearly a ton of flour and other provisions.

This company had been sent to strengthen our post. They informed us that there was a large company of apostates on the road led by Tom S. Williams. Before leaving Salt Lake some of this company had made threats that indicated danger to us.

The circumstances leading to the threats were these. The goods we were guarding belonged to the last season's emigrants. The wagon companies freighting them through agreed to deliver them in Salt Lake City. These goods were to be taken in and delivered as by contract. Some of the owners had become dissatisfied with "Mormonism" and were going back to the States. As their goods had not arrived in Salt Lake City, they demanded that they should be delivered at Devil's Gate. Quite a number settled their freight bills and brought orders for their goods and received them all right. Others refused to settle, but threatened that if the goods were not given up they would take them by force. Tom Williams' company was composed largely of this class and their backers. They numbered about fifty men. The twenty men coming to our relief were sent under the emergency. This is the way Brother Hampton's prophecy came to be fulfilled.

Tom Williams knew nothing of this company, as they had slipped out and got ahead of him and arrived long enough before him for us to get everything ready. We now had forty men well armed, the twenty sent us being picked for the occasion. As I cannot remember all their names I will simply say for the purpose they were all first-class men. Our old company were reliable. As Ben had said they would be, they were a little ashamed, but nothing farther was said, and the boys showed their repentance by doing their duties now.

Our instructions were to deliver no goods to anyone unless they presented an order from the right parties.

When Williams' company arrived they made camp near our fort. Most of our men were kept out of sight. There were rooms each side of the front door, where we had a guard placed.

A person that claimed a lot of goods had come on the evening before and presented an order that was not genuine. He had reported to his friends our refusing to let him have his goods. Soon Williams and a few others came up and said if we did not give up the goods that they would tear down the fort or have them. Williams was well known to most of us; by marriage he was my wife's uncle. I informed him that we intended to obey instructions. He raved and threatened considerable, but to no purpose. He started to his camp with the avowed intention of returning and taking the goods.

I now got my company ready for fight if necessary We had prepared port holes in front of the fort and here I stationed some of the best shots.

Brothers Hampton and Alexander took charge of our company. The company that came to strengthen us working together under their leader. Soon we saw Tom Williams approaching with his backers. As he supposed double our number, but in reality near the same. I did not wish blood shed, and fully believed that Tom was playing a "bluff," so concluded to try and beat him at the game. I instructed some of the best marksmen what to do in case shooting had to be done.

As Williams approached I went out alone and stood about thirty yards from the fort, having only my pistol. As the company came up near me I placed my hand on my pistol and told them to halt. They halted but commenced to threaten and abuse the whole fraternity sparing none. I explained our situation, being simply custodians of the goods, not knowing whose they were; but only knew who left us there, and we could not consistently recognise any orders except from those under whose instructions we were acting. My reasoning had no effect whatever, but Tom called on his crowd to say if the goods should be taken. The vote was to take them.

Now that no one may suppose that I wish to appear brave, I will say that the way I had my men placed, and the instructions given, if a weapon had been drawn on me, half Williams' company would have been shot dead before I could have been harmed.

I said to Williams just hold on one minute and hear what I have to say:

We have been here all winter eating poor beef and raw hide to take care of these goods. We have had but little fun, and would just as soon have some now as not; in fact would like a little row. If you think you can take the fort just try it. But I don't think you can take me to commence with; and the first one that offers any violence to me is a dead man. Now I dare you to go past me towards the fort.

This seemed to take them back. I meant what I said, and some of them knew my disposition, which in those days, was not the most Christian-like when a white man was before me as an enemy.

After looking at me a moment Tom said, "For your family's sake

I will spare you, for I think you d——d fool enough to die before you would give up the goods." I thanked him and said I believed as he did.

After this we had no more trouble. Many times I have thought I should have shown our force openly to have deterred Williams, but he was such a known bully and so conceited that I felt just like "taking him down a notch," and this did it.

CHAPTER 19

I am Accused of Stealing

The wagons being sent out for the goods soon began to arrive. Provisions were not in question now, as we had plenty. There was also a big Y. X. company, Levi Stewart in charge, going down to stock the road, and a company of Elders travelling with hand-carts came through from Salt Lake City. It was about one week from the first arrival until the last of these arrived.

President Young had sent me several letters containing instructions of various kinds pertaining to my duties; but one particular letter of definite instructions how to arrange many things, had not arrived. I kept waiting for it, as there were many things to do that I had no instructions about. I kept enquiring but no letter came. Finally all were in. I asked some of the older and more experienced Elders what I should do. Their answer was that they were also expecting instructions and that they were more in need of counsel than able to give it.

There were over two hundred teams now on the ground, many of the owners beginning to get impatient at the delay. I was at a loss what to do, so I went out after night and asked the Lord to help me out. I told Him I desired to do exactly what was best, but did not know a thing about it, and made this proposition that I would take my clerk with me in the morning, and when a question was asked me by any one what to do, I would tell the clerk to write down just what first came to my mind. And if that was right to please remove the spirit of oppression that I was labouring under and allow me to go back to the fort and enjoy myself with my friends. My mind was at once entirely relieved. I went and passed a pleasant evening.

Next morning without saying anything about the lack of instructions we commenced business. Soon someone asked whose teams were to be loaded first, I dictated to my clerk. Thus we continued. As fast as the clerk put them down, orders would be given, and we passed on to the next. We continued this for four days. Everything that I felt to be my duty was done. All the teams were loaded up, companies organised and started back, men detailed to remain a while longer. Elders furnished flour, and a great deal of business was done. A memorandum was kept of all this.

I hitched up a team and started for home when everything was in shape. I reached Salt Lake City a few hours ahead of the freight teams, and went to President Young's office. He was very glad to see me, expressing much sympathy and saying that if he had known of our suffering in time he would have sent us supplies at any cost. I acted a little stiff for I did not know whether my management of the last business would be approved of or not, but I was determined to defend my actions, for I knew I had done the best I could.

Soon Brother Young asked me if I had attended to everything in order before leaving. My reply was, "I hope I did but do not know."

"Well, you acted according to my instructions, did you not?"

"I don't know. I did not get any instructions, and it was pretty hard on me."

I handed him my book saying: "Here is a report of what we did; I hope it is satisfactory."

Brother Brigham asked his clerk, T. D. Brown, about the letter of instructions. Brother Brown said a few days after the last of these companies left, in looking over his papers he found a letter directed to D. W. Jones. It was the letter that should have been sent.

Brother Brigham commenced reading my report, and as he read would remark, "That is right; this is right. Well, you seemed to get along all right."

I began to feel pretty good. Finally Brother Brown was told to look over the letter, which was very large, containing many items of special instructions. My report agreed with the whole of it. This confirmed me more than ever in my faith in inspiration. Also in the honesty of Brigham Young and his counselling, for if his instructions had not been honest I would never have been inspired to anticipate them. The trouble lies with us; we many times want to dictate the inspiration, or, in other words, put forward our own ideas and desires and call them inspirations.

I met my mother-in-law in Salt Lake City and heard from my wife and two children, who were living with Father P. Colton in Provo. We started for home the next day, where I met my family after so long and severe a trip. It was with joy and thankfulness that I greeted my wife, who was one of the best and most faithful wives that ever blessed a husband.

This was the spring after what is known as the winter of the Reformation. The reformation move was doubtless intended for and resulted in good; but like everything else where good is found the devil comes along to see what's up. So it was nothing strange if while browsing around he had a hand in some of the moves of men. This I soon became satisfied was the case now, and I did not take much "stock" in what some people called reformation.

When I left Devil's Gate, it was with the understanding that I was to return there and take charge of the place as a Y. X. station, but Brother Brigham countermanded the order, saying that I had had enough of Devil's Gate for one man.

As I was so sure of going back when I left Devil's Gate I had left my gun, saddle, a wagon that I had traded for, as well as a lot of carriage springs that I had gathered up.

In these days there were many things thrown away on the plains that were of value, and it was profitable to go back with teams and gather up wagon tires and other things which had been abandoned. I spoke to Brother Brigham about this. He said he wished me to stop in the city long enough to help deliver the goods to the owners. Patrick Lynch and myself were appointed to take charge of them.

I soon learned that strange stories had been put in circulation about me. I was accused of stealing and hiding away thousands of dollars' worth of goods. As there was no communication between us and the valley how this started was a mystery, only to be accounted for by men's imaginations. So strong was the belief in my guilt that about the time the reformation was at its height in Provo, a teacher came to visit my wife, telling her that she ought to leave me and marry some good man. I could give the name of the teacher, but he is now dead so I will spare his memory. My wife answered, "Well I will not leave Daniel Jones. I cannot better myself, for if he will steal there is not an honest man on earth." I always appreciated the answer.

One family who I will also spare as *they* are not yet dead came to search my house for stolen goods but did not find any. They professed to be very sorry for having come. My wife treated them with perfect civility; no doubt they were ashamed of themselves and are to this day when they think of the indignity. While delivering their goods I was often accused of having robbed people. The goods formerly spoken of being divided to *cache* were never replaced and I had to bear the blame. Again, before the trains had stopped in the snow-storms, so I was informed by some of the brethren who stayed at Devil's Gate, there had been a number of heavy boxes emptied, the goods stuffed into sacks and the boxes broken up for firewood. The owners of course looked in vain for their boxes. Many sacks of goods remained at the Tithing Office for a long time before being identified by the owners of the goods. I believe the most of these articles finally got where they belonged. But in the meantime I was "Paddy Miles' boy," who had done all the mischief. Brother Lynch felt so indignant that he reported these accusations to President Young when I received the following letter:

President's Office, Great Salt Lake City,
June 11th, 1857.

To the Bishops and Presidents in Utah,
Beloved Brethren:

Inasmuch as there are some persons disposed to find fault with the management of Brother Daniel W. Jones while at Devil's Gate, we feel desirous to express ourselves perfectly satisfied with his labours while there, and with the care that he has taken of the property entrusted to him. He has our confidence, and we say, God bless him for what he has done. The men who find fault with the labours of Brother Jones the past winter, we wish their names sent to this office, and when the Lord presents an opportunity we will try them and see if they will do any better.

Brigham Young,
Daniel H. Wells,
George D. Grant.

CHAPTER 20

The President's Stern Reproof to My Accusers

My wife remained in the city with me during the time we were delivering the goods, some three weeks. After getting through, I, in company with W. Roberts of Provo, fitted up a team and went back to trade.

Roberts remained at the South Pass while I went down with two yoke of oxen to Devil's Gate. It maybe interesting to some to give a brief description of my trip going down, some ninety miles. Stephen Markham was in charge of the Y. X. station at the South Pass. He had nine head of good milk cows in charge which he had orders to send to Devil's Gate for the use of men stationed there. He offered to furnish me a horse if I would drive them down. This was agreeable, as I would have had to foot it otherwise.

As I could not carry provisions very well, and having money, it was supposed that I could buy bread at least, as there were trains of California emigrants continually on the road. Cups were scarce, so when I started out I had nothing but my blankets and gun. I happened to have a new clay pipe in my pocket. After asking several persons to sell me a cup and some bread and being refused, concluded to see if I could not get through with what I had. The cows all gave plenty of milk and were gentle. I necessarily had to milk them to keep their udders from spoiling. So when I would get a cow all milked but the strippings I would put the stem of the pipe into my mouth and milk into the bowl and draw the milk through. This was about the same as sucking "mint julep" with a straw. I enjoyed it immensely, being fond of new milk.

I found it so much better than eating rawhide that I ceased asking the emigrants I met for either a cup or bread. I made the trip through in less than four days; probably felt a little "calfish" but never lost my flesh or strength.

While at Devil's Gate on this trip some parties arrived from the states bringing news of the army being ordered to Utah; and that the mail contract which had been let to Brigham Young and company was cancelled, and that in consequence of this the Y. X. (Young's Express) companies were all called home. This was startling news, as all had been at peace and nothing to justify the move could be surmised. The cause of this whole raid and the result are matters of history, so I will not mention the subject at present.

After getting my stuff together two of the brethren who had stayed there during the winter accompanied me and we started back towards South Pass, making the trip in good time. My partner, Mr. Roberts, having traded to good advantage, we were soon ready to start home.

On arriving in Salt Lake City I went to the Tithing Office as I had some articles belonging there. I was informed that Brother Brigham wished to see me. I went at once to his office, not even taking time to wash my face. As I got to the outside door of Brother Young's office I met him coming out alone. After shaking hands, inquiring after my health, etc., he said, "Come, let us take a little walk. I want to talk to you." We started and went toward his barn in the rear of his dwelling. He informed me that there had been a formal complaint made against me for robbing the people of their goods while at Devil's Gate; said these complaints were made by some of the Elders in behalf of themselves and others. He gave the names of some of my accusers. He then asked, "Are you willing to meet these accusations and answer them?"

I replied, "Yes, sir, I am both willing and glad of the opportunity." At the same time I gave the names of some I wished as witnesses.

He then said, "Be here in ten days from today and we will hear these complaints."

I felt quite sore and would like to have had a little consolation from Brother Brigham, but he commenced moving about, showing me his horses and cattle and chatting till we returned to his office. His manner was kind and pleasant. He asked me about my trip and success. Also made some remarks about the army; saying that we would have a busy time soon. Said the boys were going out to meet the army and see about getting the road clear so that there would be no obstructions in the way until they got near enough to us that we could see what was best to do with them without having to go too far; that he had sent word to have everything belonging to the mail company on the road, all goods and everything "Mormon" started west as soon as possible.

It was harvest time when I got home to Provo. I felt almost sick. I had never taken to the amount of a cent anything except such as we were compelled to use, and these were always kept in account by the clerk. As I had many opportunities to take goods and hide them and no one be the wiser, and as goods had been misplaced, people were not entirely to blame for accusing me after the stories had once got in circulation. The originators of these accusations were the more responsible parties. Many of the stories originated with the man who left his keys with me. To please his family and other relatives he had collected for presents considerable stuff while on his mission. Some of these things he had given away to the brethren, as heretofore mentioned. I believe he left his trunks and keys with me in perfect good faith at the time.

After getting home he naturally supposed we would use much of his stuff and that this would justify him in accounting not only for what he had given away but for all that his good-heartedness would have caused him to do for his family. So there was nothing mentioned scarcely but what he was fetching them, provided it was not taken from his trunks. When his goods arrived and many of these fine things were missing, (one bill of fifty pairs of silk stockings among the rest) of course "Jones stole them." I carried his keys all winter in my pocket, entrusting them to no one, so of course I knew whether anything was stolen or not.

It was this same man's wife that came to search for stolen goods during the winter. There was so much rascality brought to light that winter that it was no wonder that nearly everyone except my wife and family thought I was guilty.

The emigrants, taking their cue from this brother, passed my name far and wide as a great robber. So much so that I was refused admittance into a quorum of Seventies at Provo that I had formerly been invited to join.

I returned home and worked a few days in the harvest field. I said but little to anyone about my coming trial. I was tempted at times to leave the country, for it seemed to me that I had no friends. The devil tempted me continually to believe that President Young would believe my accusers, they being men of influence. Then there was another spirit whispering to me, saying, "You are innocent; he is a prophet and will understand the truth." This spirit prevailed.

On arriving at President Young's office August 25th, 1857, I found quite a number present. I was asked if I was ready for the hearing. I replied that I did not see my witnesses. President Young answered: "When we need them we will send for them." I was then called upon to give my report and show how we had lived, what the cost of living was, etc. I had an account of all our expenditures, which amounted to about 75 cts. a week for each man. Someone remarked that we could not live so cheaply. Then began quite a discussion over our cheap living. Some were inclined to question my statement. Brother Young said to me, "Brother Jones, get up and tell the brethren just how you lived, and explain to them why your accounts only amount to 75 cts. a week."

I then made the statement that we had killed and eaten forty head of cattle that were so poor they were dying; we had lived on the meat and hides some two months; that we had not credited the owners anything for them, as we thought it was worth the cattle to eat them. That we had killed some game at various times. That was ours, no credit allowed; had lived two weeks on thistles dug from the frozen ground, no credit; one week on native garlic; three days on minnows caught with a dip-net, fish too small to clean, rather bitter in taste, no credit; several meals on prickly pear leaves roasted, no credit; several days without anything much but water to drink, no credit; some five months mostly on short rations without bread or salt. These were about all the reasons for the price being so low. The seventy-five cents per week covered all the meats bought of Indians or anyone else. All groceries, soap, candles, in fact everything used belonging to the companies, including some leather owned by F. D. Richards, who remarked to me that he was glad it was there for us to use. Brothers Jas. Ferguson and W. C. Dunbar also made the same remark about some groceries used of theirs. Not so with some others. They grieved very much over what stuff had been used of theirs.

After I got through making my statements. Brother Young asked each of my accusers what they had to say. No one answered. Then he spoke each man's name, asking them one at a time if they believed what I had said. All replied in the affirmative. He asked each one if they believed I had been honest, and taken good care of their goods. All answered "Yes."

Brother Young then stood up and said to the brethren, "You have accused Bro. Jones of stealing from you and others whom you represent, some five thousand dollars worth of goods. These accusations commenced in the winter when Brother Jones and companions were eating raw hide and poor meat, suffering every privation possible to take care of your stuff. How such stories started when there was no communication can only be accounted for by the known power of Satan to deceive and lie. These accusations continued until I, hearing of them, wrote a letter to the Bishops and Presidents, expressing my confidence in Brother Jones' labours; knowing at that time, as well as I do now, that he was innocent. I knew what Brother Jones' feelings were the other day when I notified him of this trial."

Turning to me he said, "You wanted to ask me if I thought you guilty, but I gave you no chance to ask the question. I wanted you to learn that when I decide anything, as I had in your case, I do not change my mind. You were not brought here for trial for being guilty, but to give you a chance to stop these accusations." Then turning to my accusers again, "How does this look? After charging Brother Jones as you have, he makes a simple statement, affirming nothing, neither witnessing anything, and each of you say you believe he has told the truth. You have nothing to answer save that he is an honest man. Well, now, what have you brought him here for?"

One of the complainers then asked if some of the company with me might not have stolen the goods. I answered "No; I am here to answer for all. Besides it would have been almost impossible for anyone besides myself to have taken anything unbeknown to others."

Bro. —— asked, "If neither Bro. Jones nor the brethren with him have taken anything, how is it that I have lost so much?"

Brother Brigham replied, "It is because you lie. You have not lost as you say you have."

This I knew to be correct as before stated, I had this brother's keys and knew that nothing had been taken.

Brother Brigham continued talking, chastising some of the Elders present for their ingratitude. Brother Kimball also felt indignant toward them. Finally Brother Brigham commenced to pronounce a curse upon those who had spoken falsely about me. I asked him to stop before he had finished the words, and told him I could bear their accusations better than they could bear his curse. He then blessed me, saying they would be cursed if they did not cease their talk; saying that we had seen the hardest time that any Elders ever had. While the "Mormon" Battalion suffered, they were free to travel looking forward with hope to something better; but that we were much longer under suffering conditions, as we were tied up and had no hope only to stay and take our chances.

When done speaking he asked me what would satisfy me and what demands I had to make. I told him of the refusal to admit me into the quorum at Provo, saying that if I was considered worthy, I would like a recommend so as to have fellowship there.

The following letter was given me:

Great Salt Lake City, Presidents Office,
Aug. 25th, 1857.

This is to certify to all whom it may concern, that we, the undersigned, have investigated the matters between Daniel W. Jones and the brethren who stayed with him at Devil's Gate, last winter, and those who left goods at that place, and we are satisfied that Brother Jones and those with him did the best they possibly could, were perfectly honest, and that Brother Jones has satisfactorily accounted for all the things which were taken; and they were necessarily taken to save the lives of himself and company.

We consider that Brother Jones is entitled to the praise, confidence and respect of all good men for the wise, self-denying and efficient course he pursued. And we recommend him to all as a faithful brother in good standing and full fellowship in the Church of Jesus Christ of Latter-day Saints.

(Signed)

Brigham Young,	Daniel Spencer,
Heber C. Kimball,	John Van Cott,
Daniel H. Wells,	George D. Grant,
John Taylor,	C. H. Wheelock,
Amasa Lyman,	Edmund Ellsworth,

F. D. Richards.

T. W. Ellerbeck
Clerk.

Brother Brigham said if we had set fire to the whole outfit and run off by the light of it he would never have found fault. So the trial ended and I went home feeling pretty well.

I was asked many years after this trial by a son-in-law of one of my accusers if Brother Brigham did not favour me in the trial because we had been partial and used others' goods, leaving Brother Brigham's alone.

I replied, "No, sir; Brother Brigham had no goods whatever at

Devil's Gate. Neither had his name ever showed on box or bale, therefore he could not have favoured us on that account. He decided as he did simply because he was just and right. Whether we were all naturally honest or not, we were honest this trip, at least; for there was hardly a day but what starvation stared us in the face, and we were not much inclined to pilfer dry goods anyway."

I presented my recommend to the quorum which now received me into their fellowship. After this some few came to me asking about goods in rather an accusing manner. I referred them to Brother Brigham. So far and wide had the stories gone, that many took advantage of them. One old lady, an emigrant, who went to live in Provo, played a sharp game, but was found out. She had three daughters who were all married soon after getting in. These young ladies, as is usual with English girls, had a nice lot of linen. So when the luggage arrived, in the spring, the old lady came from Provo for the family goods. She, considering her daughters provided for, and being thrifty in her nature and liking to appear well, took her daughters' linen and traded it for furniture.

The reader must know that in those days anything from a pumpkin to a petticoat was a legal tender for some amount, so the old lady had no trouble in making the exchange. She went back feeling indignant at "Jones" for robbing her daughters. She was a great tea-party woman and never missed a chance to tell of my cruel conduct, sometimes shedding tears over it.

One man who had married a daughter became a little suspicious, so he went to the city and visited the furniture dealer, and soon found the linen. He told me of the circumstance and asked me what I wished done, as he considered it an outrage. I told him it was not worth noticing, as there were so many similar things; to let the old woman and her daughters settle their own affairs, that would be punishment enough. I could tell of many more but this will suffice. Some of these stories were related during the investigation.

CHAPTER 21

The Echo Canyon War

I will not attempt to give a full account of the Echo Canyon war but will give only sufficient to connect this history.

Word reached Utah on the twenty-fourth of July, 1857, while the people were celebrating Pioneer day in Big Cottonwood Canyon that U. S. troops were on the road to Utah. As soon as this report was confirmed, and the intentions of the invaders fully learned—which were to place the Territory under martial law, on the pretext that the "Mormons" were in a state of rebellion—Brigham Young, both as President of the Church, and Governor of the Territory, commenced to advise and issue orders to meet the situation. The far-off settlements, San Bernardino in Lower California and Carson Valley, Nevada, both thrifty, prosperous places, were broken up and the people called home to Utah. There was a determined spirit manifested by both leaders and people to be ready to meet in the best possible way whatever might come. No fear nor timidity was shown. Neither was there lack of counsel, but everything that was required to be done was promptly directed and as promptly executed.

A few companies of cavalry militia were sent out to reconnoitre. Nothing official could be done by Governor Young on rumour. Finally an armed force not officially known to him was found invading the Territory of Utah. As soon as this was reported. The governor ordered General Wells to interrupt them and hinder their approach, and protect the people of the Territory from the invading foe.

The question may be asked, did not President Young and the people know that these were government troops? President Young and the people knew it was a political mob; Governor Young, not being notified officially of their coming, only knew them as an armed enemy entering the Territory. He was appointed by the President of the United States to govern under the laws common in the country. According to his oath of office, he could do no less than try to protect his Territory. Governor Young had no more right to know this army than had the sentinel on duty to know his captain unless the captain gives the counter sign. This Johnston at first refused to give, but as the sequel shows, never got in until he "hollowed turkey."

This force continued to advance. The troops ordered out by General Wells did what they could to hinder their progress toward the valleys. The situation finally became so serious that companies were ordered from Davis, Salt Lake, and Utah counties to fortify Echo canyon. I went with the regiment from Utah under Colonal Pace, and had charge of a few picked riflemen. We remained in Echo during the winter fortifying the place.

The boys on the plains made it very disagreeable for the advancing army nightly, running off their beef herd, burning their provision trains and the grass, and in every way possible impeding their progress. Finally, winter set in with severity, catching them in the mountains at Fort Bridger, where they were obliged to stay for the winter. They were short of supplies and had a hard time wintering. Albert Sidney Johnston was in command.

After this army was fully settled in their quarters, part of the Utah army returned home, leaving only enough to watch the moves at Bridger. This was a winter of business for the "Mormon" people. There was no thought of submission, everything was fully arranged for the spring work.

As soon as the weather moderated in the spring of 1858, the people commenced to move from Salt Lake City and more northern settlements, south as far as Utah County. Every house in Salt Lake City was abandoned, not a family remaining. Men were detailed to set fire to and burn everything that could be burned. The people really manifested joy in these moves. No one appeared down-hearted at the sacrifices. All was life and energy.

What was known as the standing army of Utah was organised, intending to make guerrilla warfare on our enemies and hinder their progress, while the people moved *en masse* further and further south. There had been good crops raised previous to this year; the country was full of bread stuff and fat cattle. Provisions were prepared for future use. Not much planting was done this season, particularly in the north.

A few troops were kept in Echo and along the road. I had charge of a company at Lost Spring near the head of the canyon. In the latter part of May we received orders to break up camp and come in; that peace had been made. (The part Col. Kane took in bringing about a settlement is a part of written history.) Ex-Governor Powell, of Kentucky, and McCullough, of Texas, were sent to arrange peace. They brought printed posters declaring the people all pardoned and notifying them to return to their houses. Thus we conquered a great army and nation without bloodshed.

The whole of this move was brought about by a charge made against the "Mormons" by Judge Drummond, who had been appointed from the state of Illinois. He had left his wife and family at home and brought here with him a fancy lady (?) who sat beside him in court. This coming to the knowledge of the public, Drummond was severely criticized by the "Mormon" press. At this he took offense, and laid his plans for deep revenge. He locked up his office, with the records in it, and arranged with a party to set fire to and burn up the whole. He then left the city in a hurry, pretending to be afraid for his life. Went back to Washington and reported the "Mormons" in a state of rebellion, stating that all the United States records were burned, and that he, a United States judge, had barely escaped with his life.

It is commonly understood that Secretary Floyd and his party took this report kindly, it giving grounds for a move by the army to the far west, thus weakening the power of the Federal Government financially, and moving much of the armament and military supplies, and giving the rebellion a better chance to get a good start before the necessary force could be put in the field by the government. So Drummond's report was acted upon without any enquiry whatever being made to find out whether it was true or not.

No moves back were made until the army had passed through the city. This was a sorrowful day for the soldiers. I afterwards travelled and became well acquainted with many of the commissioned officers. As is common with the army officers, they were real gentlemen, and were in no way responsible for these moves. Many of them told me they shed tears while passing through the streets of Salt Lake to see pleasant homes deserted and everything a waste; that it could only be compared to a city of the dead; and that to think they were the instruments used to cause all this made them ashamed of their calling.

The army agreed to fix their quarters not less than forty miles of Salt Lake City. This agreement was kept.

During the winter Col. Marcy went through to New Mexico to

buy mules and such supplies as could be obtained sooner than from the east. Quite a number of my old acquaintances from New Mexico came through in the spring. One Lewis Simmons, son-in-law of Kit Carson, came in charge of several thousand head of sheep. I obtained permission, of him to shear the wool from as many as I wished. This was quite a privilege, as wool was valuable.

My old friends and acquaintances were much surprised to find me in Utah and a "Mormon" but they all treated me kindly, and as often as I have met them do so to this day. Not many are now alive. I went to New Mexico when quite young, and most of my early acquaintances were older than myself; few of them but lived differently to what I have, so at the present day I am almost the only one living of the pioneers of New Mexico.

While the standing army, formerly spoken of, was fitting up, I commenced working at the saddler's trade. This I had partly learned in St. Louis before going to Mexico; had worked in the city of Chihuahua, learning something of the Mexican style of work. Some of my friends from Santa Fe wanted saddles of my make, as they had seen some good work of mine in Mexico. I made and sold quite a number of saddles to them. I now commenced to make this my business. And as "Dan Jones, the saddler," is well known, I will let this answer on that subject.

The coming of Johnston's army has generally been considered a money-making affair to this community. To me it has always been a question, for it cost a great deal to bring them. However, we made the most we could of a bad bargain, and got what we could out of the forced speculation.

There is one circumstance connected with my experience while in Echo Canyon service which I wish to put on record—the killing of Yates by Bill Hickman. This Mr. Yates was a personal friend of mine, a kind-hearted, liberal man of whom I had received many kindnesses, and his being murdered did not agree with my feelings, but I knew of no way to mend the matter, for I knew nothing of the killing till he was buried.

I was camped with a small party about four miles west of the Weber Valley and ten or twelve miles from Echo. One very cold morning about sunrise, Hickman and two others came to my camp. They seemed almost frozen, shaking and trembling in an unusual manner. Hickman asked me if I had any whisky. I told him I had not. He then asked if we had coffee. I replied that we had. "Then make us a good strong cup."

While the coffee was being made, he took me outside and asked me if I knew Yates. I told him I did. "Well, we have just buried him."

He then told about Yates being taken prisoner for tampering with Indians. And after talking quite excitedly, he said, "We have got away with him. What do you think the Old Boss," (meaning Brigham) "will say?"

Now if Yates had been killed as Hickman related in his book he would not have manifested so much interest in what President Young would say. He tried hard to draw an approval from me of what he had done. I told him I knew nothing about such modes and did not know what Brother Young would say about it.

Hickman killed Yates for his money and horse the same as any other thief and murderer would have done, and then excused himself by telling that he was counselled to do these things. I know positively that Governor Young's orders were to avoid bloodshed in every way possible. I was continually acting and around in places and under circumstances that gave me the best of opportunities to know.

During the time that Johnston's army was at Bridger, there was an effort made to turn the Indians against the Mormons. This partially succeeded, but did not last long. As they soon got tired of the treatment received from their new friends.

While in camp near the head of Echo Canyon in May, 1858, a number of Weber and Goshutes came and camped on Yellow Creek not far from our location. A few of us visited them. They expressed a desire to be peaceable with the Mormons. A meeting was appointed, they agreeing to come to our camp and talk over affairs and make satisfaction for some things they admitted having done. At this conference A. Miner presided, Abram Conover and myself acting as interpreters. I do not remember all that was said at the time. The Indians acknowledged having committed various thefts, at the same time giving their reasons for having done so.

CHAPTER 22

The Trial

Early in the spring of 1860 orders came from Washington for a portion of the troops at Camp Floyd to move to New Mexico and to explore a wagon road from Salt Lake to Santa Fe, naming the route, as selected by the map, down Little White River, now Price Creek, and crossing over the mouth of the Dolores, thence on to Santa Fe. On the old maps these rivers showed very well as far as directions went. At this time I was the only person in Utah that knew anything of the country desired to be explored, and my knowledge was limited to the old Spanish trail and some few side trails to Indian camps.

The offer was made me to act as guide for the expedition. I declined at first but finally consented to go as far as Green River with an exploring party under Lieut. Archer, and see if a wagon road could be found by way of Spanish Fork to Green River.

We succeeded in locating a road, but not down Price River. We left that river to the right, crossing the plains and striking the river at the lower crossing. It was decided to put a working force of soldiers on the route. This was the first opening of Spanish Fork Canyon. I agreed to go as far as Green River with this company, with the privilege, given as an inducement to get me to go, of taking along a trader's wagon under the protection of the command. I arranged with my brother-in-law, S. B. Moore, to go with me and take this wagon, and attend to the trading business, we being equal partners in the venture.

While working in Spanish Fork, making road, an ox was killed by a soldier. The ox belonged to a settler in Spanish Fork. Mr. Moore saw the soldier shoot the ox and told me about it. Next day John Berry, came into camp, he being president of the settlement, and in a very excited manner demanded satisfaction for the ox. The commander, Captain Selden, said that he knew nothing about the killing and asked me if I had heard anything. I told him that I knew who had killed the ox. Berry wanted the man brought forward at once. The captain told him that the man should be given up to the civil authorities at once and proper restitution made. Berry seemed to get worse and worse; said he did not want any thief to take back with him, but wanted to see him and have him punished. Captain Selden told him that the army regulations defined modes for even bad men; that everything had to be done properly. He advised President Berry to take a course to have the man either arrested or else to leave the matter to him and he would work the punishment so as to get the pay and send to the owner. Berry would not listen to any proposition whatever. Finally, I told him that he was unreasonable and that I would not point out the man to him, but would to the captain before pay-day; that I would bring the money with me on my return, and that I would leave it to Bishop Miller, the presiding bishop of Utah county, whether I was right or not.

On my return I offered to pay to Berry the amount. He would not accept it unless accompanied by a plea of guilt to a charge already preferred against me before the High Council of being a traitor to the Church, aiding and abetting an enemy to destroy property belonging to a brother and refusing to point out the guilty party when called on to do so. Taking the whole charge together it was too steep for me. That I had refused to point out the party was a fact, and I was willing to be judged on the merits of the refusal when all the reasons were stated. So I refused and was brought to trial.

The charge was read and considerable testimony given. In the charge the price of the ox was demanded. No effort was made to oppose this, but it was acknowledged and offered to be settled. At length Bishop Miller, the president, stood up and motioned that the charge be sustained. This aroused me. I replied to the Bishop's motion in an excited and insulting manner, so much so that he motioned that Daniel W. Jones be cut off from the Church of Jesus Christ of Latter-day Saints for insulting the Priesthood.

I replied, "You hold on; you cannot do it."

"What do you mean?" he asked.

"I mean I have had my say; I am done. Now you have yours, and whatever you require of me I will do. But I will not be cut off from the Church even if I have to acknowledge to the charge."

Here Joseph Clark asked permission to speak. He said he did not think the charge was sustained by the evidence; some others spoke the same. Finally Bishop Miller said to the clerk, "Read the charge again." On hearing it read the second time he said: "Oh, I do not mean to sustain the charge that Brother Jones is a traitor or anything of the kind. I had paid no particular attention to that part. All I mean is that Brother Jones pay for the ox according to agreement."

This was a close call for me, but I saved my standing and honour. If I had said nothing probably this whole charge would have went on record as it was. Inasmuch as I had offered to pay the amount sent by the captain the whole charge was thrown out.

This command under Selden was about one month working a road through to Green River. We had a pleasant time, doing well with our trading. We were treated well by both officers and men. Captain Selden was a kind-hearted officer, without any prejudices against the "Mormons," although he was of one those ordered out to wage a war against the people.

On arriving at Green River where another guide was to take my place, we found he was not there. As the man, a Mexican, had not arrived I was told that my services would be required the balance of the trip. I refused to go. Before leaving Utah I had received word from Brother Brigham that he did not wish me to go on this trip. George W. Bean told me that Brother Young had said, "Tell Brother Jones I consider him one of my good boys and I do not want him to go off into that dangerous country and risk his life for money."

I knew this to be the best of counsel, for the country was dangerous. The Mexicans of New Mexico were not over their bad feelings about the Indian slave trade. The ones who had profited by this traffic still held a grudge against "Mormons." This I had learned from some of my old associates that came through with Colonel Marcy. Both Utes and Navajoes were uncertain in those days, particularly those living on the borders of New Mexico. There were no regular mails or communications in those days between the two countries.

Not only having a desire to respect the kindly advice of Brother Brigham, but knowing the risk we would run, I declined to go farther. On refusing, Colonel Canby, who was in command, instructed his adjutant to tell me that the good of the service required me to go on as guide, and that it would be impossible for them to fill the orders from Washington without my services; that if I went willingly I should be well treated and respected and that my brother-in-law would be employed as assistant guide; that they needed our wagon and team and that the quartermaster would pay us for it.

I still refused, telling them I would run too much risk in getting back to Utah. Colonel Canby then promised me protection and mileage home, and informed me that I could accept the terms willingly or otherwise, they would have to keep a guard over me to see that I did not leave; neither would they settle with me for services up to date. I have several affidavits proving these facts. We found that nothing would do but to consent.

The main command under Canby intended to follow what was known as Lorin's trail up the Grand River, cross over and go down to Fort Garland, while a company under Lieutenant Stith was to explore the Dolores River. I was wanted for both, but as this could not be I was sent on the Lorin trail, accompanied by a sergeant and an Indian, to the junction of the Grand and Gunnison rivers, to find the road and see how the crossing was.

My hopes were that after this trip and finding the road all right to this point that I could get off and return home, but not so. It was decided that we had to go on and guide the exploring expedition through on the Dolores. I told Canby I did not know the country. No difference. My natural ability, with my general knowledge of the country, was all sufficient, so at length I gave up and went willingly. The most of the officers treated me with great kindness and respect. They knew I was a member of the "Mormon" church and often asked me questions about our religion. Many evenings were spent in chatting about Utah affairs in a very pleasant and agreeable manner.

After crossing Green River there is a desert of fifty-five miles to Grand River. The troops suffered considerable on this desert. Some few leaving the road to hunt water got lost, and one or two never were found; they either perished or fell into the hands of some hostile Indians. One little circumstance showing the need of understanding something of their language or signs in dealing with Indians happened at Green River. There were quite a number of Utes camped below the crossing. These Indians came into camp quite often.

One day I noticed a crowd of soldiers making some curious and exciting moves. I approached to see what was the matter. I saw an Indian standing, holding something in his hand and looking rather confused. The soldiers were getting a rope ready to hang him; all was excitement and I am satisfied that if I had not happened along the poor Indian would have been swinging by the neck in less than five minutes.

I could see from the Indian's manner that he realised something was wrong but could not understand why he was surrounded by soldiers.

I asked them what they were doing. They said that the Indian had brought one of their horses that he had stolen into camp and sold it for thirty dollars; that the owner of the horse was there and they were intending to hang the "d——d thief." I told them to hold on a minute, that I did not think an Indian would steal a horse and bring it into the camp where it belonged to sell. Someone answered, "Yes, he has; there is the money now in his hand that he got for the horse."

The Indian was still standing there, holding the money in his open hand and looking about as foolish as ever I saw one of his race look. I asked him what was up. He said he did not know what was the matter.

"What about the horse and money?"

He answered, "I found a horse down at our camp. I knew it belonged to the soldiers so I brought it up, thinking they would give me something for bringing it. This man," pointing to one, "came and took hold of the horse and put some money in my hand. It was yellow money and I did not want it. He then put some silver in my hand. There it all is. I don't understand what they are mad about."

I soon got the trouble explained. The man thought he was buying the horse, the Indian thought he was rewarding him for bringing the animal to camp; the owner happened along just as the trade was being made. Here ignorance and prejudice came near causing a great crime. As soon as this was explained I took the money and gave it back to the owner. No one had thought of taking the money. All were bent on hanging the honest fellow. Soon there was a reverse of feeling; most of the soldiers in the crowd being Irish, they let their impulses run as far the other way, loading the Indian with shirts and blouses. Some gave him money, so that he went away feeling pretty well, but he remarked that the soldiers were *kots-tu-shu-a* (big fools).

I have often thought there were many like these soldiers, "*heap kots-tu-shu-a,*" in dealing with Indians.

CHAPTER 23

Arrival at Santa Fe

On arriving at Grand River Stith's outfit was prepared and we were set across the river in a place entirely unknown to me. I did not even know whether the Dolores River was above or below me, and so told the officer. There was a point known as the bend of Dolores where I had been, but from where we were to that point the country was new to me. I had no definite idea of the distance but knew it must be several days' journey. This country, as the name of the river implies, was about the worst country I ever travelled through. While we were prospecting to see if we could get any sight of the river, I found a lone Indian. He had been out all alone on a stealing expedition to the Navajo Indians, had got a few horses and was on his way home to Uintah. After much persuasion and some pay, I induced him to go a day's travel and show me the river and put me on the trail if there was any.

We were about thirty miles above the Dolores where it empties into Grand River. On arriving at the river, we found a trail leading up it for only a short distance. My Indian friend described the country and trails to me so that I felt pretty sure of getting to a place with which I was acquainted.

We were ten days reaching the bend of the Dolores where the old Spanish trail strikes it, but does not cross. We only struck the river twice the whole distance. It runs through box canyons most of the way, and is unapproachable; so the wagon-road ordered explored I do not think will be made yet awhile.

By this time we had learned the character of our commanding officer. He was simply a ruffian of the worst type. I had to watch him daily, as he was suspicious of being led into ambush.

We had met one party of Indians, an old man and family. My

brother-in-law was acquainted with him, he having been one of the Grand valley company that was driven away by the Indians. This old man was of the peace party, and told Mr. Moore all about what had happened, after they were driven away. Seeing Moore friendly and talking with the old Indian made Stith more suspicious of us. He often hinted that it would be dangerous for us if we ever came across Indians in any number. This was not very pleasant, for we were in a country where a great many Indians roamed and we were liable to run across a lot at any time, but as good luck would have it, we never did. We always believed that if we had run into an Indian camp that Stith would have attempted to take our lives.

The soldiers did not like him, neither did they think as he did, but they all feared him as he had shot down some of his company. This same officer had shot and killed one man, who had given out and could not travel. This occurred on a Texas desert.

My intention was to take care of myself, and if we had met any Indians to see that I was not harmed if a good rifle could protect me. Moore and myself watched him all the time.

We arrived at the Dolores bend at eleven o'clock a.m. I recommended camping. Stith said he had not made a day's march and would not camp. I said, "Then let's noon."

"No, it lacks an hour of noon; we must travel an hour yet."

I told him I wanted time to get my reckoning, as I had not been here for some time and had come in a different direction from what I had done before and that there were many trails leading from this point further north. It was twenty miles to the next water. All this would not induce him even to noon, but he ordered the march to continue.

After going a few miles he asked me where the water was for noon. I told him that all the water we would get would take till after night to reach. He then notified Moore and myself that we were discharged, and that there was a Mexican along who knew the road better than we did. I told him allright, to pay us and we would turn back. This he refused to do, saying that he intended to keep us along in case the Mexican did not know the country; that we would be better than no guides.

We had guided this company 210 miles, through a country entirely unknown to us, in ten days' time, and the infantry with packs had never been lost or failed to get good camps. Now, after getting, for the first time, on a good trail, we were discharged for not finding water for noon on a dry desert and, as before stated, leaving water at about half-past eleven. So much for West Point discipline.

After discharging us, as he supposed, Stith put his Mexican guide to lead, Moore and myself following along and taking it easy. We were in no way concerned about our discharge, for the quartermaster had told me to get along the best we could with Stith, but if we wanted, when we got into Santa Fe, to come back and meet Canby's command, and that we need not take a discharge from Stith unless we so desired.

They now left the trail, at night taking to the left over a dry mesa; but no water was found. There was considerable suffering among the soldiers, as there was no water for coffee or cooking and but little to drink. Here the company planned to kill Stith, nearly all the company agreeing. They sent their committee to Moore and myself with the proposition that Stith and the Mexican guide be killed together with all that would not sustain the move, and that we were to guide them out of the country. This was fully determined upon and we had much trouble in persuading them out of the notion, but finally succeeded.

Next day we continued our journey, arriving at the Mancos River much later than we would have done had we kept the trail. Stith soon learned that the Mexican knew but little about the country. After crossing the river we struck a big trail where it ascended a hill. On getting on this trail Stith made some very insulting remarks, saying that now we had a guide who knew something.

On reaching the top of the hill they found that the trail scattered, being a hunting trail and not a route. This puzzled the guide, who was the one that had taken the wrong direction. I here got my ideas clear, and for the soldiers' sake, they having treated us kindly, I told Stith's lieutenant where the trail was. He informed Stith, who was now willing to listen, having lost faith in his Mexican. We soon struck the old trail. We could now have regained our positions had we wished to, but we agreed with Lieut. Bristol, who was a real good fellow, to tell him every morning, when necessary, about the trail and distance; but not to speak to Stith about anything, and go along as though we cared nothing about the road.

After this Moore and I had a pretty good time, riding along without any responsibility; hunting when we liked and taking it easy. We had many a good laugh at Stith's expense, for if we started out of a morning ahead he was afraid to lose sight of us for fear his guide would get lost.

One morning, while travelling on a nice, plain trail, up a wide, smooth flat, Moore and I started up a steep mountain side, intending to follow along the mountain ridge and kill some game. We had gone but a short distance, without any trail whatever, when, on looking back, we saw the Mexican guide and Stith had left the trail and started to follow us. Bristol was in the rear with the pack train.

At first we felt like letting them follow, but it seemed too hard on the poor foot soldiers to play them such a trick, so Steve Moore turned round and called out, "What in the h—— are you following us for?" Stith wanted to know if we were not on the trail. Moore told him his guide ought to know where the trail was—that it was down on the flat; to go back and not be following us up the mountain.

We travelled along the mountain ridge in sight of the trail most of the day watching the company. They often seemed lost and would stop and look to see if they could see us. We finally came into the trail and travelled along with the command.

On arriving at the first settlement Stith got drunk and gambled off a lot of money that he expected to cover by the vouchers I would sign before drawing any pay from him.

We were seventy miles from Santa Fe, the headquarters where we were to report to Colonel Fontleroy, the commander.

Stith continued his spree several days, so Moore and I saddled up and went on to Santa Fe alone. On reaching that place I found many old friends, among the rest, Manuel Woods, keeping hotel. He was an old hotel keeper for whom I had kept bar during my first stay in Santa Fe. I explained our situation to him, stating that we intended to wait till the main command came in. He told us to make his house our home as long as we desired, and we could have all the money we wanted besides.

My old friends, John Phillips, H. Stephens, F. Redmond, and many others, expressed themselves ready to assist us in any way possible.

We turned our mules into the government corral and went to stop at the hotel.

Colonel Fontleroy, on hearing that someone had arrived from Utah, sent for us to come to his office the next day. There had been some uneasiness felt about the company we had travelled with, and a party had been sent out to meet them. The party had gone as far as the Dolores and returned.

We had seen their tracks; I wanted to follow their trail, knowing it to be white men's tracks. Stith took them for Indians' and refused to follow me.

On meeting the colonel, he, in a very pompous manner, asked me who I was.

I replied, "Daniel W. Jones."

"Where are you from?"

"Salt Lake City, Utah."

"How did you come here?"

"On a mule."

"What is your business—in what capacity have you come?" He was now much excited and asked a series of questions before stopping.

I then told him I was a guide in government employ.

He asked, "Where are the troops; where is the command you are guiding?"

"The last I saw of them they were about seventy miles back. The commander and most of the company drunk."

"Why are you not with them?"

"I don't like whisky," was my answer.

I felt insulted by his manner in first speaking so abruptly to me, and was determined not to give him any satisfaction until he spoke to me in a respectable manner. This he seemed to see and commenced asking his questions more politely. I gave him all the information I could about the moves of the troops on the road. He now approved of my coming ahead.

When Stith arrived he made out my account and asked me to sign the vouchers. I thanked him, telling him that I did not need any money and did not wish my discharge just then. He flew into a terrible passion, saying that he could not settle his accounts unless I signed the vouchers. I replied that I had nothing to do with settling his accounts, all I wanted was my transfer back to the command. This he refused me, so we went and bought two mules on credit and went back to the command.

We met them at Taos. The quartermaster was glad to see us, as he needed our services. I took the position of both guide and interpreter, Moore continuing as assistant.

We got into the farming district about harvest time. There was no forage to be had except fields of grain. These were bought at high prices when animals were turned in over night and a guard placed around them. Often the animals would get into other fields doing some damage. The Mexicans made great complaint, often asking several hundred dollars for damages.

The pasturage generally cost from \$150 to \$200 per night. The quartermaster would generally hand me \$500 and tell me to settle. Sometimes I would be two or three hours settling, as the damage sometimes was on various patches.

The people were at times unreasonable in their demands. When I could not get a reasonable settlement would refer to the authority. I made the people understand that they could not get anything only what was just and reasonable. When they found that I understood them they became much easier to deal with.

In that country what you do today always gets to the next camping place before you do.

When all my accounts were settled for the day I would hand what money was left to the quartermaster, sometimes it would be over \$100.

One day on handing him the money he said, "Jones, you're a d——d fool"

"Why?" I asked.

"That money is already accounted for."

I did not take the hint as he expected I would, but continued to return the over-plus.

This remark to me was made in kindness, as the quartermaster was a great friend of mine and wanted me to keep the money for myself, but I did not think it right. It would never have done me any good.

When we arrived in Santa Fe, we were paid off in full up to date, and mileage allowed; but no protection was furnished for our return home. The Navajoes had just broken out and the troops had been ordered to chastise them. The good of the service now required that we get home the best we could. Aside from this we were treated in the best manner possible; provisions being given us by the quartermaster and some valuable presents by other officers.

We knew that our chances were slim forgetting back safely. To make things as safe as possible, however, we bought a good wagon and four first class mules; loaded up with Mexican and Navajo blankets and other goods believing that we would be less liable to get robbed of these goods than if we carried our money with us. We were also informed by some friends, who had lately come in from Denver that blankets of this kind were in good demand at that place. There was a great rush for Pike's Peak and miners and prospectors wanted these blankets.

CHAPTER 24

Leave Santa Fe for Home

We left Santa Fe about the 10th of September, 1860. Two young men that came through from Utah, whose homes were in the States, accompanied us on horseback. They were well mounted and we were all well armed. We took every precaution to make ourselves secure against thieves stealing our stock, or taking advantage of us in any way.

We took the open road by way of Las Vegas, Fort Union, passing along the Raton mountains and continuing on without molestation of any kind until the evening of the 23rd, when we were attacked and robbed, the particulars of which I shall give together with our trip home to the best of my ability and recollection. Late in the afternoon we arrived at a creek where we intended to camp, but found no water. We had travelled about thirty miles, and the next chance for camping was several miles further on. Some of my reflections would not be amiss here. There was some game in sight. We killed some wild turkeys. My companions were out after antelope and I was alone awaiting their return.

We were now quite out of the dangerous country to all appearances, having travelled over three hundred miles without disturbance. We were now where it was considered safe for any one to travel. Still I felt uneasy. I remembered the words of President Young and I never had felt entirely safe on the road. In my reflections I felt as though I would rather lose what I had made than be tempted to disobey counsel again, by being successful. Still I was in hopes we could keep our property, and would try and do right in the future. I asked the Lord to direct me for the best, but to spare our lives on our road home.

I had a positive feeling that we were in danger. Shortly before sundown we started on intending to make a night drive to the next watering place. After travelling a short distance we came to a hollow where a rain-storm, just passing over, had deposited some good fresh water, and where grass and fuel were plentiful. On approaching camp we descended from a ridge some three hundred yards to a flat. There was an open space someone hundred yards wide to the right of the road. We drove to near the centre of this opening. The brush around was about waist high and not very thick. I commenced gathering up fuel, the others unhitching and taking care of the animals.

After getting some dry brush ready, I was about striking a fire when we heard a noise of horsemen back on the road. The full moon was shining and on looking up we saw some eight or ten horsemen just disappearing over the ridge, going from us. As we were near the road and had neither seen nor heard any one passing, this surprised us not being able to account for the move.

Moore and myself took our guns and went up to where we had seen them, to reconnoitre. On getting to the summit of the ridge we could see the tracks plainly where they had come following after us, and on seeing us had turned suddenly and run back. They, no doubt, had expected us to continue on some eight miles farther to the creek before camping, and had run on us unexpectedly. While examining these tracks and trying to solve the mystery, we heard the noise of horses about two hundred yards from the road, and discovered a small clump of cedars in the direction, being on the same side of the road as our camp and just back from the summit of the ridge.

We decided at once that they were robbers following us; that they were tying up and hiding, intending to creep upon us afoot, being too cowardly to make an open attack. We hurried back to camp, intending to try and get to the timber on the creek. I gave orders to hitch up as quickly as possible. The two horsemen were to take the lead and run where the road was good, holding back where rough. I was to drive while Moore did the fighting from the wagon, if we were followed.

Our team was full of life, so much so that we had to change the bits on the leaders, putting on heavy curbbits, taking off the common ones with checks. This left the driving reins alone in the bits. The saddle horses were soon ready, one man holding them just in front of the team, three of us hitching as fast as possible. The mules commenced looking in the direction of the clump of cedars, now and then looking along the edge of the brush around us. I remarked that I believed they were surrounding us. Just as I was about taking the lines in hand, the team being all hitched except the wheel mules' traces, a shot was fired.

I thought it came from one of our own party, so near by it seemed. I asked, "Who was that shooting?"

Moore answered, "You know as much about it as I do"

Suddenly several shots were fired. At this the mules started on the full run. I grabbed the nigh leader. The two men with horses now had hold of them, but were not mounted. All ran together, making a half circle back to the road about where we turned out, Moore holding to the off wheeler.

As we ran the shots came thick and fast from the brush, clear along the half-circle up to the road. Just as we struck the road, crossing it to the west—our direction of travel being to the north—shots commenced coming from the left side, one striking and killing the nigh wheel mule. This stopped the team, as the leaders alone could not pull the wagon and drag the dead mule.

The shots were now coming thick and fast from all sides. The lead mules were trying to get away. I called to Moore to cut the breast strap of the dead mule so that the leaders could continue toward open ground. He made a strike or two with his knife, but while doing so the off wheeler fell dead. An instant after the off leader fell. I now had hold of the only mule left standing.

The two horsemen were just in front of the team, and when it stopped they halted also. One of them, Daniel Dafney, I shall always remember for his coolness and courage. I felt like giving the word to run and abandon the team, but knowing that we were some eight hundred miles from home, did not much like the prospect of footing it through.

Moore raised his gun to shoot. I told him not to do so, as they, no doubt, would make a rush for us if we fired. In those days muzzle-loaders were all we had. One of the horsemen had a rope knocked from his hand with a bullet. On this he said to Dafney, "It is getting too hot, let's run."

Dafney replied, "I will not leave till all leave."

Just at this the off leader sprang up, not having been injured much, only grazed across the loins. I spoke to Moore, telling him to cut the mule out of the harness, and I would do the same with the nigh one, and we would try to get away.

Dafney came and assisted each of us in getting our mules out of the harness. The most of the shots being directed toward the team, Dafney ran ten times more risk in coming to our assistance than if he had remained in front.

The lead mules were fine large animals and full of life. They were terribly frightened at the shooting, which continued almost without ceasing. Once I called to them to stop shooting; that there was no need of killing us, as they were strong enough to come and take what they wanted. This I spoke in Spanish. No reply, except a stronger volley of shots.

The mule I had hold of had never been ridden, but there was no time for "swapping horses." Each of us had heavy, old-fashioned rifles. I got a little the start of Moore, as Dafney assisted me first. My mule had a long rope tied to his neck, and when I mounted and started with the rope dragging it tangled in the harness, bringing my mule to a sudden halt. I managed to untie the rope from his neck. While doing this Dafney succeeded in helping Moore with his mule, which was almost unmanageable. We finally all got about an even start. The balls were still coming thick and fast, the robbers having advanced up as near as possible without coming into open ground. Some of them being within thirty yards of us.

Our road led to the north, but was blocked, the firing coming from every direction but the west, where there was no brush. Our animals needed no guiding. As soon as they were free to run they broke with full speed to get away from the shots. It would be hard to tell which was the most frightened, we or the mules. Most of the shooting was done with revolvers. The mules soon took the lead of the horses.

The prairie had many badger holes and broken spots and my mule came near throwing me several times in dodging them. I had not removed the mule's collar, and when I could scarcely stick on for these side plunges I ran my arm under it, taking my gun in my hand and clinching it tight. This steadied me so that I felt safe.

After running some distance my mule commenced to act as though he was wounded and about to fall. This continued for several minutes, giving us much uneasiness, but he soon recovered himself. He must have been in pain from excitement, as he was not wounded.

Moore and I were now neck and neck on the lead, going at full speed. I asked him to turn to the north and get our right direction of travel. He paid no attention to my words, so I repeated them rather sharply, when he answered, "D———n it, turn to the north yourself, I cannot turn my mule any more than a saw-log." We found we were much like the old parson who yoked himself to the calf, we were running away in spite of ourselves.

On looking back we saw that the horsemen were about twenty

113

yards in the rear. I called and asked them if their horses were under control. They answered, "Yes."

"Then ride up and take the lead."

They answered that our mules were too fast for them, so we managed to check their speed a little. The horsemen, whipping up, at length got the lead, when they turned to the north in the direction we wished to travel. Shortly after turning to the north we came to a clump of cedars. Here Moore and I tried hard to persuade our companions to stop, tie up and go back with us and creep on to the robbers, believing we could surprise and whip them. This we could not prevail on them to do. We continued on some few miles, coming to the creek bank where it was so steep that we could not cross. This forced us to go down toward the road, which we finally struck.

I now became for the first time thoroughly frightened. During the whole scene that I have been describing, I had never felt much fear. While I was untying the rope the balls came so thick that the flesh on my ribs twitched a little. Moore says he could not help dodging when the bullets flew so thick and close. Dafney laughed and asked if he thought he could dodge them.

It would have been an easy matter for the robbers to have come on and got to the crossing ahead of us, and ambushed us, as the brush was thick on each side of the road. This I fully realised and insisted that we should not take the road, but to no purpose. The others felt that we had got clear and that it would be best to keep on to the next ranch, some forty miles distant. This we reached about sunrise.

Moore and I rode all night bareback, most of the time on a hard trot.

We arrived at Zan Hicklin's on the Green Horn River early in the morning. Hicklin was an old acquaintance and treated us kindly, furnishing us with saddles and blankets, and such provisions as we could take. We stayed with him three days before we were able to travel on, being so sore from our bareback feat.

The night after our arrival Hicklin sent back a man to where we were robbed. The man reported finding the wagon all right, with a sack of bacon and some horse feed; also the dead mules and some parts of the harness, all the light straps being taken. From all the signs we judged the robbers to be Mexicans. Hicklin offered to get the wagon for us, but we felt like getting home the quickest and best way, and thought best to take it muleback. So we told Hicklin to get the wagon and keep it.

When we started on we had but little money and very poor clothes, as we were saving our good ones that we had bought in Santa Fe until we got home; but we had two first class mules, about as fine ones as are often seen, and we made up our minds to make as quick a trip home as possible. Our friends Dafney and companion were well mounted; they were going the same road as far as Denver. They got away with several hundred dollars, carried on their persons.

Moore and I had expended our cash all but a few dollars. Our friends were liberal while we travelled together paying most of the expenses.

The country was just being settled. There was but one house where Pueblo now is, besides the old shanties where the Mormon Company wintered in 1846-47. From Pueblo to Denver there were a few new farms just started. There were several cities by name but no one living in them. These were started to boom some mining camps, but the prospect failing the city also was abandoned. Some of these places are only remembered by a few of the old prospectors, never having been put upon record.

We stopped one night with quite a pleasant, thrifty settler, on the Fountain Creek. During the evening he told us that he had lost quite a number of horses, some thirty or forty head, mostly good American mares and young stock; he had spent much time hunting them and finally given them up, supposing that they had been stolen, and taken entirely out of the country.

The road from this place continued on up Fountain creek for some thirty miles then crossed over and down to Cherry Creek; estimated eighty-five miles from this place to the next station, where we could find a stopping place. This looked like having to camp out. Something we were not prepared to do. Again, we still were timid not having recovered from our stampede. We felt much better when in a safe place.

Our landlord told us of a more direct route, that he had recommended to different ones and tried to get opened through, that would shorten the distance about half from his place to Cherry City. There was no trail through, but the country looked open and favourable, and as our host had been kind to us and manifested quite a desire to have us go through, after receiving his directions and locating the points where the country showed best, we started out.

After travelling about forty miles we saw quite a bunch of horses. On approaching them, we discovered, from the brands and descriptions given us, that they were the lost stock of our kind entertainer.

Not long after seeing the horses we struck the main road, having saved many miles of travel as our route was almost direct, while the old road was very crooked. Soon after striking the road we met a train, by which we sent a note to the owner where his horses were.

After getting home we received a letter acknowledging our act and saying the animals were his. I have forgotten the name of the owner of the stock, but have often thought of the circumstance, for I will admit that we were tempted at first to try to make something out of the find.

Notwithstanding our loss and sore feelings we found much on the trip to amuse and entertain us. Two of us were Missourians—Dafney and I, the other two were Yankees. The settlers along the route were mixed, some Missourians, others eastern people. The question generally was, shall we stop with a dirty Missourian or a stingy Yankee? We finally agreed to take it time about as much as possible. Various signs were put up along the road to attract the attention of the traveller, one I remember read something like this: "Bran, coal, pies, hay, whisky, eggs and other fruit."

CHAPTER 25

Martin's Cruel Treatment of Us

We expected to get some assistance from a man by the name of William Martin, whom we were acquainted with. He had been at Provo merchandising, but had moved to Denver.

On arriving in Denver and meeting Martin, we told him our situation. He very readily said we could have what we wanted, and asked how much we would need. I told him twenty-five dollars would answer. It was about noon and he said, "Wait and have some dinner, then you can go on."

He stepped out but returned in a few minutes, asking, "Whose fine mules are those under the shed?"

I replied, "They are ours."

He said, "They are fine mules; I will give you a good trade for them." And then offered us a pair of ponies and twenty-five dollars.

I told him they were all we had left of what we had earned during our trip; that we were anxious to get home as soon as possible, and that they would carry us better than the ponies would. I knew the ponies well that he offered us. He insisted on the trade. We declined as the mules were worth at least $400, while the ponies were not worth over $75. If he gave us the $25 difference he would still get at least $300 for nothing. Finally, when we would not trade, Martin said he had no money to loan.

He had a large provision store, and I said, "Then let us have a little provisions and we will go on."

He replied that he was selling on commission and could let nothing go without the money. If ever two men felt indignant we did. We had parted company with our friends, the two horsemen. They still had plenty of money. They doubtless would have given us some had we asked them, but we were sure of getting some from Martin. I also

117

had several old acquaintances in Denver who, no doubt, would have helped us, but we felt now like asking no assistance from any person.

We had just forty cents and were four hundred miles from old Jack Robinson's camp at Bridger. We know he would not turn us away. My answer to Martin was "Bill Martin, you see these two mules; they are better animals than you ought to own. It is only four hundred miles to Jack Robinson's; they will carry us there in four days; we can starve that long and you can't have the mules. Good day."

We bought forty cents worth of cheap cakes and started out with the expectation of going hungry. As we crossed the bridge spanning the Arkansas River, the roads forked. We enquired of a lad which road to take naming our direction. He said either, but that the left hand road went out five miles to Jim Baker's ranch. Here was a chance. Jim Baker was an old friend that I had often met on the plains. I had taken care of his brother, when snow-blind, while we were at Devil's Gate, so we concluded to go there and see if Baker would be like Martin.

On arriving we were welcomed in the true, old-mountaineer style. Although grass was abundant, he turned our mules into his oat field. We told him about Martin, and he said, "Well now, I will go into town every Saturday, get drunk, and abuse Martin for this until I run him out of the country. I will never let up on him. Why he ain't fit to live."

Baker had his squaw fix us up some food; all we would take. Next morning we started on feeling much better than when leaving Denver. We met with others along the road who supplied our wants.

While at Bitter creek one of our mules got poisoned with bad water. We got him as far as Jack Robinson's camp, leaving him and getting another.

On reaching Bridger, we overtook a government outfit coming into Camp Floyd—Captain Clery and escort. The captain was on his way to relieve the then acting quartermaster. He offered to supply us if we would travel with him as they did not know the road. We travelled with him two days receiving the best of treatment from officers and men. Our route led down Provo Canyon. I had a number of acquaintances in this valley; among the number Melvin Ross who lived at the head of the valley. He was a man of considerable means. I told Moore we would go and camp with him, telling how welcome we would be. There was a sergeant in the company who knew the road from Weber. Neither Moore nor myself had travelled the road from Weber to Provo valley. We went ahead and took the wrong road so that we lost several miles in getting back to the Provo road. In the meantime the soldiers passed on and got ahead of us. This plagued us a little but we concluded to keep it to ourselves. When we finally arrived at Ross's ranch we found the soldiers had passed and were camped a short distance down the road.

Ross was out in front of his house just laying out a big fat mutton dressed. He knew me but spoke rather coolly for an old friend, but asked us to get down. I told him we would like to stop and get something to eat and stay all night, but that we were without money. He replied that we had some good ropes and blankets. I told him we needed them, as we might go on down the canyon and camp, for we were anxious to get home to our families. He said there was good camping down the canyon. I thought he was doing this simply to joke us, but not so. We finally started on, but expecting to be called back and laughed at.

Moore commenced laughing at me, saying, "That's your friend, is it?"

I said, "He'll call us back; he cannot mean this only as a joke."

Moore said, "Nary a joke; that man's in earnest."

I felt just about as bad as I ever remember to have felt. We had been running the gauntlet for several hundred miles among strangers, looking forward with great expectations on reaching friends at home. We had travelled forty-five miles since eating. This we told Ross, but not a bite would he let us have unless we gave him a rope or blanket. This seemed so mean that we would rather have travelled all next day without food than to ask anyone again.

When we came up to the soldier camp they asked us to stop and have supper. Our mules were fed oats and turned out. We said nothing about the grand (?) reception we had had, as we were ashamed to mention it. We stayed till about eleven o'clock and then went on down the canyon and laid out a short distance from several old friends and acquaintances. We dared not call on anyone; so early next morning we started for our homes in Provo, joking each other often and wondering if our wives would treat us as Ross had.

We had made considerable money; every one of our acquaintances expected us back with plenty. Of course, our wives expected us to come home benefitted by the summer's trip. But all was lost and we were ragged and worn, and presented anything but a dudish appearance. I will not do our wives the injustice to say that we felt any doubt of the reception we would receive at home. They were sisters and two

119

as good and faithful women as ever existed. We had no fears, although we made many propositions suggestive of their shutting us out.

Our reception was such as true wives always give—all the more kind because of our misfortune. I do not think I ever heard a word of regret spoken by either of them for the loss of our property, so thankful were they for our lives being spared under the great risk we ran.

I wrote on to Canby's adjutant, who, during the winter, was sent down to Washington. About the time the Civil War broke out I got a letter stating that I would get the money for our losses. But the officer attending to it was probably killed in the war, as I never heard any more from him.

Many of the military officers to whom I have related the circumstance of our being pressed into service tell me the claim can be collected; it certainly is due to us, for we have never as yet received any benefit for our services.

Acting on the suggestions of some of the army officers I got together sufficient affidavits to establish the facts here recorded making my claim according to facts. My papers were all returned to me with the statement that inasmuch as we were robbed by parties other than Indians, that nothing could be done for us.

Some have advised me to change my papers and say that Indians were the depredators, and make the claim accordingly. This I shall not do as there is enough laid to the Indians already. If I ever get anything it will be on the justice of the claim just as it occurred and not by charging it to the Indians.

CHAPTER 26

The Black Hawk War

As I do not consider an account of my home life of any particular interest to the general reader, I will give only a brief sketch of it.

On returning and settling up with Bachman and Hanks, who had furnished much of our trade supply, I found I would have to sell my home to pay them.

In 1861, I went to Provo Valley and took up land on Snake creek, where I fenced a farm, built a house, and corrals and raised a crop of wheat and potatoes and while binding wheat had to wear a heavy coat and woollen mittens as the weather was so cold. After gathering in my crop, I concluded to return to Provo and work at saddlery, expecting to go back in the spring and continue farming.

During the early spring a flood come and destroyed the road through Provo Canyon, stopping all travel. In the fall of 1862, a company was organised to rebuild the road, the funds being furnished by voluntary contribution. Shadrick Holdaway, Chas. Kenedey, and I were chosen as committee; I being selected as secretary and treasurer. Having taken the work in hand it was pushed forward with considerable force. I was greatly interested as I wished to get back to my farm and could only do so by going round by Salt Lake City and through the Park to the valley, a distance of nearly one hundred miles, while the direct route was only twenty-five miles. Neither did I wish to be cut off from Provo, which I considered my real home. Many times I found funds hard to raise, so much so, that finally, in a tight-place I sold my farm to help on the road; so that by the time the road was finished and paid for, I had no individual use for it. But like many others of my labours for public good, my pay was in the satisfaction of seeing the work finished so as to be of use. To illustrate my situation and extremes in making payments I will relate one circumstance.

The whole funds contributed were left in the hands of the contributors until wanted, all donations being named. Some donated flour, others potatoes, wood, lumber, and any and everything in the shape of produce being on the list. When jobs on the road were finished and accepted by the two other committee men, they would draw an order on the treasurer, who would have to draw on the contributors. Sometimes the means would not be just ready to the day, but almost invariably donators paid honourably. In fact I have no remembrance of a single instance where agreements made were not fulfilled in good time.

There was one company of Welshmen that took a contract amounting to twelve hundred dollars. The committee docked them, their job not being up to contract. This soured them so much that they sought to make trouble with me about their pay, allowing me no time whatever to settle up in the usual manner. After paying all but some fifty dollars, I asked a little time to see who was ready to pay that amount. I was given to understand that not much time would be allowed, so I gave them an order where I supposed it would be paid, but the party not being quite ready asked them to wait a few days and he would settle. This they would not do, but three of them returned to my house to whip me. I tried to reason with them but to no purpose. A row had to be had. I ordered them out of my house. They went out, picking up rocks and stood facing my door and abusing me, and daring me out. I grabbed a pair of hames fastened at the top with a strap. Without describing all that occurred, I did not get hurt, but paid a cow and calf for damages done to the leader of the party.

When the row was over I started to the nearest alderman to complain about myself. Just as I approached, meeting the officer in his door-yard, a man came driving his team up the street on a full run, and shouting at the top of his voice not to listen to me, but have me arrested, that I had killed a man and nearly killed a lot more. This so enraged me that I gathered up some rocks and commenced war upon him, turning him back and chasing him down the street, team and all. The alderman fined me five dollars on my own complaint, but nothing for chasing Bob Caldwell and team. For a short time there were hard feelings in the community against me. I knew that I had been both hasty and severe, and gave the cow of my own free will, and settled up with good feelings to all parties.

After the road was made passable and all accounts settled, I concluded to give up the project of becoming a farmer, and stick to my trade. In those days money was a little more plentiful among business men than before the Johnston army visited Utah. Still, much of the business was done with grain as the circulating medium. This made business rather slow, as at times I would have to load up a wagon and go to Salt Lake City, taking from three to five days, sometimes going with ox teams. I would sell my grain and return with about as much material as I could carry under my arm.

While on one of my trips for leather, Brother Isaac Brockbank made me an offer to come to the city and work for him, he being in charge of William Howard's tannery, shoe and harness factory. Considering this better than the slow manner in Provo, I moved to Salt Lake in 1863, where I continued to live and work at my trade uninterruptedly most of the time. I carried on business until the summer of 1871.

During the time I lived in Salt Lake, Connor's army occupied Camp Douglas. The Civil War was still going on, also the Black Hawk war, so known in Utah from the fact that the leader of the depredating Utes, who broke up so many of the frontier settlements of Sanpete and Sevier counties, was called Black Hawk, after the old warrior of that name.

The people of Salt Lake had many duties to perform in those days. Strong police forces (unpaid) had to be kept ready, as much prejudice and ill-feeling existed at times. There were continual threats to arrest our leaders, which caused the people to be constantly on the alert.

It is not my intention to write much in this work except that which the title justifies. Still, there are a few incidents that certainly would be of interest. For dates I am indebted to "Church Chronology."

Dec. 17th, 1864. A landing and site for a church warehouse, afterwards known as Callsville, was selected by Anson Call, on the Colorado River, 125 miles from St. George, and the land along the Muddy found suitable to settle on. It was then contemplated to send the emigration from Europe by way of Panama and up the Colorado River to this landing, which was the head of navigation on the river named.

I believe that I have heard about as much criticism and fault-finding against Brigham Young, for the effort made at Call's Landing to prepare for what the above refers to, as anything that was ever directed by him. Some few persons were advised to spend a few thousand dollars on the speculation. It failed, and they have been mourning about it ever since. I would ask how many of Brigham Young's enterprises have succeeded? His failures were but few.

I always felt to honour and respect Brigham Young, but I have thought, that men sometimes honour him more than he asked, or than common sense could expect. That he was a good adviser and generally clear headed on business matters, all who knew him acknowledge. But that he could never make a mistake would have been unreasonable to expect. The work previously spoken of might have been useless. Still I do not think it was, and will give some of my reasons for thinking so. I have been much in the far south; have watched and studied the interests and progress of the southern country and its developments. I know that President Young's mind for some reason, was much drawn towards Southern Utah, Arizona, and Mexico. The settling of St. George and other places considered desert wastes, the building of the temple, etc., all show this.

In carrying out this move, as far as it went, a road had to be opened up as far as the river. Soon this road was opened farther on into Arizona. Thus a thoroughfare such as the country would support, was opened up now clear through to some of the most fertile valleys of Arizona and Mexico. Some have been settled by our people, and others will be in time, as the best are not yet occupied.

The commencement of the Black Hawk War was in 1865. The immediate cause was the whipping of an Indian by a white man. This occurred April 9th. Next day three white men were killed by Indians. April 12th, in a battle, two more; July 14th two; July 26th, drove off most of the cattle from Glenwood, Sevier County; Oct. 17, eight persons were killed near Ephraim.

1866. Jan. 8, two men were killed in Kane County; April 12th, three more in the same county. April 20th, Salina was raided, two men killed, and two hundred head of stock taken. Place was now vacated. April 22nd, one killed and two wounded in Piute County. June 10th, two men killed in Millard County. June 24th, one wounded in Thistle valley. June 26th, one white man killed in fight with Indians, who raided Spanish Fork.

1867, March 21st, one man and three women were killed in Sevier County. Many southern settlements were alarmed on account of the raids during the spring of the year. June 1st, one killed and one wounded near Fountain Green. June 2nd, two killed on Twelve Mile Creek. Aug. 13th, two killed at Springtown.

By this time the people of Sanpete and Sevier Counties began to get into shape to protect themselves better than they were at first; so that during the years 1869 and 1870 not many were killed, but raids were still common, the Indians often getting away with stock.

Companies of home militia were sent out to guard and assist the settlements. Records shows that General Connor and his army occupied Camp Douglas during the whole time of this bloodshed but I cannot find anything on record showing that any moves were made by Connor to assist, or in any way protect these settlements in their distress. Neither does my memory furnish an instance of help being furnished by the troops stationed at Camp Douglas to the people of Sanpete and Sevier Counties.

It may be interesting to put on record some things that I do remember. For five years, from 1866 to 1871, I lived in the eastern part of Salt Lake City, directly in the exposed portion to the depredations of numbers of Connor's army. I know of many instances where the people were insulted and abused in a violent manner, often by large parties of soldiers headed by non-commissioned officers. In some instances even commissioned officers taking the lead in lawless acts.

It was often hard to tell which were the most to be dreaded, the Indians in the south or the soldiers about the city.

While the soldiers without organisation or authority annoyed us, the commander lent his influence and offered his support to our political enemies, holding his army over the Mormons as a continual menace.

The Mormons are being accused of disloyalty; possibly this is a correct and just accusation, owing to their ignorance of what loyalty means. I will not accuse any one of disloyalty, simply because I am in the same dilemma—ignorant; but will ask, is it right and legal to fit out with government supplies, tools, and animals, and take enlisted men to work prospecting for mines, for private interests, under pretence of going to protect American citizens in their legitimate business against the Mormons? Or would it be consistent to suppose that the Mormons would be able to molest these prospectors even if so inclined, when so much occupied in protecting themselves against the Indians and the more savage and unreasonable attacks of the soldiers? Again is it legal to sell to miners and freighters by the thousands, and then to allow the commissary store-houses to get fire and burn down, allowing this fire to get so extremely hot as to burn up log-chains by the hundreds.

Now the Mormons have never taken part in anything of this kind. They are called disloyal. I do decline to be sworn on the subject, but rumor says that these things were done and headed by parties who are now called intensely "loyal."

During the war with the Indians numbers of them were killed and wounded. About the year 1868 or 1869 there was some little effort made to bring about a peace. Brother D. B. Huntington had a talk with some in Thistle valley who wished peace, but many thefts and small raids were made after this, continuing from time to time. The Indians began to have a dread of some settlements as guards and patrols were out at times. One small party had stolen some stock from Provo Valley. They were killing a beef, when they were surprised and all killed. The Indians acknowledged to me that they were afraid of Provo and Rhodes' Valley people.

CHAPTER 27

I Decide to Visit the Hostile Indians

During the Black Hawk war a great many from Utah and Salt Lake Counties were sent out to repel the Indians and assist in protecting the settlements of Sanpete and Sevier counties. I never was called to go. My feelings were different from the most. Although the Indians were cruel and unjust, I could not help but remember their personal kindness and friendship for me and dreaded the idea of being called upon to fight them.

The regiment (Colonel Sharp's) to which I belonged, had already been called upon for a detail, Captain Crow and company having spent sometime in Sanpete. About the next call would have been for my company, as we belonged to the same regiment. My mind and feelings were much exercised over these matters for I could not refuse to go in my turn, as no possible explanation could be given to relieve me from the suspicion of cowardice.

Many times, in reflecting upon the subject, my feelings were to go and see the Indians personally. Although they were at war, and had been for some six or eight years and killed numbers of our people, breaking up whole districts, still I felt as though I would rather approach them as a peacemaker than as a fighter. Luckily, one day in the summer of 1871, I met an Indian that I recognised at once as an old acquaintance, Ancatowats.

To the reader, who is not acquainted with those days, it will be necessary to say that there were friendly Indians in and around the settlements who took no part in this war, but would not inform on the hostiles when they came in, in a peaceable manner, to visit them. I had often heard of this Indian—Ancatowats—being one of Black Hawk's most active raiders. When I called him by name he said he did not know me. I told him how I felt towards the Indians. Soon I got his confidence and we had a long talk. He told me all about the hostiles and others of the Uintahs who were not actively at war. He said the Indians wished they could get some of my saddles. (I had sold them a great many in former years.) Said their saddles were all gone or broken up, so that their horses all had bruised backs. He bought three saddles of me at the time. He also told me that there was a new agent in town from Washington whom he thought was a good man; that he talked good and that he also wanted a saddle.

This Indian said to me that he thought maybe I could go out with the agent and make saddles for the Indians if I wanted to, and that, as I was an old friend and had never been out to fight them, he did not think they would want to kill me. I went and talked with George A. Smith, giving him a full understanding of my feelings, also telling of the proposition of the Indian. Brother Smith agreed with me that if someone could get among the Indians and talk to them in a proper spirit it would do more good than fighting them, and said, "If you have faith to try it you shall have my faith and blessing in the effort."

I laid before him some of my plans, which he approved of, advising me to say nothing to anyone else about the business, but to use prudence and the best judgment possible. He warned me that I would have a hard job and hoped that I would not get discouraged.

I managed to see the agent and mentioned to him my desire to visit the agency, telling him that I was an interpreter. He said if I could bring a testimonial from some responsible party he would employ me, as he wished someone, who really understood the Indians and was friendly with them, to act as interpreter. I furnished the necessary paper and asked the privilege of taking my tools and some material under an agreeable arrangement. This was allowed. I closed up my business and went, in company with the agent, to Uintah.

On arriving at that place I was notified by the Indians to leave within three days or they would kill me. This I was prepared to expect, for my Indian friend in Salt Lake did not speak very positively in regard to my safety in going, but thought maybe it would be all right. This word came from Tabby, my old friend. He would not come to see me, but sent word, saying, "You are an old friend, but the Mormons have killed many of my people; you are a Mormon, and if you stay here you will be killed. Some are mad because I do not want you killed at once. Now hurry and get ready for I do not want to see you die."

I went to work, feeling first rate, and made me a saddle within the time. Some of the Indians would come where I was at work and watch me, but would not speak. I treated them with perfect indifference.

When the saddle was done an Indian wanted to buy it. I told him I could not sell it; that I had to leave or the Indians would kill me. He said he would go and see if they would not wait three days more, so that I could let him have the one on hand. I agreed. He returned in a few hours and said it was all right. Some might ask, "Could you believe him?" I answer, most certainly.

I sold the saddle starting on another, which had the same history, thus continuing for some time until I began to feel quite at home, making saddles and selling them for a good price, with the prospect of being killed every three days. There is an old saying that one can get used to almost anything except getting killed more than once.

Tabby often passed by where I could see him, but would never look towards me. I believed that in his heart he was my friend, for I was his. This looked a little strange, but, understanding Indian character so well, I knew it would not do for me to speak first.

One day Tabby stepped into my shop accompanied by his young squaw. I had my work-bench across the room so that I faced the door, all my stuff behind and protected by the bench. I kept very busy, scarcely speaking to anyone coming in. Simply selling saddles under the rule mentioned. He came up to the bench in haughty Indian style, never offering to speak. I felt almost like laughing for I knew he was playing a part, and I determined to beat him if possible, so I never even looked up from my work. Soon he laid a new butcher knife down on the bench without speaking a word. I took the knife and made a nice scabbard for it, and laid it on the bench before him. He then took a pair of stirrups from his squaw and laid them on the bench. I had a pair of stirrup-leathers made and hanging up. I took them and put them on the stirrups and laid them down as I had the knife, then went on with my work without taking any further notice.

Tabby stood straight and silent, hardly moving during this. He then took from his squaw some buckskin, and without a word laid them on my bench. I commenced cleaning up, giving my bench a general straightening. When I came to the buckskins I handled them as though they were trash in my way, and asked the squaw if she would not take care of them. At this Tabby laughed, holding out his hand in a friendly way, saying, "All right, we are friends, and it is foolish for us to not talk and be as we used to be."

He then told me that most of the Indians liked me and thought I

129

was a friend, but that "Yank" and his crowd thought I was a spy and wanted to kill me; but that if I could win him I would be all right. After this I hadn't much fear, for I did not believe Yank would kill me for he needed a saddle very badly.

I soon learned the general condition of affairs, getting information both from the Indians themselves and some of the whites at the agency. Tabby, and quite a number of the better disposed Utes, claimed that they never had been at war with the Mormons, but acknowledged that they had a very bad feeling about the killing of some of their friends under circumstances that did not justify, telling about Tabby's half-brother, who Tabby claims, was a friend and not an enemy.

I myself knew of several instances where Indians were killed, that to me looked a little crooked, and when their friends talked about these cases, I could not help but admit sometimes that they had a right to get mad. One Indian, known as Big-Mouth-Jim, took quite a liking to me and became quite communicative. He was very faithful, never deceiving me. He would tell me how the Indians talked about me; what their plans were for raiding, and gave me advice how to control their actions, by a little stratagem.

The season was getting late. Coalville was selected as the place to raid. Yank had everything arranged but could not go without a saddle as his was about used up. Jim advised me to put him off, saying that if I could do so until snow fell that he would not go and perhaps by spring I could "make him good."

There were a great many wanting saddles. More than I could possibly supply, so that it was easy to put Yank off. I allowed the idea to still prevail that I had to leave and would not sell any Indian a saddle without the understanding that I could remain long enough to make another. I was not in the least afraid, but this suited me for I had not yet made terms with the raiders. Finally snow fell in the mountains. Jim said. "Now you can let Yank have a saddle; he will go with the rest on a hunt, and not go to Coalville." About this time the greater number of the Utes were starting on their fall hunt. Yank came in offering me some buckskins for a saddle. I told him I was going home; that I was afraid when Tabby and the good Indians went away that he would kill me. He said I was a fool to think so; that I was a good man and all the Indians liked me and none of them would kill me. I then sold him a saddle I had ready.

The Indians explained many things to me about the management at the agency. Saying that the former agents stole most that the government sent them. They did not know how the new agent would be, but agreed if I would be their friend and tell "Washington" the truth, just how things were done it would be different. They believed "Washington" was honest, had a kind heart, and when hungry men came to him crying for something to eat, that he made Indian agents of them and sent them out here to the Indians. They did not think this was right for they needed all that the government gave them and there was nothing to spare for the agents to steal without leaving the Indians hungry.

Tabby said that some of "Brigham's Bishops" helped the agents to steal and this made the Indians mad, causing them to raid upon the Mormons and to excuse themselves by saying that if the Mormons did not help to steal their provisions they would have enough; but as it was, they had to steal Mormon cattle, and when the Mormons followed them, sometimes they had to fight; but would just as soon get the beef without killing anyone as to have to kill them.

The question may be asked was there any truth or reason in this? I thought at one time of writing up some facts that can be proved, giving circumstances and names which would clearly show that the Indians had reason to talk as they did. If blood was shed and the cause originated through the speculative act of some man who ought to have known better, the day of reckoning will come without my calling them to account in this little history.

After becoming acquainted with the condition of affairs at the Uintah and the White River Agency, I made up my mind to act as a friend to the Indians in trying to get something done to better their condition. That there had been a great deal of neglect and crookedness going on for years, no one could doubt. Reports were circulated that some of the government officials, prior to this time, had encouraged the Indians in stealing cattle from the Mormons, thinking that if the Indians supplied themselves with beef they could better appropriate what government furnished, than when the Utes were peaceable and not stealing. The new agent was very emphatic in his denunciations of former agents. He seemed disposed to change the management, and work for the good of the natives. He asked me to find how the Indians felt and to assist him in every way possible to get things in good order and work to make the Indians happy and contented. I felt much pleasure in the prospective work before me.

After I had been in the agency a few weeks, the agent started to Salt Lake City to buy winter supplies. He instructed me to come in and bring his team and light wagon. In a few days after his leaving, I got ready to start in. According to previous arrangements, I was to have the right to take in with the agent's team the buckskins and furs that I had received for saddles. As far as I knew good feeling existed between the agent and myself. But when I was ready to start in, the clerk then in charge told me that the agent had instructed him not to allow me to haul any of my stuff in his wagon; that I was to take the wagon in empty. George Basor, the post trader, and a Mr. Morgan, blacksmith, were going in with me. They told me that for some cause the agent had "gone back" on me. But I concluded not to "go back" on myself so I got my skins and furs ready. The clerk at first forbade me to load them in, but soon took another notion and assisted me to load the stuff into the wagon.

After the agent had left the clerk in charge, business was carried on in a very bad manner. Quite a crop of potatoes had been raised; the weather commenced to grow cold, potatoes freezing. Instead of digging and taking care each day of the potatoes dug, he would have all hands dig all they could and then try to get all hands—mechanics, cooks, and all, to gather them in after night. While working in this manner the Indians were not allowed to help, but at the same time the most of these potatoes were expected to be eaten by the Indians. Many other things as foolish were being done daily. I kept a memorandum, intending to report to the agent according to my agreement with him.

About the time Mr. Basor, Mr. Morgan and myself were ready to start in, the first severe snowstorm of the season commenced. We had quite a hard trip getting into the valley.

CHAPTER 28

Our Terrible Journey and Sufferings

On arriving in Salt Lake, in company with Mr. Morgan, the agency blacksmith, who had been discharged by the clerk because he refused to put long, sharp corks on the agent's team, which would have cut them while floundering through deep snowdrifts—such as we would encounter on the road—which any experienced man knows is correct. But the clerk, like many others, felt that a little authority must of necessity make him wise, thought differently. On reporting the clerk to the agent, we were considerably surprised at his answer to us. He told us that the clerk suited him, and if we did not like him we could stay away from the agency. I told him that Tom Layton was a fraud on honesty and good sense, and if he felt to uphold him, he was a different man from what I supposed him to be. I wanted to know why he instructed me to notice how the affairs were conducted and report facts, which I had done and could prove all I said, and then treat my information in the way he did.

The agent told me he did not want me any more and would discharge me from his service and forbade me going to the agency. I answered that whether he discharged me or not, I had business at the agency, and calculated to visit there whether he wanted me to do so or not. He replied that it was now late in the season and that he expected much trouble in getting his supply-train through that was now about starting from Heber City with flour and other provisions, and that he forbade my going with them. He then rather derisively remarked that he did not think that I would be able to make the trip, that he thought it would be about as much as he could do with the government to back him up, to get back to Uintah; and hardly thought any one else would try the trip so late in the season.

I told him there was not enough snow for me yet. But after a while when travelling was good, I would call over and see him. I had already studied out my campaign for the winter.

Before leaving the Uintah agency, I had promised the Indians that I would return and do all I could for them. They wanted me to try and get the place of trader. There were many things they wanted that they could not get. Among the rest children's woollen shirts and dresses of various sizes. My wife went to work, with the assistance of some of our neighbours, (particularly that of the Sisters Brower of the 11th Ward) and made a lot of such as were needed.

The agent left sometime in November. The trip had never been made in the winter by anyone, as the snow often fell from fifteen to twenty feet on the mountains that had to be crossed. So when I spoke of going many of my friends considered me a little crazy.

I knew the work before me, that I had so much interest in, and that was making permanent peace with the Indians, could only be accomplished by keeping my word with them, and gaining their entire confidence; so I determined to go or perish in the attempt. I knew that I was engaged in a good work and fully believed that I would be preserved and strengthened according to the undertaking. I knew the country I had to travel was rough in the extreme, with high mountains and deep rough canyons. Following the road would be of no use, as it would be entirely covered with snow several feet deep. So I made up my mind to wait until mid winter when the snow was deepest and take as direct a route as possible.

With the assistance of Calvin Ensign, I constructed a sled of peculiar and original pattern. One thing was certain; unless good sleeping arrangements could be provided, we would perish at night. The sled was long enough and of size and shape so that two could sleep in it by lapping our feet and legs to the knees, each one taking his end. We took in provisions goods and bedding to nearly four hundred pounds weight.

My wife assisted me in every way possible in getting ready, with a kind cheerful spirit, manifesting no uneasiness whatever. As I have before mentioned whenever my labours were among the Indians, she sympathized with me fully. Eight days before I started, a son was born to me. My wife was confined to her bed when I started. I waited as long a time as possible, but there was now plenty of snow.

I started Jan. 12th, 1872. I hired N. Murdock of Provo Valley, to take my sled to Heber City. I had not yet found any person to go with me, expecting to procure someone in Provo Valley, as there were a number of hardy, venturesome persons living there who were in the habit of going out for days on snow-shoes, hunting elk and trapping beaver. On arriving there I found Bradley Sessions, a Mormon Battalion boy, willing to undertake the trip. I told him all I wanted him to agree was, that if we perished on the trip he would agree with me that we would not grumble, but die uncomplainingly; that under no circumstances were we to give up or turn back.

He said, "All right, I will stay with you." And he did.

Brother Sessions furnished me with a pair of snowshoes. I had prepared almost everything else needed for two before leaving the city, so that we were soon ready to start.

On leaving Heber City we took the most direct road over the pass leading down into the west fork of the Duchesne, then down to the main stream intersecting the government road, not far from where it crosses this stream. The divide is too steep for a wagon road, but part of the way up had been used for carting timber down to a mill near the foothills. There was a sled road some few miles out from Heber City to this mill. Brother John Duke hauled our sled that far with his team; here we made our first camp, in an old house. I had taken from the city a large, strong dog with the idea of having a camp guard, as wolves and other wild animals were in the mountains.

We had a few light tools along with us for repairing our sled in case of accident, and Brother Sessions wished to take along a few beaver traps. Our load already being heavy, and the traps awkward to load among our bedding, as our whole load of goods were arranged in convenient shape for a bed, we concluded to make a sled and harness our dog to it to pull the traps. We got some choke-cherry sticks with crooked ends and spent the evening making a rig for the dog. When harnessed up next morning, he acted rather unruly.

We found the snow lighter than we expected. The winter had been continually cold, the snows deep and not yet settled or packed. But we had started out to stay with it and did not intend to give up. We found it impossible to move our sled on the snow until a road was packed. Accordingly we would take a few handy articles on our backs, and with our snow-shoes, five feet long and some fifteen inches wide, go forward tramping a trail wide enough for our sled, the dog following with his load. After tramping a mile or two we would return and bring up our sled.

The main trouble we had was with our dog chasing the little pine squirrels, running after them sled and all, and getting overturned, or hung among the trees. We would have to straighten him out. We did not like to thrash him for fear he would run off, as he seemed a little disposed to get away from us.

This tramping road and having to double on our tracks was very laborious. Many times even after tramping the road the way was so steep that it took all our strength to move the sled a few rods at a time, but when an easy grade was reached, we walked along quite easily with our four hundred pound load.

We were five days in reaching the summit. When there we could look back and see Heber City, some twenty miles distant. This looked a little trying to us as our provisions were wasting away very fast.

Our dog seemed to understand the situation and rebelled. I had hard work to conquer him. Heretofore we had coaxed him along, but it now became necessary to make him mind as bolognas were getting too scarce to feed him more than his share. We crossed the divide at the head of the West Fork of the Duchesne. The weather was so cold that we were afraid to halt for dinner until we had descended quite a distance from the summit. Once we halted among some dry trees intending to get dinner, but the wind blew so cold that we were forced to swallow a few bits of frozen meat and go on.

We naturally expected that the descent would be much easier and more rapid than pulling up the mountain. In this we were mistaken, owing to the wind blowing the light snow from the mountain tops which settled down into the canyon. Much of the time we had to tramp and make road before we could move along. Sometimes the whole bottom was covered with willows, the tops sticking out and holding the snow up so light that we had to cut and tramp them into the snow before we could move our sled along. While passing the narrows, we had to make a dug way for quite a distance, still we pressed forward. Neither could we abandon our sled or goods, for the sled was our salvation to sleep in. Almost any night we would have perished with cold without our bed-room.

The goods we were taking were promised, and the influence I desired to gain with the Indians would greatly depend upon successfully reaching them with the outfit. When I made them the promise I expected to go out with the agent and take these things with me; but when he forbade me going it only raised my ire and I was determined to go.

By the time we reached the main fork of the Duchesne, our provisions were about gone. Game cannot exist in the high mountains during the coldest part of the winter. Nothing had been met. We hoped to find something on reaching the river. We camped near some springs that ran into the stream, finding places where the river was open. We hoped to catch some fish for supper. We cast our hooks, but had no bites. We continued to fish until near dusk. We had travelled eight days without rest, but agreed if we could get something for supper, to lay over and call it Sabbath. We finally gave up fishing.

Brother Sessions got to camp a little ahead of me. I followed, feeling very much discouraged, I thought of course we would have to go to bed supperless. It was becoming quite dark, and suddenly I heard a shot that made me feel happy. Directly another was fired. As I came up Bradley was reloading his shot gun and remarked, "We've got supper and breakfast. Here are two pine hens."

At that the third one came flying along, knocked Sessions' cap off his head and lit on the ground just in front of him. He shot, saying, "There's dinner." We had a few crumbs of crackers and a small piece of bacon. We soon had a fine stew of one of the chickens giving the dog his share. The dog had by this time become quite well trained, and a great favourite also, pulling his sled with nearly one hundred pounds load on it.

We laid over next day, catching several fine trout. We had not yet suffered for food, so we ate heartily, knowing that as long as we kept our strength we were all right, that it would be time to starve when forced to it.

When we left camp, we had a few fish; enough for one meal, and one small meal of crumbs and a few bits of bacon. We agreed to try and make a good drive down the river that day and not stop for dinner; and if possible reach the road where we hoped to find the snow hard. The snow was now harder than in the mountains. We could move along slowly without tramping a road and were making very good time.

About noon I became very hungry and remarked to Sessions that the man who works has a right to eat. He replied, "That's what I think."

We halted, took out our little stock of food, and ate it all except the fish.

About the time we had fairly started on, we discovered a mountain sheep on a high point of the mountain. Sessions grabbed his rifle, telling me to try and keep the sled in motion so as to attract its attention and he would have some meat for supper.

I continued tugging at the sled, moving a few rods at a time. Bradley climbed the mountain at a rate of speed that could not well have been done by a hungry man. Still it took quite a while as it was a long way up. I could see the sheep, but Sessions kept out of its sight. He had now got well up the mountain, I heard the rifle crack and saw the sheep fall. I felt happy again and moved up to some dry cedars at the foot of the mountain and had a fire ready for a roast by the time Sessions got down the mountain with the meat.

After roasting and eating what we wanted we moved on down to old Fort Duchesne, now abandoned. We cut up our meat, which was very poor, being mostly skin and bone; jerked the flesh which was but little, boiled the bones and ate very heartily.

Next morning we were both sick. I took the dog and his sled and went down to the government road, a few miles distant. The travelling was tolerably good. We fed the most of the meat to the dog as it seemed to weaken us to eat it.

After resting one day we moved down to the road, camping near an old house. We had hopes of finding something stored here that we could eat, but nothing whatever was found. The house was open and no wood very near, so we camped where there was plenty of dry timber standing.

We were very weak, our stomachs being out of condition and nothing to eat except the jerked meat, which only made us sicker to eat it. It was an intensely cold evening. We became chilled and hadn't strength to cut down trees to make a good fire. There were a few dry willows but they would only make a temporary blaze. Each of us tried to use the ax but we were as weak as little children. I never felt so used up before. I felt as though we would perish, I knew if we went to bed in our exhausted, chilled condition we would be in danger of freezing; for no amount of clothing will warm a person under such circumstances, but, like the ice, the more blankets you wrap around the colder it keeps. Some may doubt this, but when far enough chilled there is danger in going to bed. I have had to get up and make a fire more than once to get thawed out.

Our condition seemed almost hopeless; so much so that I found the tears running down my cheeks before I thought what to do. This weakness made me a little angry with myself At last I told Bradley to gather as many willows as possible. The wind was blowing almost a blizzard, but we were in the timber and tolerably well protected.

I got our coffee pot ready and made a lot of strong coffee. We drank of it and ate a few bites of the meat. The coffee seemed to almost intoxicate us, giving us strength. We pitched in like strong men and cut down trees and made up a roaring fire, got well warmed up and went to bed and slept soundly.

Next morning we were quite feeble, but felt safe as the travelling was now of a different kind from this point, for forty-five miles to the agency. The road was open for teams; in fact, in many places, the snow was clear from the road which was now muddy and heavy; so we stored our sled in the old house, left our snow-shoes, strapped a pair of blankets on the dog and started on. We had nothing for breakfast, and a march of two days was before us. We were so determined to keep our pledge not to complain, that we never spoke a word regarding our situation, simply doing what we had to and moving on just as though all was right.

We had our guns but no game came in our way, and we were too weak to risk a step out of our direction on an uncertain hunt. We never spoke of the thought until afterwards, but our last hope was to kill our dog, which would have seemed almost like killing a human being, for he carried a heavy pair of blankets on his back when we were too weak to carry them ourselves. Again, our condition would not be materially helped by unpalatable dog meat. We were more sick from bad food than starved. Our condition grew worse and worse. Each of us was attacked with flux in a most violent manner.

I remember well of looking ahead several times a few rods and picking out some object by the side of the road and thinking it looked a more comfortable place to die in than where I was. Sessions told me afterwards his thoughts were the same. First one and then the other would pass on a little way and stop; not a word was spoken. My feelings were to move ahead as long as a mite of strength lasted.

We continued on in this way until about the middle of the afternoon. Our progress was slow. We had fell in together and were moving along at a snail's pace, when Sessions stooped down, picked up something, and in a joyous tone exclaimed, "Here's life." And breaking in two an ear of corn handed me half of it. We commenced eating. I ate mine cob and all, chewing it a long time before swallowing. Never before or since have I tasted anything so sweet and strengthening. It seemed to penetrate to the end of my toes. We were strengthened immediately and commenced to walk at a regular, even pace, in good travelling time.

About the time we had finished eating this, I discovered another ear, picked it up and divided it, saying, "Here is more life." Our sickness ceased entirely and we continued travelling until near midnight. We arrived at a good dry camp, gave the last scrap of meat to the faithful dog, feeling that we were good for next day's tramp, food or no food.

It was a good long day's travel. The next morning we left our blankets hung up in a tree, measured our gait, and agreed to keep it up, setting our time to arrive at the station about sundown. At times I was tempted to cry "enough, halt," but it seemed as though we dared not stop for fear we could not get up steam for another start. So we kept up our gait all day and till nine o'clock at night.

When we arrived at the trader's quarters, owned by George Basor, whom I was well acquainted with, and who still lives in that region. George started back and in a serious manner asked, "Is this Dan Jones' ghost, or Dan himself?"

I answered, "I am Dan, and d——d hungry."

He grasped my hand, laughing, and said he saw it was all right, for Dan always came into camp hungry.

While we were at supper, some of the boys went over to the agent's office and told of our arrival. They came back and said that the agent and clerk declared they intended to kill me on sight.

I do not wish to be considered a boaster, in truth I leave many things untold that I might tell, only I despise a braggart and do not wish to appear as one. I was too hungry to let this report stop my eating. When I got through, I picked up my shot gun, putting a few extra navy balls into it and told the boys I was going over to the office. Some of them wanted to go with me, but I preferred going alone.

Men often get the name of being brave and fearless from such occurrences, but in this case I will tell just how I felt and what my reasons were, and I think many others feel the same under similar circumstances.

I consider suspense or uncertainty the most disagreeable condition in the world. I did not wish to be annoyed by fear or dread of being killed and I deemed it best to get that off my mind at once, as I was tired and wished to rest. Again, I wanted freedom to be at the agency unmolested. Then I did not much believe that the intention was to kill me, for men who really intend to kill scarcely ever send word of their intentions. All this passed in my mind, so it was not any great bravery on my part.

On reaching the office I knocked, and was told to come in. I had my shotgun ready. Their pistols lay in front of them. I was asked what I wanted. I replied that I wanted to know whether it was to be war or peace.

The agent answered, "I guess it had better be peace."

"Peace it is then," I put my gun down and shook hands with both.

I was kindly treated and accommodated in many ways by the agent, after this, while at the agency I got a team from him to bring in the sled and goods.

Chapter 29

I Visit the Indian Camp

The Indians were greatly pleased to see me. It is well understood by all who are acquainted with Indian character, that they are undemonstrative as a rule, except when angry, especially the warriors. Many of them said I was a strong man and had good legs. They admired my companion, saying they knew him and knew he was a good hunter.

The most that I desired for a few days was to rest and eat. Sessions soon got filled up, but it seemed to me that I never would be able to satisfy my stomach for having punished it so with the sickly mountain sheep. There was plenty to eat at the trader's quarters. The agent was kind, giving us all the potatoes and milk we wanted; these being about the only articles the trader was lacking. The dog was in about the same fix as myself, he tried to eat everything on the reservation, but finally got satisfied by getting at a barrel of tallow, one day, and eating, as we all estimated, about ten pounds. Reader, remember this was a large dog.

Basor, the trader, would not cook for me. He said a man that ate as much as I did would have to do his own cooking. So one day while alone, I made up my mind to conquer my hunger. I cooked a good square meal for three of us, waited a little while for the others then sat down and ate the whole of it. I did not feel hungry again for several days. After getting this difficulty over, I told the Indians I would visit their camp and have a talk with them. A time was appointed, and Tabby, the chief, sent a man and horse for me. The camp was some eight miles from the station. When I reached their camp, there were about fifty of the principal men of the tribe present. "Captain Joe," of Thistle valley, was there also. I always considered him like some of our political white men, not very reliable.

I was informed by Joe that I could talk. I spoke to them about half an hour, telling them that, notwithstanding all the trouble and war, the good Mormons were still their friends; that Brigham had always desired peace and was sorry that any of his people wanted to fight the Indians. After saying what I thought was safe, for I knew the delicacy of the subject, as some of the Indians had been killed by such as professed to be Mormons, and I was careful not to push the subject too far in my first attempt, I desired to hear Tabby talk.

I knew he was much respected by his people, also that he was not inclined to war, but had accepted the situation and let things run, neither taking an active part in killing and stealing, nor making any great effort to stop the war. He was very sore about the killing of his half brother while a prisoner. I, myself, considered this somewhat treacherous on the part of those who did it.

Capt. Joe seemed to think he must do all the talking for the Indians. No one else spoke. Joe urged me to say more. I told him I wanted to hear Tabby. The old fellow laid down, as much as to say, "I will not take part in this." The act nettled me considerably, and I told Joe I would not talk unless Tabby did. Tabby grunted out that he was an old man, and chief; that Joe was a little captain and young, and was good enough to talk to me. This made me mad. I got up and told Tabby that I was more of a man than he or any of his men ever were; that they had been born and raised in Uintah, and none of them had ever been brave or strong enough to cross the snow mountains, but had laid there shut up winter after winter like women; that I had done what none of them could do, and had done it to keep my word with them; that they had agreed if I would be their friend and tell "Washington" their grievances that they would listen to me and make peace.

When I got through, Tabby got up and said, "You talk big for a boy. I know you have strong legs and a good belly, for I have seen you eat. But I want to know where your grey hairs are, that give wisdom. You had better wait a few years before you talk." I really felt small under this sarcasm. He further said, "You have spoke about the Indians stealing from the Mormons. I can answer that by saying some of the Mormon Bishops helped the agents to steal what 'Washington' sends us. While some of Brigham's Bishops steal, I do not. Neither does Tom and many others; but we have staid at home and worked and hunted. It is the bad Indians that will not listen to me, that steal." He then named some twelve or fourteen present whom he said stole from the Mormons and made the trouble.

He continued, "I have told them it is wrong; now you may talk to

143

them and make them good if you can. I am not bad and do not steal, so you do not need to talk to me."

I held several meetings and cultivated on every opportunity the personal friendship of the Indians, especially the raiders, talking kindly to them and gaining their confidence and good-will. At length, one night, the bad Indians were induced to talk. They related many things about their raids; each in turn told something of his experience, entering into details. How they felt, and giving the causes of their ill-feelings. Each taking his turn in talking, said that hunger often caused them to go on raids to get cattle to eat, always making the statement that the agents stole what "Washington" sent them; that Mormons helped the agents to steal; that the Sanpete Mormons had stolen their country and fenced it up. The lands that their fathers had given them had been taken for wheat fields. When they asked the Mormons for some of the bread raised on their lands, and beef fed on their grass, the Mormons insulted them, calling them dogs and other bad names. They said when the Mormons stole big fields and got rich, other Mormons, who were poor, had to buy the land from them, they were not allowed to steal it from the first owners, the same as the first Mormons stole it from the Indians.

I have often wondered how these statements will be answered. They are still open. I never could answer them like many other propositions I have had to meet while labouring among the Indians. I have had to give it up acknowledging that they had been wronged. All I could do was to get their hearts set right and then teach them magnanimity.

Some may jeer at this idea, but I have found more nobility of character among the Indians than what is common among many whites, even Mormons included.

In explanation of their accusing some of the Mormon Bishops of helping to rob them, it had been told to them how the agents managed to get certain ones to sign false vouchers for flour and beef. Whether this was true or not the Indians fully believed that it was. I found evidences afterwards that at least looked like their accusations were well founded. All who are acquainted with Indian character know that a trader who deals liberally with the natives can hold a great influence over them. The Utes were great traders at that time, having a great many skins and furs to barter. They urged me to come and trade with them. This could only be done by buying out the trader and getting the appointment. So I bought out the trader, conditionally, with the hopes of getting the post tradership. In this I failed.

The friendship of the agent was only politic for the time being. His endeavors to keep me out of the situation were successful. Mine to bring about a permanent peace and get the Indians better provided for were also successful, probably much more so than if I had been allowed the trader's position. After visiting with the Indians and gaining considerable influence over them, getting them to promise peace, provided the Mormons would be friendly again, I commenced preparing for my return home. The Indians wanted me to go back and talk to the Mormons and see positively what they said and how they felt, especially in Sanpete valley, where the war had been the worst. They wanted to be assured that the Mormons would not kill them, provided they came in to visit and trade as in former times. I agreed to find out and return again and see them, and bring a few more things they wanted.

There were two men, John Sessions and David Boyce, at the agency that wished to come in with me. We brought in five hundred pounds of buckskins. This, with our provisions and bedding, made about seven hundred pounds. On this trip the snow had settled and we moved along all right. The dog hauled most of the time two hundred pounds. We thought this a big load, but I afterwards learned what a load was for a large dog.

In justice to my Indian friends, and one in particular, I will relate one incident. Just before leaving, an Indian, Toquana, came to me and asked me if I did not want a horse. I told him that I had finished trading and had nothing to buy a horse with, and that I did not particularly need one as we would run the sled out on wheels until we struck snow, then we could haul it very well.

His reply was, "I do not want to sell you a horse. You are a friend, and are doing hard work for our good. I want you to live and keep strong; I do not want you to wear out. I know your legs are good, and I want you to keep them good to go over the deep snow where a horse cannot go. I have got a good, gentle horse that knows how to work; he is strong, can go through snow up to his breast. You take him, let him pull your sled just as long as he possibly can, then maybe you can find some place on the hill side where the snow is not deep; turn him out and if he lives I will get him, and it will be all right; if he dies, he will die mine, and I will know he died to help my friend, and that will be all right. I do not want anything at all, no presents or anything. I want to do this because I feel like doing it."

I took his horse, worked him about eighty miles and then turned him on good grass where there was but little snow.

CHAPTER 30

Treaty with the Grass Valley Indians

On my arrival in Salt Lake City and after disposing of my furs and skins, I made arrangements for the money to pay the trader, George Basor, for his stock of buckskins, amounting to some two thousand dollars. The arrangement was to close the bargain by a certain date, provided the purchase was made.

I found the dog so useful in pulling a sled that I determined to get hold of some more large dogs and train them. To do this I would be delayed a few days; so I got David Boyce, who had just come in with me, to take Ring, the old dog, with a sled load of one hundred and fifty pounds, and a $2000.00 check and make the trip alone. Boyce, travelling on Norwegian snow-runners, made the trip through in good time. This trip of Boyce's I consider one of the most heroic of any, as he travelled alone one hundred and fifty miles, passing over twenty feet of snow, with no one but the faithful dog for company.

On getting my dogs, four in number, trained with sleds for each, I took my son Wiley, thirteen years of age, and started again for Uintah, taking about four hundred pounds of goods for the Indians. I was careful to take a good supply of provisions on this trip. I hired a young man from Heber City, by the name of Hickins, to go with us. We made good time over the mountains. Our dogs behaved tolerably well, as I had trained them before starting.

Boyce, who went through with the express, found the horse, loaned by Toquana, all right. He packed the goods on him, after getting to hard ground, went on to the agency, transacted the business, got a yoke of cattle and a light wagon, and came out and met us at the snow line. So everything went off smoothly on this trip. On my arrival at the agency, I found it would be impossible for me to get the trader's position and be true to the Indians. What I had started to do for them would make the agent my enemy, so I concluded to stick to the peace-making, let it cost what it might.

On getting the Indians together and talking to them, we came to a full understanding and agreement. By this time they had come to believe in and trust me implicitly. I agreed to procure all the evidence I could in regard to irregularities on the part of the agents. Such evidence I had been gathering up for some time, to make a report to Washington in their behalf, and do all I could to get them their rights. There was not much provisions at the agency at this time for the Indians. Only a few sacks of flour. I assured them that if they would come in and visit the Mormons, that they would be glad and would not fight them, but would treat them as friends, as was the custom before the war.

This finally was agreed upon. I knew that some move of importance, sufficient to cause the government to take notice, had to be made. So it was arranged that all the Indians should leave the reservation and refuse to return until they were furnished with supplies, and a better system of provisioning them devised. They hated the agent as he had acted very insultingly to some of them. They urged hard that I would send in evidence of his wrong-doing, and get him removed. I told them maybe they would get a worse one, but they insisted that there was no danger.

I did not agree with the idea of the Indians. The present agent had not been long in position, and from what I knew and had heard about former agents, he was not nearly so bad as some of his predecessors. In fact I believed him capable of making a very good agent when once posted on the duties of his office.

My interests were entirely centred on doing the best for the Indians I possibly could, also that the people would be relieved from their depredations.

The furs and skins that I had bought from the old trader amounted to some twenty odd hundred pounds. The ground was now bare for some seventy-five miles; the snow being still deep for about the same distance. I bought a wagon and team from the trader, loaded all up and pulled up to the snow region, where we turned the team out, loaded up our dog sleds and, by making an average of three return trips, moved our whole load six miles each day. Our dogs were fed mostly on beaver meat, caught by trapping in the streams along the route.

On nearing Provo valley I went ahead to get teams to come out and meet the dog train a few miles from Heber City. It took two light wagons to contain our load. We made the trip down Provo Canyon and camped one night near American Fork. I had been from home longer than was expected; there were no means of communication and I felt very anxious to get home as I believed my family would be uneasy about me.

At that time the terminus of the Utah Central was at Draperville. I started out early in the morning on foot to make to the train by 8 o'clock, some eight miles distant. I had been working on snow shoes for most of the winter; I was now on good dry road and was wearing Indian moccasins. I was feeling well and in good trim, so I had but little fears of making the distance in time.

After travelling a short distance I heard a wagon approaching. On looking around I recognised a gentleman who had always professed great friendship and interest in my labours among the Indians. It occurred to me that I would see if he would ask me to ride without my making the request. He drove by without turning his head. I made up my mind that although he was driving a nice fine travelling team, to beat him into the station. This I did. He drove quite fast, but I kept in sight of him all the way, passing the team about a mile before reaching the station.

As I went by he spoke to me, saying he had not recognised me before. I replied that I was in a hurry and could not stop. One of his horses suddenly failed, causing them to halt. This friend (?) probably never passed a footman afterwards without thinking of the circumstance.

The reader will now have to make a little allowance, as I am writing entirely from memory, and there was so much crowding upon me at this time, I will have to go ahead and write as it comes to my mind, regardless of dates. I have heretofore been able to place incidents in regular order tolerably well; possibly I may, in writing the next few months' history, get a little mixed as to which first occurred, but not as to facts.

Soon after my arrival in Salt Lake City I called on Governor Woods and told him something about the condition of affairs at the Uintah agency, informing him that, owing to the fact that there was no flour or other provisions at the agency, it was the intention of the Indians to leave there. Mr. Woods agreed to assist me in bringing the matter before the proper department. My intention was to visit Washington to see in person the Secretary of the Interior, in behalf of the Utes; I had sufficient evidence to show cause for complaint. Advising and persuading the Indians to leave the agency was entirely my own work;

I was satisfied that nothing would be done unless some move was made worth noticing.

I had, as before stated, visited the people in Sanpete county and got their consent for the Indians to come in. The Indians were now on the road and would soon be located in Thistle Valley, where they had agreed to stop. I was to meet them there as soon as they were in, get things in shape and then, if necessary, go to Washington. About the time the Indians got in Secretary Delano arrived in Salt Lake City, passing through on a visit. Seeing his name among the hotel arrivals, I called to see him and made my business known. He treated me with much respect, making many inquiries about Indians and Indian agents in general, admitting that the government had more trouble with them than any other officers in the service, and asked me what I thought was the reason of this. I said the wages were too small; that no man could support himself, especially in an expensive place such as agents generally had to occupy, on the pittance the government allowed them. This often forced them into dishonest speculations. Mr. Delano admitted that my explanations looked reasonable.

After listening to what I had to say for the Indians, he said if I could bring him such testimonials from some of the government officials as would warrant him in noticing me as an honourable man he would listen to and cause action to be taken on my report. I told him about my conversation with Governor Woods and his seeming interest in the welfare of the Indians. Mr. Delano sent for Governor Woods. In the meantime I went to a prominent lawyer, Mr. R———n, whom I knew to have much influence with the officials, and paid him a liberal fee to make out the necessary testimonial and get the needed endorsers. This did not require much time. I presented my papers to Secretary Delano. He said he would have the matter investigated and advised me to see Mr. G. W. Dodge, who had lately been appointed special agent for Utah and Nevada, and report to him and inform him of the condition of affairs.

When I called on Mr. Dodge he seemed much interested and agreed to go to Sanpete Valley and visit the Utes on their arrival, promising me that he would see that they were cared for. I agreed to meet him there. Accordingly, when the Indians were encamped in Thistle Valley, not long after my arrival in Salt Lake City, I went to Fairview, where I met Mr. Dodge. A party of us accompanied him to the Indian camp, some fourteen miles distant. Several hundred Indians were there. This was quite a move. For several years most of the

Indians had been at war, stealing, robbing and killing. Now they were all in to visit their old acquaintances as friends. Many of the settlers had seen their friends and kindred killed by these same Indians. If any mishap had occurred I would have borne the blame, as I had been instrumental in bringing this move about.

On arriving at the camp Mr. Dodge seemed a little lost. It was the first Indian camp he had ever visited. He professed great friendship. The Indians said to me: "He talks good, but his eyes have dirt in them."

A number of the leading citizens of Fairview and Mt. Pleasant went over. The meeting with the Indians was friendly. Each party really desired peace. Mr. Dodge appointed a meeting to take place in Fairview next day, where he desired to see all the chiefs and have a big talk with them. There were some thirty of the principal Indians came over. Douglas, of the White river Utes, who spoke English, being at the head.

Mr. Dodge had employed several interpreters to assist in the talk. He wished to be fully understood. For some cause he seemed to rather slight me as interpreter; so when the meeting was opened Mr. Dodge commenced and made quite a speech, and called on one of his interpreters to explain what he had said and invited the Indians to reply. The speech was interpreted, but the Indians said nothing. Then another speech was made and another interpreter explained with the same results.

Finally, Mr. Dodge was determined to make an impression. He began and told the Indians of his love for the red man; and of his big heart that swelled so large that all the ties of home and friends could not hold it back, but it had grown in him till it had reached clear out to the wilds of the Rocky Mountains, penetrating into the camps of the much abused natives; that he was here as their friend, sent here by "Washington" to see that all their rights were respected and grievances redressed.

Still there was no answer from the Indians. Mr. Dodge was now almost exhausted. The Indians recognised me as their representative and were intent on silence until I was noticed. Finally I said to Mr. Dodge: "With your permission I will talk a little to the chiefs present. I have been acting as their friend and I think they will talk if I request them to."

He said he would like to hear what the principal men had to say. I told the Indians to explain to Mr. Dodge why they had left the agency and what their desires were. Several then spoke in turn, recounting how they had been defrauded out of the government appropriations;

that if they could have their rights they could live in peace. Douglas, being the last speaker, did not use an interpreter. He said:

> The man from. 'Washington' talks good and makes good promises, and I hope it is all true, but I am afraid it will all be a lie pretty soon. 'Washington' has sent to us a heap of men, All of them talk good when they first come but in two or three moons, most of their talk proves lies. Some in two moons, some in three, some in six. One man's talk was good for one snow; then it was a lie, same as the others. This man here now, looks like the man who lasted two moons. Maybe the talk is all good, but I think in two moons may be it will be all lies. I know Washington means to be good to us. His heart is good, most too good. He has many hungry men come to him for something to eat; they have slim faces and long beards and look hungry; and they cry and tell Washington they have nothing to eat. Then Washington gets tired of their crying and makes them agents and sends them out here, and they take all Washington sends us. I don't think this is right. They ought to send men who are not so poor and starved, then they would not take our flour and we would have plenty.

This is Douglas's speech in substance. Mr. Dodge did not reply farther than to say he would see to their wants.

From Sanpete we went down to visit the Indians in Grass Valley. They had been stealing had taken quite a band of horses lately. They were not of the Uintah tribe. On visiting them, a treaty was made, the agent agreeing to make them some presents. The Indians agreed to bring back the horses.

I knew very well that no treaty would be considered by the Indians until the goods promised were delivered. I told Mr. Dodge so. He said the government had not furnished him with any goods, neither would they get any till he could send to New York for them. I told him I had goods along with me that he could have. Some $350.00 worth. He said he was not authorized to pay more than New York prices, and freight. I replied, "You can take mine now, and when you find what New York prices are, you can pay me."

He took my goods, enough to ratify the treaty. The Indians kept their contract to bring in the horses, but I do not know whether Mr. Dodge ever learned what New York prices were or not.

CHAPTER 31

They Threaten to Kill me

During the time the Indians were in Thistle Valley, there were a number of persons mean enough to sell them whisky. This was a dangerous business, and I did all in my power to stop it.

After returning from Grass Valley, I camped near the Indians in Thistle. I also visited the Sanpete settlements and watched the moves and did what I could to keep peace. There were quite a number opposed to the Indians being around and expressed themselves quite freely; but the greater portion of the people were desirous of peace. The whisky selling was the great evil, likely to bring on trouble at any time. Finally, through threatening the whisky sellers with prosecution, I succeeded in frightening them off, all except one man at Moroni, who still had not given up the business. Douglas and some fifteen others obtained whisky from this rascal, sufficient to get well started on a drunk, then came on to Fairview, went to where they had been in the habit of getting whisky and wanted more. Here they were told by D.S. that Jones had stopped him selling whisky and that none could be had without a written order from him.

The Indians had just enough to fire them up for more, so they struck for my camp, twelve miles distant, in full charge. No one was with me but my son Wiley, then about thirteen years of age. Soon I was charged upon by three or four drunken Indians, demanding of me that I should give them an order for whisky. I told them I would not. One Indian had a pencil and paper. He offered it to me, saying: "You must now write, or we will kill you." Still I refused. Others were now arriving. Soon the whole crowd was upon me; all were excited and just drunk enough to be mean.

I told my son to sit still; not to move or say a word. This he did, not seeming to notice what was going on. Many times it looked as

152

though my time had come, for numerous guns were aimed at me at different times, seemingly with the full intention of pulling the trigger. When one Indian would fail to shoot, another would crowd in with his gun aimed at me, saying, "I will shoot if you don't write." Many of them took hold of my hand and tried to make me write, but I was determined that I would not.

Finally, I became so overcome and weary with the excitement and effort to resist their demand, that I almost became indifferent to life. It really looked as though I might get shot. So I begged them to be still a minute and hear me; then, if they wanted to, they could kill me. All became quiet. I told them that I had always been their friend and was now working for their good; referred to the hard trips across the snow mountains to do them good, and that I would still like to live, as I had not finished the work I was doing for them. And it was as their friend that I had forbidden anyone selling them whisky, because it made them fools and bad men—so much so that they were now abusing me, the best friend they had; that I had agreed with God to be their friend and never shed any of their blood; and that I would die before I would sign the papers, and if they killed me God would not be their friend.

I was now so exhausted and sleepy that I could scarcely keep awake, although it was mid-day. So I told the Indians I was tired and would lie down and go to sleep, and if they were determined to kill me to wait till I was asleep, then put their guns close to my head, so I would not suffer much, telling them I asked this as their friend. I spread my blankets on the ground, laid down and I am sure it was not more than two minutes till I was sound asleep. My little son still sat silent.

After sleeping quite a while I felt someone pulling at my foot. On looking up I discovered that most of the Indians were lying around me asleep. My son was also sound asleep. The Indian pulling at me asked me to get up and sell him something he wanted. I told him I was too sick to get up. He insisted, but I was determined to be sick. Soon others tried to rouse me, but I knew as long as I lay in bed I was all right. Finally all the Indians left. I now wakened Wiley and asked him about how the Indians acted when I went to sleep. He said that one after another came near and looked at me without saying a word. Then they all laid down around me and went to sleep; that finally he got sleepy and also laid down.

I concluded to play them a little game for this, for I knew when sober the Indians were faithful to me, and I did not want another experience of this kind. Wiley watched, and whenever an Indian approached I would cover up—sick. We had a lot of trade, but I was too sick to do anything. When they wanted to know what ailed me I told them my heart was sick; that it felt so bad I could do nothing. This continued day after day till the Indians became really uneasy, for fear I would die. Finally, Tabby and others came and made me presents of buckskins and beavers and begged me to forgive the Indians who had threatened me, saying that if I would live and be their friend they never would say whisky to me again. And if they ever got drunk they would go away to the mountains and not come near me. I finally got well, much to their joy. To show the danger I was in, a few days after this affair two Indians were killed in a drunken row among themselves.

Soon after returning to the city Mr. Dodge seemed to change his tactics. He informed me that it was his intention to order the Indians back to the reservation at once; and that he would make me no promises whatever. I told him the Indians expected something as there was nothing at the reservation when they left except a little flour. The most of the Indians from Uintah were now camped near Nephi. Mr. Dodge went out there and pre-emptorily ordered them back to the agency.

Tabby told him they would not go back until there was something sent with them as they would as soon die fighting as to starve. The Indians had agreed with me that they would not fight but would hold out as long as they could, but would give up and go back if pressed. I had been forbidden to go among the Indians any more under penalty of arrest for inducing the Indians to leave the reservation. I began to feel a little uneasy when I heard now Tabby had talked, that he had forgotten his promise to me. I tried to get permission to go and see the Indians, offering to guarantee that they would go back peaceably if I could have a talk with them, but was still refused the privilege.

The condition of affairs was telegraphed to Washington. Much excitement prevailed. Many persons blamed me for getting the Indians into the settlements, and some favoured their being whipped back. A good many sensational stories came from Sanpete, the Indians being accused of many things they did not do. The telegraph operator of one of the settlements was knocked in the head by someone. This was laid to the Indians. It afterwards proved to be a white man that committed the deed.

I was working continually to counteract these stories for I had faith in the Indians. The only thing I dreaded was the selling of whisky to the Indians by some of the settlers. A drunken Indian is dangerous under any circumstances. Finally a commission arrived from Washington to inquire into the affair. I had already offered some affidavits I had, to Mr. Dodge, to prove some things against the management of the agent at Uintah, but he had not taken them from me. Mr. Dodge fully expected that I would offer these in evidence before the commission, but I had become convinced that the agent was a better man than the one who had been appointed to superintend affairs; so I told Mr. Dodge that I had concluded to say nothing more about the agent.

He flew into a terrible rage, and said I would have to go ahead; that I could not back out as he had made a contract, with a Mr. Popper for several hundred beef cattle that were then being sent to the agency for the Indians; and that unless the agent was prosecuted and turned out, the government would not sustain him in what he had done, and that if I did not go ahead, I would be prosecuted for libel. I asked him what he would make out of it, and told him if I had said anything against the agent I would apologize for it, and that I did not intend to interfere in the agent's business any more.

I had learned enough to know that the Indians would get the cattle, but Charles Popper had quite a time getting his pay for them, but finally did.

The superintendent was now down on me fully and completely. So when the commission met in his office. General Morrow being present (I was watching all the moves continually), I walked in. Mr. Dodge ordered me out. I replied that I was an interested party; that I represented the Indians and did not intend to go out: that there was a sign outside the door which allowed me, as an American citizen, to walk in, and that my business was such as warranted my coming in. General Morrow said he would like to have me stay, so permission was given me to remain.

The question being considered was whether the Indians should be induced to return to the reservation by telling them they were to have plenty of provisions, or whether an order should be given the military commander to force them back with arms without any promise being made them. I made the best fight I could in behalf of the Indians, but I said nothing against the agent at the reservation. Dodge could not, as he had no evidence in his possession, so the agent was not brought into question.

Mr. Dodge was very angry and desired war, and worked until he

155

won, getting an order issued to General Morrow to take his troops and drive the Indians back. Now, some might think I had done all I could, but I was determined not to give up. So on going out into the street I asked General Morrow if I could talk to him. He said, "No, I have no time. I have to go and whip these d——d Indians back to the reservation." Still I did not give up. I felt almost desperate, for if the Indians had resisted, it would have reflected on me for getting them away from the agency. My intention was, if necessary, to go and see them and take the consequences.

General Morrow and some other officers mounted their horses and started for camp. He was hardly in his quarters before I was there. I had been to his house before and been introduced to his wife. When I called, the general treated me pleasantly and asked what he could do for me. I told him I had called to see his wife; that I wanted to get her to help me to try and persuade him not to make war on the Indians if it could possibly be avoided. I believe General Morrow thought me a little crazy. Finally he promised me that he would not fire a gun until I had the privilege of going and talking to the Indians. I now felt satisfied for I knew that they would listen to me, as they had pledged themselves to take my advice. It was not the intention of Mr. Dodge to let the Indians know that anything would be sent immediately to the agency; but as I had learned about the beef cattle I intended informing them.

I went and talked with D. B. Huntington. He was pretty well posted on what I was doing and was in sympathy with me. He was a good interpreter and was not known by Mr. Dodge. Dimick went out and explained my situation to the Indians, that I had been forbidden by Mr. Dodge to visit them; that I did not want them to resist but to listen to General Morrow and go back to the agency peaceably. The Indians met at Springville, where General Morrow listened to them. I was not present but kept track of all the moves. The Indians were perfectly willing now to return and made no offer of resistance. Several hundred sacks of flour as well as the beef cattle mentioned, were sent out. The Indians were now happy. So far my aims were accomplished. Peace had been made and confirmed between the white people and hostile Utes. Government had taken notice of their condition, and provisions had been sent. All this had been done on the stir I had been the means of making.

The agent at Uintah was not consulted and nothing had been done in his name or by his authority; neither was he in any way implicated, as not one word of testimony stood against him. So he ignored the cattle purchased, came in and bought supplies, and went on as usual with his agency business. Mr. Dodge was censured and dismissed from office for getting up all the trouble.

There were several attempts made to get some papers I had in my possession, but I kept them for future use, if needed. I never have heard of any material trouble between the Mormons and Utes since that time. The agent took hold in good shape and the Indians afterward spoke well of him. During this whole business I worked without counsel or advice from any one, except the advice first given by G. A. Smith. I acted as a trader most of the time, but my main business was to establish peace. It cost considerable time and money, and when I got through there was a debt of some $1200.00 against me at Z. C. M. I. Brother Brigham ordered the account sent to him for settlement.

Several years after this, whilst living in Arizona, I received a letter from a former friend of the agent, asking me for the papers I had, saying that with them and what they had, they thought they could make a case against this same agent. I replied to them that if they had to go back so far for evidence it was clear to me that the agent was doing pretty well; that I had not heard of the Indians complaining of late years and that I had no papers for them. So long as the Indians were satisfied I cared nothing for disappointed speculators.

CHAPTER 32

The Killing of an Indian near Fairview

After the Indian troubles were settled I was advised to move to Sanpete valley to try and keep an influence for peace with the whites as well as the Utes. The authorities of Sanpete County, together with the greater portion of the people approved of my labours, and were glad that peace was now made, whilst some of the more captious found fault and used their influence to bring about a collision hoping thereby to get the Indians killed by setting the troops upon them. I believed then and still do that some things laid to the Indians was the work of white men and designed for effect.

In justice to the Indian side of the question, I will say that most of the annoyance was done by drunken Indians, a party of which attacked the herd boys coming into Fairview, killing one of them. This was supposed to be a personal affair as these same Indians passed other boys about the same time without molesting them.

Some time after peace had been considered fully established an Indian was murdered in cold blood by a party of whites going out after wood from Fairview. The body was covered up but was finally discovered by the Indians. The killing was cowardly in the extreme, and more treacherous than anything I ever remember done by the Indians. The exact number I have forgotten, but some six or eight young men were going out to the cedars for wood. They met a lone Indian coming in from Thistle Valley on his way to Fairview.

At that time this was nothing unusual. The wood haulers spoke friendly to the Indian, and asked him to go with them into the cedars, and as soon as they loaded up he could ride into town with them. The Indian had no suspicion of anything wrong, and I do not believe the wood haulers at first thought of killing him. He went out into the cedars, staying around while the loading was going on. After a while someone suggested that it would be a good chance to kill the "d——d Indian" and hide him away, others assented. So much was said that the Indian, who understood some of their talk, became uneasy and started to leave. At this one of the party shot him. All being armed with pistols now took part and, as the Indian ran, the whole party fired at and succeeded in killing him. They buried him among the cedars, covering him mainly with brush.

When the Indians discovered his body they came to me feeling very badly. The Indians really desired peace. The murdered Indian in fact belonged to a band that never had been of the worst. I was now living in Fairview. I was greatly mortified and scarcely knew how to answer, for I was aware it would be natural for the Indians to seek blood for blood, and it was a little surprise to me that they stopped to consider, but as they had come to me I took courage and commenced talking, reciting a great deal of the Indian history from the earliest settling of Utah, acknowledging that the first blood shed was that of an Indian on the Provo bottom, also admitting that they had often been wronged; referred to the hard labour that I had done in crossing the snow mountains, and how I had got them beef and flour and made good peace between them and the Mormons, and how true the Indians had been to me, and how sick my heart now was that this had occurred.

I was not acting, for it was a cruel thing, besides being so senseless. Finally, when I had got the Indians to feel that I fully sympathized with them, I said to them, "Someone has to be the last or this killing will never cease. Now as some persons, without cause, have killed one of your people. If you kill a Mormon to pay for it, won't some bad Mormon kill another Indian? Then when am I ever to see good peace? If you will pass this by and let this be the last, I don't believe there will be any more killing; for when the Mormons know that an Indian was last killed they will be ashamed, and the men who killed your friend will be despised by all good people."

At last these Indians consented and agreed not to kill anyone in retaliation. I have never heard of their breaking this promise. I would ask those who are so down on the "treacherous Indians" to think of this.

My labours with the Utes were now almost ended. I had already been asked to get ready to go to Mexico on a mission. An account of which will be given in subsequent chapters.

CHAPTER 33

The Salt Lake City Election in 1874

One item of home history that I took a small part in I will mention. At the August election of city officers of 1874 there was an attempt made by the U. S. marshal to control the polls. This was disputed by the municipal officers. Maxwell, the U. S. marshal, had a large number of deputies sworn in. Milton Orr was at that time the regular deputy and took the active control of the special deputies. This election occurred soon after the passage of the Poland Bill.

The Liberals were on their "high heels" and believed that they had now the right and power to put down Mormon rule in Salt Lake City. During the day there was continued contention who should act as police or protectors of the polls. The marshals interfered continually, and when the police attempted to do their duty they were arrested by the deputies and taken before the U. S. Commissioner and put under bonds. Several times during the day the spirit of lawlessness ran so high that a collision seemed inevitable. The police acted with great coolness and forbearance, only working to keep the polls unobstructed, but making no resistance when insulted or arrested, neither acting against the rioters so long as they kept clear of the polls. Many times during the day men would yell out that the Mormons had run this country as long as they could, that their day was done, boasting, swearing and defying the police to help themselves. This was immediately in front of the City Hall, some of the mob even crowding into the hallway.

Late in the afternoon the mob became so aggressive and the polls so obstructed that people wishing to vote could not get in. The marshals headed this obstruction. The police seemingly had no power to keep order. Captain Burt sent word to Mayor Wells asking for instructions. Mayor Wells soon appeared on the ground and managed to work his way through the crowd and get into the door of the polling room. The regular police were mostly on the inside of the city hall at that time. The mayor commanded the crowd to disperse and leave the entrance clear. This he uttered by authority of his office. There were possibly two hundred persons in the crowd. The room was full and the doors completely blocked and the sidewalk crowded. Many were in the street and more coming, cursing and yelling. Some of the leaders, now more or less intoxicated, when the order was given to disperse, instead of obeying, made an attack on the mayor. They were led by Milton Orr, who seized hold of Mr. Wells and attempted to drag him from his position. Mayor Wells resisted this move. Several others now caught hold of him, tearing his clothes.

I was just at the outer side of the sidewalk in company with George Crismon. As we saw this violent move against the mayor we started through the crowd, George taking the lead. And I always remembered his expertness in opening a way, for we were soon on hand. The noise was so terrific that I had to put my mouth close to Mr. Wells' ear. I asked him which way he wished to go. The jam was on both sides of him. I naturally supposed he wanted to get away, for the mob seemed to want to rend him in pieces and were doing their best to accomplish it.

Brother Wells answered, "I do not want to go either way. I shall stay here if I can; you help me to keep my place." Brother Crismon did all he could to keep the mob off. I caught Brother Wells around the waist and held him against those pulling at him. His clothes were badly torn in the scuffle. While this was going on. Brother Andrew Smith, of the police force, managed to get near us from the inside. He called to me to push Brother Wells to him.

I said, "He don't want to come in."

Brother Smith said, "Never mind." At the same time reaching and getting hold of Brother Wells, telling me to shove him in. This we did. I always believed that Mayor Wells would have died before he would have given way to the mob of his own free will.

As the mayor went in the door was shut and I was crowded outside with the mob. I now felt quite small, jammed into the doorway, all alone with the mob. I could see no friend near me, so I kept very quiet. Soon Mayor Wells appeared on the balcony of the court house. He looked rather dilapidated, but in a clear, steady voice commanded the rioters to disperse. At this they only shouted the louder, cursing and defying his authority. He then turned to Captain Burt and said, in substance: "Captain Burt, disperse this mob and clear the side-walk of obstruction" The mob had given way from just in front of the hall door, as the balcony was immediately over it and those under the balcony had crowded out so as to get a view of the mayor.

In a moment after the order was given Captain Burt stepped out onto the side-walk in front of the hall door, followed by a few regular police. Addressing the crowd immediately in front of the polling room, he commanded them to disperse.

Instead of obeying the order, the mob, with a howl of defiance, rushed at the captain, who stood with his arms folded. I was looking from a slight elevation, being on the doorstep, and powerless to do anything but watch, so that what I am writing is just as I saw it. As the mob rushed at Captain Burt he let drive with his police club; instantly others of the police pitched in. I have seen a good many knock-downs, but men fell as fast for a short time as I ever saw them. Most of them were U. S. marshals. The police were making a clearing toward the door where I was jammed in. The mob almost instantly gave way. They were so taken by surprise at seeing their leaders falling that many who were seemingly brave as lions a minute before took to their heels and ran away. During all this not a shot was fired. So rapid and thorough was the work of the police that I was a little afraid of getting hit myself and called out to Capt. Burt to set 'em up. One fellow that was knocked down fell against me as I was getting out.

All the police were arrested and brought to trial before the commissioners, but were cleared. There were many sore heads but no one killed. The man's name who did the hardest hitting that day never came up, and without his permission I will not mention it.

Sometimes when I see the Latter-day Saints insulted, accused and put upon by their enemies as they now are in the year 1889, I think of the good old days when we did not bear as we do today. Especially when it is put forth as though we are cowed and dare not say our souls are our own. Often when noticing some of the young Mormons of today, (1890), who are toadying to the Gentiles and listening to their flattery, I cannot help but contrast their spindle-legged, dudish build, their supercilious looks, their effort to ape the infidelity of the day, etc., with the sturdy, faithful boys who went forth in the defence of their fathers in the days of Echo Canyon, and many other duties of the early days. Now why is this? There is too much luxury, indolence and false education. Many suppose that education consists in conjugating verbs. My grammar says, "Man is a verb—that is, man is made to do, and grammar says a verb is a word to do." Hence, man should be a verb and not a worthless, do-nothing noun—a name of a thing.

CHAPTER 34

I Report to President Young that I am Ready

According to the request made by President Young I bought a lot and had a good, comfortable house built in Fairview, Sanpete Co., expecting to make that my future home. The house was not yet complete when I was called upon by Henry Brizzee, about June, 1874, who told me that President Young wished to see him and me at his office to talk with us about a mission to Mexico, saying that President Young understood that we spoke the Spanish language. I had expected this call to come some time. I had both desired and dreaded the mission. My desire was from a sense of duty. My dread was owing to the power of Catholicism that I had seen prevail in that land, while living there from 1847 to 1850.

At that time no man dared pass in front of a church without raising his hat. Anyone doing so was most sure to be pelted with stones with a possibility of having his head broken. A priest passing along the street demanded the uncovering of the head by all who met him. A person's life was in danger unless acting promptly in conformity with all these customs. To offer a word against their religion would be almost certain death.

That the country had been revolutionized and religious freedom declared I had not learned. I only remembered what I had seen. I felt a dread that tried me severely while on my way to the office; but before arriving I had formed the resolution to "face the music." My reflections were: This mission has to be commenced by someone and if it is necessary for the extreme sacrifice to be made, just as well to be me as anyone else.

On meeting President Young, he told us that the time had come to prepare for the introduction of the gospel into Mexico; that there were millions of the descendants of Nephi in the land, and that we were under obligations to visit them. Asked us if we were willing to prepare for a mission. We told him we were. Nothing very definite was arranged at the time. Brother Young said he would like to have some extracts from the Book of Mormon translated to send to the people of Mexico; advised us to get our private affairs arranged, also to study up our Spanish and prepare ourselves for translating and report to him, and when the proper time came and all was ready he would let us know. Some suggestion was made about visiting the City of Mexico as travellers and feel our way among the people.

Brother Brizzee and I visited together often and talked about the work before us. We began to study and prepare for translating. My own feelings were that it would require considerable study, although I understood Spanish quite well. Still to translate for publication required a more thorough scholarship than either of us possessed. I often thought how good it would be to have a native Spaniard to help us.

Some few months after the notice to get ready, Brother Brizzee called at my house, accompanied by a stranger whom he introduced as Mileton G. Trejo, a Spanish gentleman from the Philippine Islands and was an author and a traveller. After conversing for some time with the gentleman I became hopeful that he was the one needed to assist in the translation, which afterwards proved to be the case. Senor Trejo told me that he had been induced to come and visit the Mormon people partly through a dream. His account, to the best of my recollection, was that while discussing religion with a brother officer of the Spanish army when stationed on the Philippine Islands, he remarked that he believed the scriptures literally; that he did not think anyone had the right to privately interpret or change them. His comrade told him he would have to go and join the Mormons who lived in the interior of America; that he had learned about them from his wife, who was an English lady, she having heard about the Mormons and their doctrines in England.

This caused Senor Trejo to reflect and study about the people, so much so that he made it a subject of prayer. Finally he dreamed that if he would go and see the Mormons he would be satisfied. Accordingly he sold out all his interests in the Islands, together with his commission, etc., bade farewell to his people and friends and came to this country a stranger, not knowing anyone or enough of the spoken English to ask for a drink of water. Unfortunately, he was introduced to President Young by a party that did not stand very high in the estimation of Brother Young. I have forgotten the name of the one introducing him. This had rather an unfavourable effect upon President Young, and it was a long time before he gave him his confidence. Trejo never resented the suspicion, only said: "He will know me some day."

Brother Brizzee took Trejo home with him to live. He commenced studying hard, reading and translating the Voice of Warning the best he could. He acquired very rapidly an understanding of the English language, and being a graduate of the highest schools in Madrid, as soon as he got a clear understanding of the text he could write the same in Spanish, his native tongue.

Here I wish to correct an error that exists in the minds of a great many who suppose that Spanish is not the language of Mexico. Pure Spanish is the language of Mexico just the same as pure English is the language of the United States. Just as the uneducated speak bad English, just so the uneducated Mexican speaks bad Spanish. Anyone learning Spanish correctly will scarce perceive the difference when talking to a native Spaniard, a Mexican or a Californian.

Senor Trejo soon became convinced of the truth of the gospel and was baptised by Brother Brizzee. After qualifying himself somewhat, he commenced on the *Book of Mormon* at our earnest solicitation. My house being completed, I moved my family to Fairview, Sanpete county. Brother Trejo expressed a desire to be with me. He said I understood the written language somewhat better than Brother Brizzee. Brother Brizzee had associated more with the people than I had and talked quite fluently and understood Spanish very well, but had not studied the written word so much as I had. It was arranged with good feelings all around seemingly, that as soon as I was settled at home that Trejo would live with me and we would work together translating. When Brother Trejo came, I rented an office for him where he would be undisturbed through the day. In the evenings we would read and correct together.

In the spring Brother T. returned to the city. I began to feel like reporting to President Young, for we had everything ready, as it seemed to me, to do something. With this before me I came down to Salt Lake City, met Brother Brizzee and told him how I felt. His answer was that he was sick of the whole business; that he had been up to the office to see Prest. Young and could not get a hearing.

At this time Prest. Young was much harassed by lawsuits of various kinds. I felt disappointed at the answer and asked Brother Brizzee if we had not better keep on and do all we could, and probably Brother Brigham would know when we were ready, but I got no promise from him. I told him I intended to keep to work as long as I saw anything to do; and when I felt fully ready I would report. I concluded to remain in the city for a while so as to be near Trejo to encourage and help him. He had commenced to carefully rewrite the whole manuscript of the *Book of Mormon*, having translated it entirely. He had improved so that by this time his understanding of English was pretty good. He seemed thoroughly interested in the work. He had now expended what money he had brought to the country with him.

I shared what money I earned with him and kept him going the best I could until some time in June, 1875, when he came to me and said he would have to quit as he could not live longer without an income of some kind, and he did not want to accept of me as he knew I was not able to spare him means to live on. This confirmed me in the thought that the time had come to report to Brother Brigham, so I told Brother Platt, the man I was working for, that I was now going to see Prest. Young or *camp* with him till I did see him and report.

I went up town and saw Brother Brigham going into the "Old Constitution" building, followed and spoke to him. He asked, "What are you doing?"

"I am hunting you," I replied.

"Well, what do you want?"

"I want to report to you. You told me to come when I was ready, I am now ready."

"All right, go up to the office, I will be there right away."

When Brother Brigham came in he asked what I had done. I told him just about what had been done, and explained Trejo's situation. Brother Young had never heard a word about his labours; asked if I could vouch for him. I told him I could vouch for the work he was doing, that it was good and getting to be correct. Brother Young was somewhat surprised and very much pleased. He asked me what Henry Brizzee was doing. I replied that I had made my own report and preferred that Brother Brizzee would do the same. Brother Young said he intended to release Brother Brizzee from the call for reasons that were sufficient, and said that he would have him notified accordingly.

Brother Brigham advised me to have printed about 100 pages of selections from the *Book of Mormon*, and get them ready to take to Mexico, and be ready to start about the 1st of September, remarking that the Church funds were low at the time.

I told him I could soon raise the money on subscription if so authorized. Accordingly I received the following letter:

Salt Lake City, June 1st, 1875,

To whom it may Concern:

Elder Daniel W. Jones, the bearer of these lines, is hereby authorised to solicit and receive subscriptions to be applied toward the support of Brother Gonzales while he is translating the *Book of Mormon* into the Spanish language, and such other Church publications as it may be found advisable from time to time to translate into that language. As Brother Gonzales's labours, as above mentioned, promise to be productive of much good, it is hoped that the Saints, so far as able and willing, will aid toward his comfortable sustenance while translating, and also to defray the cost of publishing his translations that are desired to be done by November next.

Brigham Young.

President Young handed me a blank book, saying, "Take this, get what subscriptions you can, and what is lacking I will furnish." He dictated the following heading:

We the undersigned agree to pay the amount subscribed opposite our names to be used for the purpose of defraying the expenses of translating and publishing the *Book of Mormon* and other Church works into the Spanish language.

Salt Lake City, June 1st 1875.

(Signed.)

Edward Hunter, John Sharp, Z. Snow, Feramorz Little, J. T. Little, G. W. Crocheron, Geo. C. Riser, Wilba Hayes, D. Day, W. C. Rydalch, T. Taylor, J. C. Cutler, George Goddard, Erastus Snow, George Dunford, A. C. Pyper, Andrew Burt, R. Campbell, Laron Pratt, Jos. Bull Jr., John Priestley, James Anderson, A. McMaster, R. Mathews, W. J. Lewis, H. W. Attley, Benjamin Judson, Geo. Margetts, O. S. Thomson, John B. Kelly, W. H. Perkes, Jno. Kirkman, Charles Livingston, John Y. Smith, Jas. Livingston, Lorenzo Pettit, Jeter Clinton, W. Grimsdell, P. A. Schettler, J. H. Picknell, Jacob Weiler, Thos. Maycock, T. F. H. Morton, Jas. Eardley, J. P. Ball, E. M. Weiler, A. C. Smith, Angus M. Cannon, Martin Lenzi, Geo. Crimson, D. Miner, Hyrum Barton, N. J. Gronlund, Robt. Dixon, J. M. Pyper, J. R. Winder, J. B. Maiben, Millen Atwood, Francis Platt, F. B. Platt, P. A. Shreeve, B. Y. Hampton, William

Goforth, William Hyde, Alex. Burt, W. Woodruff, A. Woodruff, Wm. G. Phillips, T. O. Angell, United Order Tailors, D. W. Evans, John Nicholson, Joseph Bull, J. Jaques, T. C. Taylor, T. McIntyre, C. Denney, J. Tingey, S. Roberts, W. H. Ogelsby, Emma S. Kelly, George Buckle, N. H. Rockwood, Wm. Nevee, J. B. Hawkins, Mrs. M. A. Leaver, E. D. Mousley, R. B. Sampson, Thos. Roberts, Robert Aveson, Lucy Pettit, Rosana Pettit, J. C. Kingsbury, A. M. Musser, A. H. Raleigh, James Leach, Robt. C. Fryer, Wm. F. Cahoon, Jos. E. Taylor, E. M. Cahoon, S. A. Woolley, J. M. Benedict, John L. Blythe, R. J. Golding, Geo. W. Price, N. V. Jones, J. Morgan, T. McKean, T. G. Webber, Jas. Sanders, Orson Hyde, H. S. Eldredge, W. H. Hooper, W. C. Neal, John S. Davis, Geo. Q. Cannon, C. R. Savage, Geo. Lambert, Morris & Evans, Geo. Teasdale, Thos. Jenkins, G. F. Brooks, G. H. Taylor, T. Latimer, S. P. Teasdel, J. M. Bernhisel, Ann Peart, E. F. Sheets, J. C. Rumell, Jas. McKnight, John Needham, C. Crow, C. J. Lambert, J. McGhie, Mathias Cowley, Mary Bingham, Emma S. Kelley, Ludwig Suhrke, Chas Shumway, Christian Hendrickson, Johan Vink, Jas. Whitehead, Paul A. Elkins, Geo. Curtis, J. D. Cummings, 17th Ward per Bishop Davis, 16th Wd. per G. Riser, 15th Ward per T. C. Griggs, 1st Ward per Bishop Warburton, 10th Ward per Bishop Proctor, 11th Ward per Bishop McRae, Hyde Park per S. M. Molen, Moroni, Sanpete Co., per Bishop Bradley,

Names of Bountiful Ward, Davis Co.

Anson Call, Joseph Noble, David Lewis, Geo. O. Noble, Alfred Burmingham, Stephen Ellis, Thomas Waddoups, Samanthe Willey, Elizabeth Barlow, John Telford, John K. Crosby, Peter Moore, Wm. Lewis, P. G. Sessions, Henry Rampton, James Wall, J. Kynaston, John Moss, Daniel Wood, J. N. Perkins, Enoch Lewis, J. T. Botrell, J. H. Barlow, Daniel Carter, James Wright, Wm. Henrie, F. T. Whitey, Benjamin Ashby, Mary Ann McNeil, Patty Sessions, Cordelia M. Barlow, Jas. Kipper, Benjamin Peel, William Knighton, Eric Hogen, Joseph Moss, Wm. Salter, John Easthope, Richard Duerden, Samuel Smedley, Wm. Atchinson, Joseph Wilkins, Arthur Burmingham, Israel Barlow, Sarah Nicholas, Sarah Easthope, Lucy H. Barlow, Heber Wood, Thomas Briggs, Daniel Davis.

Kamas Ward per Bishop S. F. Atwood, 8th Ward per J. M. McAlister, Payson Ward per J. M. Coombs, Provo City per P. M.

168

Wentz, Nephi City per Bishop Grover,

SMITHFIELD, CACHE CO, (PER J. S. CANTWELL,)
WITH FOLLOWING LIST OF NAMES.

George Barker, Edward Wildman, Silvester Lowe, Catharine M. Sorenson, Harriet Meikle, Alice Doane, Niles C. Christianson, Christiana Ainscough, Joseph Hartan, John Plouman, Wm. A Noble, Stephen Christianson, Jens C. Peterson, Jane Coleman, Sarah Langton, Robt. Thornly, Jane Harton, Niels Tooleson, Jane Miles, Jane M. Miles, Mary Swenson, Samuel Roskelly, John F. Mack, Thomas F. Mather, Lars Tooleson, James Mather, Frank Lutz, Lars Sorenson, Elizabeth Knox, Lars Swenson, Hanna Toolson, Peter Neilson, Carl Johnson, Diana Hendrickson, Frdk. B. Thybergh, Thomas Smith, Lars Mouritzan, Ola Hanson, Benj. Lloyd, Caroline Christianson, Preston T. Morehead, Euphemia Bain, Adeline Barber, Louisa Barber, James Mack, Wm. G. Noble, David Weeks, Robert Meikle, Saml. Hendrickson, Betsey Collett, Neils Gylenskogy, Wm. Thornton, Mary Roberts, Mary Moritzon, Hannah Olsen, Ann Mary Weeks, Mary Ann Noble, Laura W. Merrill, Penella Gylenskogy, Elizabeth Heap, Lena Nielson, Hans Peterson, Mary Hopkins, Mary Ann Mather, Matilda Kelsey, Andrew Tooleson, Niels Nielson, Jens Christianson, Charles Jones, Elizabeth Roberts, Besides obtaining donations in Smithfield Brother Cantwell solicited help from several other settlements.

Richmond Ward, Cache Valley, per Bishop Merrill.

LOGAN CITY, (PER J. H. MARTINEAU.)

Jens Hansen, Klaus Klausen, Olof Hansen, Geo. Baugh, H. R. Cranney, J. H. Martineau, C. J. Larsen, H. Thatcher, Chas. Laudberg, E. Curtis, W. B. Preston, John Anderson, T. Lockyer, Rasmus Nelson, Thos. Morrell, R. Gates, F. Hurst, R. D. Roberts, T. B. Cardon, Josiah Hendricks, Hans Anderson, H. Nelson, Chas. Martensen, John Jacobs, Osro Crockett, B. Ravsten, M. H. Martineau, P. Crone, Geo. Hymers, John Ormond, J. Sandberg, W. Partington, H. R. Hansen, John C. Larsen, Jas. Merrill, Thos. Fredricksen, Lars Hansen, L. R. Martineau, H. Flamm, Alex Allen, J. Hayball, Geo. Merrisson, H. Ballard, R. Maria Nelson, Anna Larsen, W. J. Davis, John Thomas, Robt. Davidson, J. P. Tuevesen, J. Knowles, Joel Ricks, Jr., J. Quinney, Wm. Trapp, C. D. Fjelsted, H. D. Hansen, Ann Davis, C. C. Jensen, Bodil

169

Hansen, Ann Hobbs, Frank Larsen, Davis Rees, Gustave Tommason, Pleasant Grove per Bp. J. Brown, Hyrum Winters, Wm. H. Green, J. B. Clark, C. C. Petersen, A. Warnick, D. Thorn, B. Harper, D. Adamson, M. P. Peterson, Wm. Marrott, Thos. Winder, Olive Thornton, John P. Hayes.

SPANISH FORK.

Magnus Bjearnson, Jeff Demick, Elizabeth Boyack, Niels P. Madsen, Mrs. Isaacson, Marijah Mayor, C. Jacobson, Paul Jensen, Hans Regtrul, Christena Ghrame, A. P. Nielson, C. Christiansen, Sarah Brockbank, Jas. G. Higgenson, August Swenson, Anna P. Jensen, Jens Nielsen, Hans Olsen, Peter Nielson, Mrs. George Sinnett, Isabella Rockhill, John Moone.

LEHI CITY.

William Thomas, J. Houldsworth, Wm. Goats, S. Empey, E. H. Davis, George Kirkham, Isaac Chilton, —— Ball, P. Christophisen J. W. Morton, Wm. Clark, Mons Anderson, Abel Mathews, D. Thurmond, John Johnson, Wm. H. Winn, John Zimmerman, Elizabeth Bushman, Wm. L. Hutching, Edwin Standing, J. W. Taylor, Mrs. Knudson, John Austin, Sarah A. Davis, Ellen Rolf, Chas. Barnes, G. Gudmundsen John Andreason, Elisha Peck, Oley Ellingson, John Bushman, Jens Holm, Jane Garner, N. P. Thomas, F. Ericesen, A. F. Petersen, Peter Petersen, ——Hawkins, John Beck, T. R. Cutler, J. Goodwin, Andrew A. Peterson, James L. Robinson, Ephriam City per Bp. Peterson, Springville Relief Society, Parowan per Jesse N. Smith, Brigham City per A. Nichols, C. J. Lambert, Centerville Ward per Wm. Reeves, H. S. Ensign, Manti City per J. C. Brown and Charles Smith.

The names given are all that I can furnish from the list as taken at the time and preserved in the same book given me by President Young. A few names are not plain, so I have to omit them. The donations ranged from ten cents to ten dollars. When the wards are credited, no list of names were sent.

The people were so ready and prompt that it took but a short time to collect the amount needed. In all my travels I have kept this list, as the people helping, seemed to me like particular friends.

I was not long in raising the amount needed, some $500.00, and contracted with the *Deseret News* office to publish one hundred pages. A committee was appointed to make the selection. I called for them when I was about ready for work but nothing had been done. On mentioning this to Brother Brigham, he picked up a *Book of Mormon*, saying: "Take this, go home and get a few days' rest. Read the book and when you feel impressed to do so, mark the places and they will be the proper selections, for you have the spirit of this mission and you will be directed aright."

On arriving at home in Sanpete County, I commenced reading and studying, expecting to have but a few days at home, then to soon leave on a very hard mission. My wife and family were kind and loving and I enjoyed home as much as any one could. A few days after my arrival Bishop Tucker, of Fairview, and others wished me to go with them to explore Castle Valley. On this trip I read and made most of the selections, afterward approved of and printed.

The first indications of the Pleasant Valley coal mines were discovered on this trip by Lycurgus Wilson. Also the country known as Emery County was prospected for settling.

I once noticed a rail road guide book, where General Johnston was given credit of opening the road down Price Creek Canyon. This is not correct. No road was there until the rail road was worked through. Captain Seldon took a party up Spanish Fork through a short canyon to the east of Price Creek. According to the best information in my possession, the credit is due to Sam Gilson for first penetrating and passing through Price canyon.

After spending about three weeks I returned to Salt Lake City. The selections being approved, work on the printing was soon commenced. There being no one competent to judge of the translation, Brother Brigham asked me how we proposed to prove to the satisfaction of the authorities of the Church that the translation was correct. My proposition was to take a book in English we, Trejo and I, were not acquainted with, let Trejo translate it into Spanish, then I without ever seeing the book would take his translation and write it into English and compare it with the original. Brother Brigham said that was fair. He asked me if I was familiar with "Spencer's Letters." I said I was not as I had never read them. He sent me to the historian's office to tell Brother G. A. Smith to let Trejo have a copy and do as I proposed. On furnishing our translation as agreed upon, Brother Smith laughingly remarked, "I like Brother Jones' style better than Brother Spencer's. It is the same in substance, but the language is more easily understood."

Brother Trejo was instructed to carefully rewrite the selections and get them ready for the printers. We were advised to call upon Apostle Taylor and ask him to advise us as he had been in charge of the publishing of the *Book of Mormon* into the French language. Brother Taylor said he did not think we could do the work; and he would rather have nothing to do with it. I told him we had been appointed by the highest authority that there was in the Church to do the work and we believed we could do it and make as good a translation as any that had been made. Two others of the apostles were present. Whether they remember this or not is a question but I am satisfied that Brother Taylor never forgot my answer.

When the printing was commenced, Brother Brigham told me that he would hold me responsible for its correctness. This weighed heavily upon my mind. So much so that I asked the Lord to in some way manifest to me when there were mistakes.

Brother Joseph Bull allowed us an extra reading of the proof. The printers did not understand a word of Spanish and could only follow literally the copy. They soon, however, acquired an idea of the spelling that made it easier than at first.

The manuscript as written by Brother Trejo, was at times rather after the modern notion of good style. When I called his attention to errors he invariably agreed with me. He often remarked that I was a close critic and understood Spanish better than he did. I did not like to tell him how I discerned the mistakes.

I felt a sensation in the centre of my forehead as though there was a fine fiber being drawn smoothly out. When a mistake occurred, the smoothness would be interrupted as though a small knot was passing out through the forehead. Whether I saw the mistake or not I was so sure it existed that I would direct my companion's attention to it and call on him to correct it. When this was done we continued on until the same occurred again.

President Young gave us all the encouragement and advice necessary. Brothers George A. Smith, G. Q. Cannon and Orson Pratt also manifested much interest in the mission, as well as a great many others, who contributed means to pay for the publishing of the book.

CHAPTER 35

The Missionaries for Mexico

While the work of printing was in the press, the brethren wanted to go on the mission were selected. It was agreed instead of going by rail road and ocean to Mexico, that we would fit up with pack and saddle animals and go through and explore Arizona on our trip. At this time there was but little known by our people of Arizona. Even Salt River Valley was not known by the head men. Hardy, able-bodied men of faith and energy were wanted for the trip. Besides myself there were selected, J. Z. Stewart, Helaman Pratt, Wiley C. Jones (my son,) R. H. Smith, Ammon M. Tenney and A. W. Ivins.

The book of one hundred pages was now ready, being bound in paper.

About the 1st of September, 1875, we appointed to meet at Nephi and start from there with pack animals. Two of the company, being in the extreme south, were to join us at Kanab. We left Nephi about the 10th of September, and with our books, some two thousand packed on mules, we started out. We had a good outfit for the trip. The people of the settlements, as we passed along, assisted us in every way. Some additions were made to our outfit. One place, Cedar City, gave so much dried fruit that it became necessary for us to have another pack mule, which was readily furnished. We stopped a short time at Toquerville, where Brother Ivins joined us. From here we went to Kanab where our company was completed by Brother Tenney joining.

The route chosen was by the way of Lee's Ferry, thence to the Moquis villages, Brother Tenney having been to these villages some years before, was to be our guide to that point, after which we were to make our way through an unknown country the best we could. Our instructions were to explore the Little Colorado.

Some few years previous to this a large company had been called to go and settle Arizona. They had penetrated beyond the Colorado some forty-five miles, but finding no water had all returned except one small company under Brother John Blythe, the names of which as far as obtained are, David V. Bennett, William Solomon, Ira Hatch, James Mangrum, Thomas Smith and son. These remained doing all they could to carry out the design of the mission, until circumstances caused their honourable release. Their history and experience there would make quite a chapter, but I cannot claim the right or memory to record it.

One little incident I will relate, to show how I came to be called to explore Arizona in connection with this mission to Mexico, which could have been made in an easier way than travelling so far with pack mules. I was in President Young's office one day when several others were present. Brother W. C. Staines came in and was telling about having heard a Brother McMaster, of the 11th Ward, related a remarkable occurrence whilst on this first Arizona trip. Brother McMaster's statement, as told by Brother Staines, was that there were several hundred persons, with teams, in a perishing condition. They had passed some forty-five miles beyond the Colorado and no water could be found. Someone had gone on up the Little Colorado and found that entirely dry. Brother McMaster being chaplain went out and pled with the Lord for water. Soon there was a fall of rain and snow depositing plenty of water for the cattle, and to fill up all their barrels. They were camped in a rocky place where there were many small holes that soon filled up. In the morning all were refreshed, barrels filled up, and all turned back rejoicing in the goodness of the Lord in saving them from perishing. They returned to Salt Lake and reported Arizona uninhabitable.

After Brother Staines had finished, some remarks were made by different ones. I was sitting near by and just in front of Brother Brigham. I had just been telling him something about my labours among the Indians. He said nothing for a few moments, but sat looking me straight in the eye. Finally he asked, "What do you think of that Brother Jones?"

I answered, "I would have filled up, went on, and prayed again." Brother Brigham replied putting his hand upon me, "This is the man that shall take charge of the next trip to Arizona."

Not long after crossing the Colorado we were overtaken by an Indian bringing us a telegram from President Young, sent to Kanab, directing us to visit Salt River Valley as he had been informed something about it since our departure. This changed our intended direction somewhat as we were intending to make toward the Rio Grande, a country that I was acquainted with.

On arriving at the Moquis villages, the Indians were much pleased to see us, and were very friendly. Their country and villages have been described so well and often that I will say but little about them. They are a peaceable, honest class, dwelling in villages that have a very ancient appearance situated on high bluffs, facing a dry, sandy plain and distant some sixty miles from the Little Colorado River. The Indians farm by catching the rain water which runs down from the hills, and conduct it upon the more sandy spots; thus gathering moisture enough to mature beans, pumpkins, early corn, melons and a few other early vegetables. They have a number of peach trees that grow in the sand ridges, bearing a very good fruit of which they dry the most. They save and eat every thing they possibly can. They own quite a number of horses, sheep and goats. They seem to be happy, well fed and contented, making some blankets and clothing of a rude kind.

As there may be readers of this work more interested in the travels and the country through which we passed than the mission in which we were engaged, for their benefit I will describe our outfit and mode of travel. On leaving Kanab there were seven of us with saddle animals. Brother Pratt rode a contrary mule. We had some fourteen head of pack animals. Our books were in convenient bales for packing. All our provisions, which were ample, were put up in uniform-sized canvas bags. There was one mule for water kegs and one horse for kitchen traps. The latter was well suited for his position, for nothing would excite him. We had to depend entirely on the grass to sustain our animals, as we could not carry grain for them. In the early travels of western explorers grass was the only feed. It was much more fresh and abundant than at the present time. Now throughout the western country almost every watering place is occupied by the ranchman's cattle.

At night our animals were hoppled and turned out. When any danger was expected we would guard them. If there was no danger we went to bed and hunted them up in the morning. Sometimes this was quite a labour. We had one span of mules that seemed determined to get back to Utah. We tried many times to hamper them, sometimes with seeming success, but they soon learned to travel side or cross-hoppled, or one tied to the other.

Most of us were old travellers, that is, we had all had considerable experience in handling animals in camp, but these mules showed more cunning and perseverance than any we had seen before. Once they travelled with hopples some sixteen miles. I happened to strike their trail first. After tracking them about five miles I found Ammon Tenney's saddle horse with a few other animals. I managed to catch the horse, and with nothing but my suspenders for a bridle I followed on alone until I overtook the mules. They tried to run away from me, but I managed to head them back and drove them several miles before daring to take the hopples off. The horse I was riding was quite sharp backed. By this time, not like the king who cried "My kingdom for a horse," I thought, "My kingdom for a saddle."

So I commenced to study how to make one, and succeeded finely. I took off my overalls, pulled some hair out of the horse's tail and tied the bottom of the legs together, then pulled the grass and stuffed the overalls full—both legs and body. This formed a pad fast at both ends but separate in the middle. This I placed lengthwise on the back of the horse with body end forward so that I could hold the waistband end together with one hand to keep the grass from working out. Under the circumstances this made me quite comfortable, and I drove the mules back to camp all right. My companions laughed heartily as I rode in, but acknowledged that I was a good saddler.

A few nights after we were discussing these mules, Brother Tenney proposed that we tie each mule to the other's tail. This worked like a charm. We had no further trouble, as they simply followed each other round and round and got their fill of travel without going very far from camp.

There was some uneasiness felt by Brothers Tenney and Ivins about meeting the Indians who had killed Dr. Whitmore, as they had never come in to make peace with the Mormon settlements. As we neared the Moa-abby we were all somewhat anxious and kept a good look-out. Brother Tenney knew these Indians well and said he would be able to recognise them from any others. The Navajoes who had formerly been hostile were now at peace and coming in to trade for horses; but the Indians dreaded were still supposed to be on the war path.

On arriving at the Moa-abby we camped near the edge of some willows, keeping a good watch. We made an early camp shortly before sundown. Brother Tenney, who was on the alert, suddenly said, "Here they are. We are in for it."

At this time about twenty Indians on horseback showed themselves some two hundred yards from us. They came somewhat slyly out of the willows. Brother Tenney recognised them at once as the hostiles. I told him to make friendly signs and tell them to approach, as he talked their language well. I told the rest to be ready but to make no moves. Brother Tenney and I stepped unarmed out from the willows and walked a little way in the direction of the Indians. They approached us slowly. Brother Tenney told them to come on as we were friends. We stood waiting for them to approach us. When they came up we shook hands and I was introduced as a Mormon captain who was a great friend to the Indians; one who never wanted to fight them and had a good heart for the Indian race. Really I felt no fear, for we were sent out as messengers of peace to this very people. Still I believed in being prudent and not giving them a chance to get the advantage of us, for this band of Indians were noted for their treachery even by the other Indian tribes.

Like most Indians, they wanted to know if we had anything to eat. I told them we had, and if they would do as I wanted them to that I would give them a good supper. They agreed to do so. I showed them where to make their camp, some twenty-five yards from ours, in an open spot. I told them that my men were not acquainted with them and were a little afraid, and that they must not go near them, but that Brother Tenney and I knew them and were not afraid of them. I told two of the Indians to bring some wood to our camp, which they did. I also told them to get their wood and water and turn their horses out with ours, and get everything ready before night, so that they would not want to leave their camp after dark, as our men might be scared if they moved about then. We had an abundance of provisions, so we gave them a good, hearty supper.

Brother Tenney and I talked with them until bedtime. They said they had desired to make peace with the Mormons but were afraid to come in. I agreed to give them a paper next morning stating that we had met them and that they desired peace. Our party laid on their arms all night watching these Indians. None slept. They kept faith with us and not one of them stirred during the night. We had breakfast early in the morning and sent two of the Indians to bring up our animals. We gave them some more provisions, wrote their recommend and then started on, leaving the Indians cooking their breakfast and we saw no more of them. I never heard of them committing any depredations afterwards.

CHAPTER 36

We Push Forward on Our Journey

We visited a few days with the Moquis, who received us very kindly. After taking into consideration our instructions to visit Salt River Valley, we tried to hire an Indian to pilot us across the country to the Little Colorado River, wishing to strike it at the nearest point. We were told that there was no water on the route. No one seemed to want the job to guide us. Finally an Indian was found who said he would go for a certain number of silver dollars. We agreed to give him his price. We packed up, filled our water kegs and started out in the afternoon. The guide was to come on in the morning and overtake us.

We travelled a few miles and camped. Next morning the guide came up, but demanded more pay. Finally we consented. We had travelled but a short distance when he demanded another advance. This we did not feel inclined to make, so Brother Tenney told him we could get along without him. He then turned back. There was no trail. We took a southerly direction trusting to our own judgment to get through.

After travelling a few hours we approached near some hills where the country looked like there might be water. We turned off from our direction, went up into the hills and found a spring of good, fresh water. We refilled our kegs and watered our stock. It was somewhat difficult as the banks were steep and the water was a foot or more below the surface.

All our stock drank except a little Mexican burro that would not approach the spring. We all got around him and pushed him up to the brink several times but he would slip away from us. We knew he was thirsty, but, donkey-like, he would not drink. At length we grabbed hold of him, lifted him clear from the ground and put him in the middle of the spring, where he stood quite still but would not drink; so he beat us after all. We named the spring Tussle Jack. I doubt if anyone has been there since.

On leaving this place we were forced by the formation of the country to bear in a westerly direction. Soon we struck dim trails. Following along we came to some water holes in a ravine but passed on. The trails soon giving out we again turned south. At night we made a dry camp; travelled next morning about two miles; still no trail. We found some water, but it was barely sufficient to water our animals. We continued travelling all day without a trail. Towards night we came to a large, dry wash with cotton woods growing along it.

Having heard that the Little Colorado was subject to drying up, we thought this was perhaps the dry bed of the river. If so, we were in a bad fix for there was no knowing when we would reach water. Brother Ivins having a good horse rode out on a high hill to look for signs of the river ahead. The sun was just setting. He helloed back that he could see the river a few miles further on. This news was received with a shout of joy. We started on, travelling with the stars for guides. The country became quite rough and broken, and it was with much difficulty that we finally descended from the bluffs to the river bottom. We had to travel some time before getting to water.

We struck the bottom at a bend of the river where the direction of the stream was the same as our direction of travel. At length we got to water where grass and wood were plentiful. All felt happy, for here we knew by information that we would soon strike the main road leading to Prescott, Arizona. We had a map of this road and country. We had been travelling for some time through a strange country, but little known, some of it, even to the natives. We now felt as though we could get along with less anxiety. We remained a few days looking at the country further up the river so as to be able to report to President Young, which we did as soon as we found a chance to mail our letters. We now took the wagon road leading from the Rio Grande to Prescott, followed a westerly direction and soon reached the Mogollon mountains.

The first night out from the Little Colorado we camped at a mail station which had two men in charge. They gave us considerable information about the country. Next day we reached Pine Station, a place then deserted. Here we met two men from Phoenix, Salt River Valley, a Dr. Wharton and a Mr. McNulty. They had come out to meet their families, who were moving into Arizona. The night was cold and stormy. Next day was the same, so we laid over and had a good visit with these gentlemen. They were two of the most prominent men in Phoenix. McNulty was county clerk for several years. They both still live in the country. They were always kind and friendly to our people and never forgot our first friendly acquaintance in the lonely camp on the wild mountain road.

We left our letter at the first mail station. We got the direction from these gentleman as to the shortest and best road to Salt River, and as there were no natives to visit or country suitable for settling before reaching Phoenix, we concluded to take the shortest route. We were now travelling through a country that was considered somewhat dangerous, more from outlaws than Indians. The Apaches having been driven from their former haunts were now occupying the reservations at Bowie, San Carlos and Camp Apache, where they had recently been located by the management of General Crook. While crossing the Mogollon mountains the weather was quite cold. As we descended toward the lower valley the temperature changed very rapidly, instead of overcoats we soon hunted shade trees.

We were much surprised on entering Salt River Valley. We had travelled through deserts and mountains (with the exception of the Little Colorado valley, a place which we did not particularly admire) for a long ways. Now there opened before us a sight truly lovely. A fertile looking soil and miles of level plain. In the distance the green cotton wood trees; and what made the country look more real, was the thrifty little settlement of Phoenix, with its streets already planted with shade trees, for miles. Strange as it may seem, at the time we started, in September, 1875, the valley of Salt River was not known even to Brigham Young.

Our animals were beginning to fail, as they had lived on grass since leaving Kanab. We bought corn at four cents a pound and commenced feeding them a little. Although Salt River Valley is naturally fertile, owing to the dryness of the climate, there is no grass except a little coarse stuff called *sacaton*.

We camped on the north side of the river. On making inquiry, we learned that Tempe, or Hayden's Mill, seven miles further up the river, would be a better place to stop for a few days than Phoenix. C. T. Hayden being one of the oldest and most enterprising settlers of the country, had built a grist mill, started ranches, opened a store, blacksmith, wagon shop, etc.

As we were passing through Phoenix, we met a few Indians, Maricopas and Pimas. I called one of them to me, and asked him if he understood Mexican. He said he did. I told him who we were and that our mission was to talk to the natives, that we wished to get the Pimas and Maricopas together, over on the Gila, and talk to them. He said, "All right, how much will you pay me to go and notify them?"

I replied, "We will pay you nothing. We are not travelling for money; we are here more for the good of your people than for our own. You can go and tell them or not, just as you please."

He said that he understood who we were, and would go and tell the Indians about us. On arriving at Hayden's place, we found the owner an agreeable, intelligent gentlemen, who was much interested in the settlement and development of the country, as well as friendly toward the Mormons, he being a pioneer in reality, having been for many years in the west, and could fully sympathize with the Mormon people in settling the deserts. He gave us much true and useful information about the country and natives. Here we traded off some of our pack mules and surplus provisions. We had already traded for a light spring wagon, finding that the country before us could be travelled with wagons. We remained here a few days, camping at the ranch of Mr. Winchester Miller.

His barley was up several inches high, but he allowed us to turn our animals into his fields, and treated us in a kind, hospitable manner. The friendly acquaintance made at this time, has always been kept up. Mr. Miller was an energetic man, and manifested a great desire to have the Mormons come there and settle. He had already noticed the place where the Jonesville ditch is now located. He told me about it, saying it was the best ditch-site on the river. What he said has proved true. We wrote to President Young describing the country.

After resting a few days we started for the Gila, striking it at Morgan's Station. This was near the lower villages of the Pimas. The Indians had heard of us and wanted to hear us talk. We did not say much at this place, but told the Indians we would stop at Sacaton, the upper settlement, and have a good long talk with the people; that there we hoped to meet all the leading men of the tribe. Next day we travelled up along the north side of the River Gila, passing a number of the Pima villages, talking a few words and giving out our appointment. Most of the way there was no road, and sometimes it was rather difficult to get along with our carriage.

We arrived that night at Twin Buttes or Hayden's trading station. Here quite a number of Indians came to see us, and we had a pleasant talk with them. It was here I met for the first time an Indian named

Francisco Chico, who spoke Spanish quite well. This man will appear again in this history.

Next day early we arrived at Sacaton. There was no feed, except a little grass among the thorny brush on the river bottom. There was a trader here, doing quite a business. I went to his store and asked him if he had any hay or fodder for sale. He looked at me in surprise and said, "Mister, that is something the country don't produce."

"Then what are travellers to do that wish to stop over here for a few days?" I asked.

"There are no travellers with any sense that want to stop over here. You had better pack up and go on. You can get fodder up at Juan Largos' near Florence, but there is none here."

I answered, "Well we want to stop, and will have to put up with what there is. I see there is a little grass among the brush. We will have to feed all the more grain. We can get plenty of that, I suppose."

"You had better not stay." He said, "If you turn your stock out they will be stolen from you. I have lived here ten years; am friendly with the Indians, but they are the biggest thieves you ever saw. I tell you not to trust them. There are some poor people now in camp down there, two men and a woman. The d——d thieves have stolen their stock and will not fetch it back unless they pay them five dollars a head, and as they have not got the money they are in a bad fix. The Indians will serve you the same way."

We concluded that here was a chance to commence to work and do some good. We made camp in an opening among the brush. Soon quite a number of Indians collected around camp. I told some of them to take our animals and watch them until night, then bring them in for their corn. We put a bell on one of the animals. I told the Indians not to take them so far we could not hear the bell. We went back to the trader's for some grain. I told him what we had done. He said I was like other "smart Alecks" that had just come among the Indians; but that we would be in the same fix as the party was who had lost their stock. I told him we would not lose one of our animals; but that I believed I could induce the Indians to return those they had stolen from the poor people. He said, "You must be either crazy, or in collusion with the Indians."

I told him we were neither. At feeding time all the animals were brought in. After feeding them they were again turned over to the Indians. Next morning all were brought in. This being the day appointed for the meeting, about ten o'clock the Indians commenced gathering. We found an excellent interpreter in Francisco Capulla. He seemed quite intelligent and ready to comprehend what we told him. We talked quite a while with the interpreter before requesting the people to listen to us. Finally there gathered between three and four hundred.

We were told that all the captains had arrived and were ready to listen to what we had to say. I told the interpreter to explain to them what we had been telling him. He talked quite a while in the Pima tongue, in an earnest, spirited manner. When he got through, a few remarks were made by some of the old men. The interpreter told us they were much interested in what they had heard and wished me to talk more, and tell them about their forefathers. Said they knew nothing about them, but that they always understood that sometime there would be those coming among them who knew all about these things.

I now felt it was my time to get the animals which had been stolen from the poor travellers. These people were sitting in sight, looking very much disheartened. I pointed to them and told the Indians it made me feel sorrowful to see those poor people there, and that it weighed on my heart so that I could not talk; and that I wished some of the young men would go and hunt their stock up. I never hinted that I thought they had stolen them away. After this there was some little side-talk among the Indians. The interpreter asked me to go on and talk to the people. The Indians got very much interested when I commenced to explain to them the *Book of Mormon*. (I will here say that in all my labours among the Indians I have never known of one failing to be interested when the *Book of Mormon* was introduced.) These Pimas were intelligent and capable of understanding all we said to them. I then again referred to the disagreeable subject, telling them that I still felt grieved. One of the chiefs spoke up, asking me to go on, as the stock had been found and were being brought to the owners. I now felt free to talk and gave them much instruction.

Brother Tenney being a good interpreter, having had much experience among the natives of Lower California, explained with much clearness the gospel of repentance to these people. A good spirit prevailed and the Indians manifested a desire to be instructed, acknowledged their degraded condition, and said they wished the Mormons would come to their country to live and teach them how to do. We all felt well paid for the hardships we had gone through, for we could see here was a chance for a good work to be done.

183

We were in no way annoyed. Our animals were watched and brought in regularly to feed. When we got ready to start on everything was in good shape. We bade the Indians goodbye, promising that the Mormons would visit them again and some of them would probably come and live in their country.

The trader never knew how to account for our way of doing with the Pimas. From here we went a day's travel farther up the Gila to Juan Largos' villages.

Juan, a Papago Indian, presided over quite a settlement of his people. His son was educated so as to read. We gave him a copy of our book. These extracts from the *Book of Mormon* we had been presenting to a few of the Indians, and some of the Mexicans, on our road. Many years afterwards, the Indians showed me these books. They prize them highly.

At Juan Largos's the people came together and we taught them the same as we had the Pimas. Francisco Capulla went to this village with us. He became much interested in our teachings. His home was in Sonora; he was here only on a visit. I have often heard of but have never seen him since. We found that many of the older Indians on the Gila, remembered the Mormon Battalion that passed through their country in 1846.

CHAPTER 37

My Talk with the Natives

On leaving the Gila our route led to Tucson. We crossed the eighty-five mile desert where the Battalion suffered so much for water. When we crossed there were two wells furnishing good, pure water. One, two hundred feet deep, where there was a small stock ranch and station. For support, the owner sold water to travellers.

At Tucson we received a letter from Brigham Young, from which I will give a short extract, dated, Salt Lake City, November, 8th, 1875.

"Since your departure from Salt Lake City on your way southward, more than one hundred and fifty have been called to aid in the building up of the Kingdom of God, in various parts of the earth. Among these, a party have started in charge of Elder James S. Brown, who intends to winter somewhere in the neighbourhood of the Moencoppy (without a more suitable place is found) and from there spread out as opportunity offers."

At Tucson, we found quite a number of white residents. This old town has been so well described by many writers, that I will simply say, it never was, is not now, and never will be much. Its only merit is in its being so very old; some two hundred and seventy-one years. Our intention had been to go from Tucson to Sonora. But at the time there was a hot revolution under way, and everything was in confusion. There was no safety whatever for anyone entering the country.

We had a letter of introduction from C. T. Hayden of Tempe to Gov. Safford who resided in Tucson. We had a pleasant visit with his Excellency. Mr. Safford is much respected by the inhabitants of Arizona, he having been the framer of the Arizona public school system, which is acknowledged to be excellent. From the governor we received a letter to Mr. Jeffries, the Indian agent at Apache Pass. We were invited to preach in the court house at Tucson, and had a good attendance and attention.

The *Police Gazette* had me pictured out as being rotten-egged by a lot of women, while preaching in a town in Arizona. Tucson was the only town we preached in, in Arizona, while on this mission. So much for sensational reports.

Owing to the unsettled state of affairs in Sonora, we concluded to go farther east and visit El Paso and then go into the state of Chihuahua. Our mixed outfit, both wagon and pack animals were inconvenient; and as the roads were good, we concluded to get another wagon. Having sold some of our animals we had money to spare, so we bought an excellent wagon from the quartermaster, at the post, near Tucson.

We now had a good outfit. Our wagons took the place of the pack animals, but we retained our saddle horses.

The next place of importance, to which we looked forward with some anxiety, was Fort Bowie. On arriving there, we presented our letters to Jeffries, who was in charge of the reservation at Bowie. But the Indians seemed to be in charge of both Jeffries and several companies of soldiers stationed there, for the Indians did about as they pleased.

It was considered somewhat risky to pass through the Apache Pass. According to an agreement made at Beaver with D. H. Wells to be careful, we camped a day's travel this side of the Indians, and with one of the brethren went in to see how things looked. I felt a little uneasy. The Indians were under no control whatever, save that of self-interest. The government gave them everything they wanted, and more. They had provisions of every kind so abundantly, that a great deal was wasted. They had all the guns and ammunition they wanted, and were allowed to raid at will into Sonora and Chihuahua. It was generally believed that they were encouraged by some of the whites in their raiding. When I talked with the agent he said we were safe enough if we did not happen to run across any drunken Indians on the road; but as the weather was cold and disagreeable, he did not think any of them would be out. Advised us to stop at the mail station near the fort and not turn out any animals.

We went back to camp and reported All felt like we would be safe. We all had faith in being protected for we were on a mission, not of our own choosing. We got in next day all right. Our animals needed shoeing so we concluded to lay over a day. I had a great desire to talk to these Indians, believing that they would listen a little. I made some inquiry of the trader who had been with them for some years, about their traditions. He said they had none, only to murder and steal. This I found afterwards to be a great mistake.

I asked Mr. Jeffries, permission to talk to the Indians. He rather jeeringly replied, "I don't think you can get them to listen to you, I am the only man they will talk to."

I answered, "All I ask is your permission and if they won't listen to me, all right."

He said, "Go ahead, I guess you can't make them much worse than they are anyway."

I inquired if any of the Indians talked Spanish. Their interpreter, a drunken little Mexican, offered to interpret, if I would pay him, saying that that was his business, and that no one had a right to talk to the Indians except through him. I told him that the agent had given me the privilege of talking to them; that I was not working for money, and that I did not intend to pay for any interpreting. He then pointed out an Indian that spoke tolerable fair Spanish.

I approached the Indian and spoke to him. He answered quite short and asked what I wanted. I told him that what I wanted to say to him was for his people's good; that if he would listen to me a few minutes, he could then judge.

He looked me in the eye for a moment and then said, "All right, say what you please."

I asked him if the Apaches had any knowledge of their fathers, counting back many counts. He answered that they had lost that, and did not know anything about them.

I showed him one of our books, and informed him that it told about their old fathers. At this he got up and called to a lot of other Indians that were loafing around. Some thirty or forty soon gathered around me. I commenced and explained considerable to them. They were growing quite interested when the agent was seen approaching.

They seemed to understand that my words were not for the agent's ears, and manifested as much by their remarks, so I changed the subject and said that the Mormons had also sent us to look for country to settle, as we were growing and wished new country; that we would perhaps settle near them; that we were friends to the red man and hoped the Apaches would be friendly with us.

The agent had approached near enough to hear this talk. He stayed around, giving me no further chance to explain the *Book of Mormon* to them. He made some remarks to call their attention away from me.

I could see plainly that he wished me to stop talking, so I told the Indians we would meet again sometime. I felt that I had made a little impression for good upon them.

Sometime after this I had a good long talk with the Apaches, which I will give an account of in the proper place. We had a vague idea of the western portion of Chihuahua, where the Mormons are now settling, but could get no definite directions, as we met no one who seemed to know much about the country. So we concluded to continue on the main road to El Paso. Nothing of interest occurred on the way. All went well with us.

We drove into Franklin, a small town on the American side of the line, opposite El Paso. The main question now was, how will we be able to pass the custom house and get our books and outfit over the line into Mexico. Many persons had told us that we would never be allowed to pass, as Catholicism ruled in that country and they would never permit us to enter with Mormon publications. Our hopes were in the overruling Power to help us. None of us pretended to have wisdom for the occasion.

We were standing in the street about noon. I was talking to a gentleman, telling him that we wished to pass over the line at once with our outfit. Our mission was to Mexico, and we felt like going ahead and getting in. We intended to remain there until spring. It was now January.

While talking with the stranger he said, pointing toward three men passing: "There go the custom officer and postmaster; the other man is a good interpreter. The post master is an American, but is a great friend of the custom officer. They are going into the post office now. They have just been to dinner and will be in a good humour. You had better go at once and see them."

I went to the office and inquired if I could see the custom officer. I was invited into a back room where the three sat smoking. Politeness is the rule in that country. I was asked to take a seat and offered a cigar. The custom officer inquired through the interpreter how he could serve me. I told him I was travelling with some others, seven in all, and we wished to cross over into Mexico at once, as we desired to winter there. He asked about our outfit, then our loading. I told him it consisted of the necessary utensils, provisions, clothing, etc., for travellers. Then a lot of books we intended to distribute *gratis* through the country.

He wanted to know what class of books they were: if religious. I told him they were. He said he would rather have some good novels; that he did not care much for religion, but asked what denomination we represented.

I told him, "Mormons."

At this all three burst into loud laughter, the post master and interpreter making many jesting remarks to the officer, and saying to me, "Yes, he will let you in. You are all right. You will get in."

I was a little puzzled, not knowing whether this was favourable or otherwise.

Soon the custom officer turned (as yet I had not spoken a word of Spanish) and said directly to me, "Well, I guess I will have to let you in. I have just been telling these gentlemen that I am a Mormon in principle, and that I wished some of them would come along. That I thought your religion the most sensible of any. You will do good in Mexico, and you shall cross over. I will fix it so you will not have to pay a cent."

I now thanked him in his own language and said we would try and act so as to retain the good opinion he had of us and our people.

We shook hands as friends. He kept his word entirely, and we crossed over at once, rented quarters and got ready for the winter's campaign. We were the first Mormon missionaries that entered Mexico. This was in January, 1876.

CHAPTER 38

We Find Some Friends

We arrived in the Republic of Mexico on Friday. It was not long before everyone in El Paso knew of the arrival of Mormons. We were stared at, but nothing occurred until Sunday that indicated anything unusual. On Sunday we concluded to go to the Catholic church, the only one in town. The building was crowded. We stood in a group near the entrance. There was quite a jam of people around as, and many furtive glances and dark, wicked looks were directed toward us.

About the worst element in Mexico can be found in Paso del Norte, or El Paso. Padre Borajo (pronounced, borah-ho) officiated. After the usual services of tingling bells, kneeling before the cross and various performances common in a Mexican Catholic church, services were over. The *padre* who was quite old and lean (something very unusual for a priest; most of them being rather corpulent) mounted the stand, and in a very impressive manner, commenced to warn the people against us.

These were his words in substance:

The world's history gives an account of great plagues that have visited the world from time to time. Mankind has been subjected to great calamities, such as wars, storms, cholera, small pox, great drouth and floods. We of this land have been subjected to many plagues. The murderous Apaches have made war upon us for many years. We have had our ditches and dams destroyed by floods, so that some seasons we have had to suffer hunger. "We have had many revolutions and thousands have been killed. Lately we have had the grasshoppers come and destroy every green herb and product. But all these things have made war only on the body of the man. None have had a tendency

190

to destroy the soul.

Now of all the plagues that ever visited the earth to curse and destroy mankind we have the worst just come to us and there stand the representatives of this plague. Look at them. Their faces show what they are.

Thanks to God we have been warned in time by the Holy Pope that false prophets and teachers would come among us.

These men, (pointing to us), represent all that is low and depraved. They have destroyed the morals of their own people, and have now come here to pollute the people of this place. (I thought if that was so we had a hard job on hand.) They have no virtue. They all have from six to one dozen wives. Now they have come here to extend the practice into Mexico. *I denounce them.* Yes, here in the presence of the image of the Virgin Mary, I denounce them as barbarians. . . . . And I want you all to get their books and fetch them to me and I will burn them.

As Brother Tenney was not present, I was the only one of our party who perfectly understood his words. I began to feel as though it would be best for us to get out of the crowd before the spirit got too high, as some fanatic might be tempted to slip a sharp knife in among our ribs.

We managed to work ourselves gradually out of the crowd which filled the door yard for several feet. When clear we walked straight way to our quarters, where I translated all that had been said. It was taken down at the time and to the best of my memory was about as here given. We could not help but be amused at the old fellow's vehemence, and our first introduction to Mexico.

For some days after this when women in the streets would see any of us coming, they would jump into the first door and close it and then look out through what all Mexican houses have in their doors—a peep hole. Some of the women who ran from us were of the class that do not often scare at a man, yet they acted as though they dreaded us.

We managed to pass quietly along never seeming to notice these actions, but often had a hearty laugh when we got to our quarters.

On enquiry we learned that the laws of Mexico, under the new constitution, required all religious services to be performed in a structure recognised as a church building.

One liberal-minded gentleman, Esperidion Sanches, gave us much information. He said the law simply required the presiding officer of a town to recognise a house for the occasion, and put the police to protect it; but if the civil authority was under the influence of the priests, they could baffle us and forbid us preaching in any house except a regular church edifice, erected solely for religious worship.

Sanches told me the Jefe Politico of Paso del Norte, was an affable gentleman but a strong Catholic, and he doubted if we would be able to get the privilege of holding meetings. When we called upon the gentleman he told us that he understood the law forbade any religious services performed except in a house especially erected for religious purposes.

I tried to reason with him. He listened to me patiently, but said no difference how unreasonable the law might seem we would have to submit. I then asked him if the law defined any particular material to be used, or size, or shape the house should be built, that possibly we might take it in hand to build a church. This he could not answer.

I visited him several times but to no purpose. The laws forbade all street preaching. I felt determined not to be beaten. There were a number of the better class of citizens visited us and protested against the way the priest had talked about us, saying that none but ignorant fanatics would sustain such talk.

This gave us an opportunity to explain our mission and principles to many that would not have listened if it had not been for the *padre's* rabid talk. Finally an idea occurred to me. President Young had presented me with a good new set of saddler's tools before leaving Salt Lake City. He had said that they might help me out sometime when nothing else would. So I called once more on the Jefe Politico. He was always patient and polite.

After talking a while about the meeting house I told him I had given up the idea of holding meetings until I went to Chihuahua and saw the governor. This seemed to please him for he desired peace, and he was afraid for us to attempt holding meetings in Paso del Norte, as the people were much under the influence of priest-craft.

I asked him how he would like a saddle shop started. He said it would be a good thing; that many people needed saddles and had to pay a high price for them; that he thought I could do well making saddles; in fact much better than preaching, as no one would pay me for preaching, but would be glad to pay me a big price for a good saddle.

When I talked with my companions, showing my plans, all agreed with me. So we rented quite a large house for a saddler shop. I hired a bench and vise, put up my tools, bought some timber and went to work making saddle-trees. My son Wiley assisted me.

Soon the people began to call in to look at my work. As there was no law against conversation, especially in one's own house, we soon got to having quite respectable audiences and the spirit of friendship grew up toward us.

Some of the brethren went over on the Texas side, to Ysleta, to winter where the stock could be fed more cheaply than in El Paso.

Brothers Tenney and Smith, did not want to go on into Mexico, so we agreed that they should have the privilege of labouring in New Mexico among the Pueblos and Zunis, and then return home. As they never reported to me, all I know about them is what I have learned from others. Brother James Brown took charge of that field of labour.

About this time I received the following letter:

Salt Lake City, U.T.,
January 22nd, 1876.

Elder D. W. Jones, El Paso, Texas,

Dear Brother:—I was more than pleased to receive your favour of the 10th inst., and was much interested in its contents, not to say amused at your account of the oration by the *padre*, as an introductory greeting into Mexico. Like you, I doubt not but that the opposition bodes good for you, and the success of your mission. I feel that it would be wise for you to visit the old original blood as much as possible. Let the Catholic church alone; if its members wish to hear the truth, expound it to them as to any other people, but do not debate with them. And as to the curses of the priests, you need not regard them as much as you would a mosquito, in the season of the year when these insects trouble.

Be cautious in your labours and movements; do not court opposition, but move steadily on, presenting the truths of the gospel to those who will hear you, and inviting all to become partakers of the gospel of the Son of God. You have the faith and prayers of all that you will be able to do a good work, and I have no doubt but that you will see me again in the flesh yet many times.

Brother James S. Brown has returned from his visit to Arizona.

193

He left the brethren of his party building a fort at Moencoppy, 20 x 40 feet. Whilst in that country he, with three others, went a long distance up the Little Colorado River, from the Moencoppy, passing up beyond where you crossed. He fully substantiates the statements made by yourself and the brethren of your party with regard to the desirability of the upper valleys of the Little Colorado as settlements for the Saints.

We have called about two hundred brethren, whom we think of dividing into companies of 50, to settle on the Little Colorado and adjacent country. These brethren will mostly be ready to start by the 1st of February. A most excellent spirit prevails with regard to this mission amongst the brethren, and numbers more would have been willing to have gone had they been wanted. We shall send down a grist and saw-mill during the summer. Among those called is Elder Lot Smith, who will have charge of one company of fifty.

Since my letter to you of Nov. 8th, addressed to Tucson, we have had a very peaceable and quiet time. Judge White set me at liberty, soon after, from the unjust imprisonment of Judge Boreman for contempt. Brother Reynolds has again been tried, convicted for obeying the law of the Lord and sentenced to two years' hard labour in the U. S. House of Correction at Detroit and $500 fine. He appealed and was admitted to bail. The appeal will come up in June.

Brother Cannon has been seated in Congress; his contestant has not made much of a show yet. I notice by the telegrams that Mr. Christiancy, senator from Michigan, has introduced a bill to provide for challenges to jurors in trials for bigamy and polygamy; that it shall be sufficient cause, for the rejection of a juror, that he has more than one wife living, or that he *believes* it morally right for a man to live with more than one wife. Well, the faster it comes the sooner the end will be.

Our legislature is now in session with plenty of work provided for it. If the members feel it consistent or necessary to attend to all that is suggested they will have to be very wary and prudent, or our ever watchful enemies will introduce some bills that, if enacted, will prove snares and pitfalls. They will have to work for nothing, for Congress has allowed the U. S. Marshal to spend the appropriations for the payment of the legislature and passed a law prohibiting the legislature from passing any act to pay themselves out of the Territorial Treasury.

The new building of the Z. C. M. I. is a great success. It is lighter than the most sanguine expected. It presents, now that the elegant front is on, a most handsome and imposing appearance. We expect to commence business in it about the 7th of March.

My health is generally good; occasionally I catch cold and then I suffer from rheumatism. I hope the temple at St. George will be sufficiently near completion at die end of February to enable me to go down at that time and dedicate the lower portion.

With love to yourself and all the brethren associated with you, and with constant prayers that you may enjoy all the blessings that in your heart you can righteously desire, and that abundant success may crown your labours, I remain

Your brother in the Gospel,

Brigham Young.

I did very well with my saddle work, earning enough to assist some little in keeping up expenses. The brethren with me were all diligent and acted in a manner to create a respect for our people and religion.

We had meetings quite often on the American side of the river, that were generally well attended, and good order prevailed during the whole winter, with one exception.

We were informed one Saturday that there was a crowd of Irish Catholics that intended to rotten egg us the next day, Sunday, if we attempted to preach in Franklin. I told our informers, that we expected to preach and hoped the Irishmen would change their minds.

There was an old acquaintance of mine, Tom Massey, who knew me in Santa Fe. Tom told these Irishmen that he did not know what religion had done for me, but unless it had done more than is common, they would not meet with much success, and advised them not to try it.

Massey was a saloon keeper and gambler, and was considered authority on all questions that had to be settled with the knife and pistol, and I think his advice had some effect.

However, next morning when meeting opened there was quite a large audience. About the time I commenced speaking the Irish gents came in, sat down near the door, and soon began groaning.

I walked down near them and told them that I was capable of making all the noise necessary, provided the audience wished to hear

195

my noise, but if they preferred theirs to mine they could say so, and I would give them the floor.

Several in the audience called for me to go on and told the disturbers to keep quiet. They made no more disturbance. This gave me a good text and I explained plainly the gospel of repentance; referred a little to my experience in that country when a boy. I could talk plainly as there were persons present who had known me and knew that I was rather a hard case in a rough-and-tumble-go-as-you-please fight.

I told them our doctrine required us to forsake all of our evil ways and to be willing to bear all kinds of persecution meekly; that I had endeavoured to school myself in these principles and hoped that I had succeeded; but that I was not quite certain yet; and that I hoped I would be spared the trial for a year or two longer before having to be thumped for my religious belief as I might not be prepared to take abuse with a submissive spirit.

In explaining Mormonism I said that the gospel did not debar a person from any pleasure he desired to enjoy. Brothers Pratt and Stewart followed and spoke on the first principles of the gospel.

After meeting was dismissed the leader of the disturbers met us at the door. He asked me to go and take a drink with him. I told him I did not drink liquor.

"Then you go back on your own words, do you?" he questioned.

I asked him what he meant. He said "While preaching you made the statement that your religion allowed you any pleasure you desired."

"Yes sir, but drinking whisky is no pleasure to me and I do not desire to drink any."

"Well, do you ever eat anything," he asked.

"Yes, we are all good eaters."

"Well then come with me to the hotel and I will pay for a good dinner for as many of you as will come."

Brother Pratt and some others went along. We had a good dinner and when we went to go our friend said, "If any body bothers you let me know and I will lick them for you. I like to fight but would rather fight for you boys than to fight you. Goodbye."

To finish this,—some ten years after as I was sitting at the dinner table at Pueblo, Colorado, I noticed a man looking across the table at me. I soon recognised him as my Irish friend.

I spoke and asked if he knew me. "Yes, I know you. How are you?" he asked, reaching across the table and shaking hands with me.

"Have you ever thought of me?" I enquired.

"Yes a thousand times."

I told him I had often thought of him, and with a few more words we parted. I feel an interest now in this man and would be glad to meet him again and know his name.

I can say that I have often observed, in the course of my experience, that every man, even the worst, has something good about him if properly treated.

CHAPTER 39

Justice in Early Days

I will give you a short account of the actions of the first authorities of Franklin as given to me by the main actor, that the "tenderfeet" of the present day may know a little of the experiences of early days.

When Franklin first established itself as a town, Judge Jones was elected mayor and Ben Dowel marshal. Soon after organising a number of roughs came in and started to run the town, defying the officers. This would have been all right and possibly admired a few days before the organisation, but now order must be kept and the laws vindicated.

A warrant was issued and the marshal and posse approached the rioters. A man was killed, but the outlaws kept possession of the street and defied the officers. Something had to be done.

The dockets show that these men were arrested, brought to trial and found guilty of murder in the first degree; that the court sentenced them to be shot; that Ben Dowel and others were ordered by the court to execute the orders.

Accordingly the orders were duly executed, and Dowel and his assistants, the judge being one of the party, proceeded to shoot four of these condemned men on the street in front of the main saloon of the town. They were buried, as the records show, and the costs of court and all proceedings duly recorded.

Judge Jones showed me the record and explained how it was done. I never heard any complaint about the proceedings but, on the other hand, Judge Jones and Ben Dowel were very much respected by the average citizens of the country.

During the winter Brothers Pratt and Stewart remained most of the time at Ysleta. Brother Ivins helped me make saddle-trees, took care of the stock, and made himself generally useful. I worked most of the time in the shop, my son Wiley helping me. We boarded with a Mexican family, Santiago Vega, who treated us very kindly, often posting us on what was said of us.

The Mexican people are great riders and fond of a good saddle. This gave me a chance to talk to the people. All seemed friendly. Even the priest who had given us such a setting up came and patronised us. We also distributed a few books. We tried quite hard to get a hearing from the natives that lived in and around El Paso, but the priest kept such a watch upon our moves that we had but little chance.

These natives are known as Pueblos. Never having mixed with the Spanish blood they are still pure blooded Indians. They are generally poor, occupying lands owned by the rich. They desired to hear us and appointed meetings, but were warned that if they listened to us their rents would be raised or they would be driven from their lands. So we had to let them alone, seeing their situation.

The brethren held meetings often at Ysleta and adjacent towns. One family, by the name of Campbell, who resided at San Elesario, opened their doors to the Elders, treating them with great kindness. This family afterwards joined the Church.

After recruiting our animals and feeling that we had done about all the good in our power in El Paso, we determined to make a move into the interior and go to the city of Chihuahua. We were told that the governor, Senor Ochoa, was a very liberal-minded man and not under priestly control, and that he would be very likely to allow us the privilege of preaching.

I wrote to President Young regularly. We received letters from him in return, giving us kind encouragement and instructions.

I reported to him our finances, which were getting short, stating that we intended going on and working our way through the best we could. We received a postal card directing us to wait till we heard from him. When we did hear it was in the shape of postal orders for money sufficient to bear our expenses for some time.

Before leaving El Paso I called on the Jefe Politico. I had hoped that I could get some kind of a letter from him that would assist us in getting introduced into Chihuahua.

The Jefe had the reputation of being a very kind and affectionate father, extremely fond of his wife and children, so I called on him at his residence. He received me kindly and expressed regret that we were going away. Said that he had had his opinion changed about the Mormons. "From the way in which your company have acted I think the Mormons would make good citizens, and I would like to have you remain."

I told him our duty was to travel through the country and visit with and explain to the people our principles and make friends with them, in anticipation that some of our people would, in time, come into his country and make homes; that they were now coming this way; that we had, on our trip found country and reported back the same, and that we had received word that several hundred were getting ready to follow upon our tracks to colonize the places already reported.

"Well" said he, "all you will have to do will be to do as you have done here. When you first came we all thought you bad men. You have stayed here and behaved yourselves in a manner that we now look on you as good men and respect you. You can do the same wherever you go."

I replied "Yes, you are right, but it will take a long time. We desire to visit a great many places. I have a good kind wife at home whom I love dearly. I have a number of little children near the ages of yours here. I love them; they are fond of me."

He looked at me a moment and then said; "That is so. I understand your feelings and will give you a letter that will introduce you to the governor, or wherever you go, and you do not need to wait three months to introduce yourselves."

He gave us the letter, stating that we were gentlemen of good behaviour, etc., etc.

We bade goodbye to our numerous friends and started to Chihuahua in the latter part of March.

By this time it was known throughout the state of Chihuahua that Mormon missionaries were in the country. The reception given us by the padre had also been heralded abroad. This caused the more liberal minded to sympathize with us. Wherever we stayed we were kindly treated. We managed to keep posted where to apply and who to avoid. The liberal people notifying us against the rabid Catholics.

The first day's travel from the Rio Grande brought us to a station where water was supplied in a large tank. A few soldiers were stationed here as a guard against the Apaches that sometimes raided the ranch. This was an important camping place, being the only water found on a 75 mile drive. Grass was plentiful and travellers often camped here for their teams to rest.

We were now in a country where our stock would have to be

carefully watched every night. Our custom was to feed grain, hopple the horses and take turns guarding them through the night. It was my turn to go on guard. The animals were eating their corn. Grass was good all around the camp. The night was very dark, the brethren were singing. I got interested in listening and delayed a few minutes attending to the stock. When I went to take charge of them, they were all gone. I gave the alarm.

One man remained in camp to keep up the fire and the rest of us spent until midnight hunting, but nothing of our stock could be seen.

I went to bed feeling about as miserable as anyone ever did. The fault was my own. I had been very strict; so much so that some of the brethren had felt hurt at times. I had been so careful of all our outfit. Now I felt, after all my strictness I had been the one to lose the stock.

Next morning we could see bunches of stock in every direction, but ours could not be found.

At length Brother Ivins and my son found their trail and followed it some ten miles. They were afoot and the trails showed that the animals were being driven off, so the boys returned and reported. I went to the station to see if I could get help. The commander said it was his business to lend assistance and that he would do all he could for me. I told him I wanted a good horse as I was a trailer.

The commander, myself and two others were ready in a short time. Orders were given for five others to follow our trail, bringing water and provisions. We went to our camp. I told the brethren that I would not return without the stock.

The commander wanted to know of me how long I wished to follow the trail. I told him until I got the animals or died trying. He said he never left a trail as long as one man stayed with him.

The agreement was if I did not return, the brethren were to hire a team, return to El Paso, and report to Brother Brigham.

As soon as we struck the trail the Mexicans decided that the animals had been stolen by Apaches, as we could see plainly that there were barefooted tracks along with ours. The trail was quite plain until we reached a low mountain range. Here the formation was rocky and no trail could be seen.

I had taken the lay of the country in the distance and picked out the point where I was satisfied the animals would have to go. So, while the Mexicans were looking for tracks, I made for this pass.

On reaching the summit of the rise the country opened out somewhat level. I made a circuit and soon struck the trail. I was now alone, but on calling the others heard me and soon came in sight. I started on a gallop. One of the party, riding up, overtook and complimented me on my ability to trail.

As we rode I looked back and saw a signal fire. I asked what it was for. My companion said, "The captain is now satisfied that the Apaches have your stock, and that is a signal fire for some more men to come on and follow our trail, bringing water, as there is none for three days in this direction."

He proposed riding a little slower till the captain came up. I felt more like going faster.

There was a clump of cedars in sight in the direction we were going. As we neared it the Mexican said, "There are your animals; the thieves have gone in there and we have got to fight." We looked back, but no one was now in sight.

The Mexican asked, "What shall we do? Will you fight?"

I told him I would, if necessary, and for him to take out on one side, keeping out of gunshot, I would go on the other and we would get beyond the cedars and keep the thieves from running the stock off.

We were in a wide flat, with mountains on each side. We rode clear round on the run and met. We saw no sign of thieves. Soon five men, with the Mexican captain, came up.

We approached the cedars cautiously and found all the animals bunched, but no thieves. We made a careful survey of the country and found the tracks of the thieves, where they had gone off in another direction. The captain asked if I wished to follow them. I was too thankful to get the stock, so I told him to let them go; that they had had their trouble for nothing.

We arrived at our camp about sundown, having ridden nearly forty miles. The commander charged us nothing, but we made the soldiers a present of a few dollars, which they accepted very thankfully, as a Mexican soldier serves for almost nothing and boards himself.

Our animals were never molested afterward. There was quite a number of teams camped around at the time, and there was considerable interest shown, as most all thought it was the Apaches that had stolen our animals, but it was doubtless thieves who had taken them expecting to get a reward for fetching them back.

When we returned, the captain told them it was no use for any one to steal my animals, unless they rolled up the tracks as they went along, for if they did not I would find them. And added that "the Mormon" was the best trailer he had ever seen.

Months after this when hundreds of miles from this place, Mexicans would speak of the circumstance and quote the words of the captain. We were something strange in the country and all our movements and actions were watched and talked about so that wherever we went we found the people seemed to know all about us.

CHAPTER 40

Interest Aroused Concerning Us

Before writing any further account of our travels and experiences in Mexico. I will explain as briefly as I can the cause of the mission being called and the expectations entertained by many.

The *Book of Mormon* teaches us that the gospel is to be carried to the remnants, that is, the natives of America (Indians.) The promise is that the natives will receive the gospel and rejoice in it.

The census of Mexico shows that there are over six millions of pure blooded Indians or descendants of the ancient races inhabiting this country. Now when this mission was opened a great many became enthusiastic over the prospects and expected great things of us, the first missionaries to Mexico. I remember writing to my wife while in El Paso, referring to this spirit, telling her that many would be disappointed in the mission, but that I should not; that I should be satisfied even if we did not baptise a single person; that our mission was more as prospectors going through to prepare the way, and that President Young so understood it. We were to be governed by circumstances and not to feel disappointed if we could get to distribute our books and learn about the country and make friendly acquaintance with the people. That was all that would be expected of us on the trip. This was our calling. We were not sent to baptise and organise branches, neither were we forbidden to do so. That was an open question to be decided upon according to the openings made.

There were two parties in Mexico, the Catholics and Liberals. We kept our eyes open for the latter as we were always safe with them.

When we reached the city of Chihuahua, I desired to find a stopping place with a Liberal. The Liberals of Mexico believe in religious liberty, please don't think they were like Utah Liberals(?). We did not wish to seem partial to either, and did not like to make a direct enquiry. I was well acquainted with the old customs of this place, having lived there for some time, so we drove up near the Catholic cathedral. I knew that any good Catholic, passing in front of the church, would take off his hat, but a Liberal would pass along with his hat on.

In 1847, when I was there, *all* had to take off their hats, or run the risk of getting a good pelting with rocks. But it was not the case in 1876, the time I am now writing about.

I soon noticed a large, fine-looking man coming along who did not raise his hat. I asked him to direct us to a good *maison* or hostelry. I felt sure he would send me to the right place which he did, to the *maison* San Francisco. A *maison* is a large building with rooms, corrals and stabling where you can rent accommodations and sustain yourself, generally with stores of provisions kept by the proprietor to sell to travellers, connected.

On arriving and taking rooms and stables, I went to the landlord and told him we had left our money at El Paso, to be expressed to us, and we wished him to credit us for a few days for such provisions and feed as we needed. He said, "No sir. I will not do that."

I was "stumped" and did not know what to do as we had but a few dollars with us. Our outfit was first class and valuable, and we had not expected to be refused.

While I was wondering in my mind what to do, the landlord stepped into a room and soon returned with a large, well-filled pocket book, and handed it to me saying. "There is money, take what you want, and when yours comes, you can return it. If I should sell you things on credit, you might think I took advantage of your circumstances and charge you more than if you had money. Take what money you want, look around and buy where you can do the best."

I thought how very different from the average white man whether Gentile or Mormon.

The landlord proved a true gentleman in every respect, giving us much useful information and treating us kindly during our stay.

As soon as we got cleaned up and rested a little, we called upon the governor and presented the letter received from the Jefe Politico of El Paso. He received us kindly, saying that he had heard about us, and laughingly said he had heard of Padre Borajo's speech and hoped we were not so bad as the *padre* had represented us to be.

Governor Ochoa was an intelligent, liberal-minded man and was much respected. His name is still held in respectful remembrance in Chihuahua. He was known to be truthful and honest. He was quite learned and understood well the condition of Mexico.

After explaining our reasons to him for visiting Mexico, he said he was glad to have us come among them; that he believed our principles taught to the people would do them good. He also said that he was well acquainted with the lands of Mexico and would give us all the information he could to help us understand them properly, so we could report correctly to Brigham Young.

The governor recommended us to the Jefe Politico of Chihuahua who furnished us the public cockpit to preach in. Printed notices were circulated. The editor of the official paper gave us a favourable notice.

In the evening, at the time of meeting, quite a respectable congregation had gathered. The cock fighting was still going on, but soon closed. Many persons there at their national sport remained to hear us.

As I was the only one who could speak in Spanish, Brother Tenney having gone north, I had to do the preaching. It was quite a task but I knew the native politeness. No Mexican will ever jeer a foreigner if he tries to speak their language. They will listen attentively and try to understand. I understood Spanish quite well, but had never spoken in public and, no doubt, made many blunders. However, our audience seemed pleased.

When meeting was over many came and shook hands with us and said they liked what had been preached. One aged blind man who had held a discussion with the Bishop of Durango, said he had been preaching our doctrine for years. He showed us a report of his discussion. The old fellow, although very poor, had made a name that is known far and wide. No one could answer him. He came to our rooms next day and talked for a long while. We gave him some of our books to distribute. He lived at Jabonero, southwest from Chihuahua some two hundred miles. He said the honest people of Mexico would believe our words. The old man manifested a great desire to have us go to his town. I have never heard of him since, but we were all impressed with his honesty.

By invitation we visited Gov. Ochoa several times. He explained fully to us the condition of government lands. He said the Mexican government made big offers of land to colonizers, but the fact was, they had no good land; that all desirable tracts for settling were covered by old grants with titles. He desired us to say to Brigham Young that if he wanted lands for his people they must be bought from the owners; and for him not to be deceived by any offers coming from the government of Mexico. He said their offers were polite and looked pretty on paper, and sounded well when listened to; and he really believed that if they could do as they offered to they would.

"The Mexicans are naturally kind and polite, but inasmuch as they have neither land or money," he said laughingly, "you must take the will for the deed."

This I reported to Prest. Young on my return home, who received it as a fact, and remarked: "Why should there be good lands left in the heart of Mexico, when they had given out grants clear into California, New Mexico, Arizona and even into this territory?"

We remained some three weeks in the city. A great many persons called upon us, some to enquire about our religion with sincere interest, others for mere curiosity. Among our visitors were some notorious robbers from Arizona who visited us often. We could not avoid them as they passed for gentlemen, and really acted as such. One was a small, heavy-set Dutchman, who seemed to know all about the big mail robbery on the southern route in 1875, as also about the robbing of Golinsky, of Silver City. The other was a young man from Silver City who robbed an old Dutchman of some fifteen hundred dollars, not far from Mecilla, while they were travelling together.

The old man had been to California for five years, had mortgaged his farm, or bought it with a mortgage given as security, he had saved the money to pay up and was on the way home full of joy to meet his wife and children. He had travelled all the way from California on horseback and alone, not even a pocket pistol to protect himself. He carried a fifteen hundred draft and some little money. He looked quite poor. No one would have suspected him worth robbing.

This young man got in company with the old fellow and they travelled and camped together. The Dutchman confided his good luck to the lad, who could not stand the temptation but made the old man give up; the boy rode ahead and got across the line, changed his draft and skipped. We saw both while in El Paso. The old man came in hunting the robber, where we heard his story. The young fellow told my son Wiley all about the job, and expressed himself sorry, saying he was of good family but was now ruined for life.

In talking to the people we found that many adhered to and respected their ancient traditions. They also retained a respect for their native lineage. This spirit prevailed strongest among the Liberals.

The power of Catholicism had been broken and a new constitution adopted under the leadership of Juarez, who had overcome Maximilian. Juarez was a pure-blooded Indian. His most active helpers and the main portion of his army were composed of natives. So at the time we were there it was respectable to be called Indigine, or native. This class received the *Book of Mormon* readily and manifested much interest in the same.

While in Chihuahua we sent out copies of the book, five in a package, to each town and city throughout the republic, wherever there was a mail.

The clerks in the post office assisted us for three days. All their spare time they were packing and directing. Each package was directed to the officers of the place with a request to read and distribute them among the people. We sent to all the head officers of the different departments a package. I received letters of acknowledgment from some of the principal men.

Among the rest Sr. Altamarano, a full-blooded native and a high officer of state; I got several letters from Doctor Rodacanaty professing to have had a vision showing him the truth of the *Book of Mormon.*

CHAPTER 41

We Prepare to Return Home

After finishing up our work in the city of Chihuahua we decided to visit the western portion of the state.

We had received information that a great many natives lived in the Canton de Guerero. This district commences about one hundred and fifty miles west of the city of Chihuahua and extends into the Sierra Madre mountains. The greater portion of the inhabitants of Guerero are natives known as Tarumarie. Many villages of these people are located in the valleys near the mountains.

There are many towns and villages that retain the old Indian names. Towns that were there when the Spaniards first came into the country have come under Catholic rule. Cathedrals were built and a few Spaniards settled among the people, mixing with them. (In some settlements most of the mixed blood claim relationship to the *padres*.) In this way Spanish civilization somewhat modified the habits of the people, but did not do away with them entirely, for in most of these towns pure Tarumaries inhabit districts, retaining all their ancient customs and language.

This race of people are much respected throughout the state of Chihuahua, and it is considered rather an honour to be related to them. We concluded to make their country our next stopping place.

Bidding goodbye to our friends in Chihuahua, and particularly to our good old honest governor Antonio Ochoa, we started west. Our route led through a country that was very sparsely settled, owing to the lack of water for irrigation. The city of Chihuahua is located in a rough, barren country, which continues for some thirty-five miles going west.

For several days' travel there is nothing very inviting to the eye. But on reaching the higher country toward the head waters of the Aras

River, a tributary of the Yaqui, the country became more inviting. We continued our journey, passing settlements and ranches daily, leaving with each a few books and talking a little with the people near where we camped.

Nothing of importance occurred on the road except the mending of one of our horse's hoofs with rawhide. The hoof had been badly cracked for some time. As we were descending a rough, rocky hill the horse stumbled and struck his foot against a boulder so hard that the hoof split clear open up to the hair. We had much difficulty in getting him into the settlement a few miles ahead. We offered to sell the horse but could get only one dollar offered for him. We could not well leave him neither had we money to spare to buy another.

Mexicans are great people to use rawhide, and I had learned from them to use it in many emergencies.

As we were going to bed Brother Pratt remarked: "Brother Jones why can't you use rawhide on John, (the horse) or does this case beat you?"

The question put me to thinking. So in the morning I obtained a suitable piece of rawhide from a Mexican, took the horse to a blacksmith who put some tallow and burnt horn into the opening of the hoof, then seared it with a hot iron. I then took the rawhide and fitted it nicely over the whole hoof, lacing it behind and underneath. The blacksmith fitted a shoe and nailed it on, driving the nails through the rawhide which now formed the outer crust of the hoof. We let the horse stand in a dry place until the next morning when the nails were tightly clinched.

We laid over one day to see how this would work, then continued our journey. The horse travelled as though nothing had happened, and finally, when the hide came off after we had travelled some six hundred miles, the hoof was entirely healed up. This may not be interesting, but might be profitable to some, and for that reason I relate the circumstance.

On arriving at the village of Concepcion, (the principal town of Guerero,) we enquired for a good place to stop, and were directed to Don Eselso Gonzalez, where we soon made arrangements for the necessary accommodations.

Don Eselso furnished us good quarters with a large hall attached, had it seated with benches brought from the bull pen which he owned. We held several meetings that were well attended and much interest was manifested by some, while all treated us kindly.

One man, Francisco Rubio, really understood and believed the *Book of Mormon*; as once in meeting he took it in his hand and explained it in a more lucid manner, especially the part relating to the Saviour's appearance on this continent, than I had ever heard before. Individually, I received new light from the native.

From what I have seen now and then among the natives I sometimes think that the people called Latter-day Saints are only half converted. I have seen and felt more warmth of spirit and faith manifested by natives than I ever saw by white Saints. Even the Apaches told me that they would not wait long for the winding-up scene, when they once had power and authority from God to act in His name. That faith, which will yet remove the powers of evil from around the Saints, will come largely from the remnants. I think we will need them in our work and should be looking after them some little and not altogether after money.

We deposited our money with Don Eselso. Many times getting articles from his store, and when we went to settle up for house rent and other things, he would not take a cent, but insisted on presenting us with some dried meat and other stuff, jokingly remarking that he could not sell it anyway.

While here we visited Arisiachic, the principal Tarumarie town. The trail was very difficult. We were well received. The chief called the people together and we had a long talk with them. They were very much pleased with our visit and hoped we would return some day.

We remained in Concepcion about three weeks. Held several meetings which were well attended. Many people visited us to learn of our doctrine. We were fully convinced that many believed in the truth of the *Book of Mormon*, yet we had no spirit to offer baptism.

By this time some of the brethren began to manifest a desire to return home. At first I felt a little disappointed, but I can look back now and see that our mission was properly a short one. We were united in one idea, and that was before any great work could be done in this country it would be necessary to colonize among the people.

As to the spirit of the people, we all agreed, also, that it was favourable, so it was deemed best that we work our way toward home, visiting the various settlements on our way.

We left many warm-hearted friends at Concepcion, some testifying to having a perfect faith in the *Book of Mormon* and expressing a strong desire that the Mormons would come and dwell among them.

On our way home we turned off from the road at Tejoloquechic west to visit the towns of Matachic and Temosachic, the last a place containing some five thousand inhabitants. The people of these towns received us not only kindly, but many of them manifested great faith in our teachings. They often insisted on giving us something for our books, saying we had a long way to travel and would need something to help us on our journey.

At Matachic Tomas Tribosa opened his house to us and we had a large congregation. We talked freely and plainly to the people. Many persons had told us that we would be all right so long as we let the subject of polygamy alone; but if that was ever taught the women would knife us.

This night, while speaking, I felt impressed to talk on the principle of plurality and explain plainly the doctrine. There were quite a number of women present. After meeting was dismissed I went to the end of the hall where the women were. Many of them came and shook hands with me and said they would rather their husbands would do as we taught than as many of them did. No one seemed offended in the least.

Wherever we held meetings permission had to be first obtained from the civil authorities. When we arrived at Temosachic, the proper officer for granting this license was out of town. A man was sent four miles for him, it not being certain whether he would be found or not.

While we were arranging to send a courier, the priest of the settlement came up. He expressed the hope that we would be able to find the officer. Said he desired very much to hear us and asked if the *padre* at Chihuahua had offered his church to us.

I told him he had not. He said he wished he had set the example, then he himself could invite us into his church, where a license would not be required; but he did not like to risk being the first to open a Catholic church building to us.

"But," said he, "you must come down tonight (it was now about noon), and I will have a good lot of my people together. There is no law against friends sitting down and talking on a decent subject. I want to ask some few questions if you will answer them."

I replied that we would come. We conversed for some time and the *padre* seemed quite interested.

We were camped some three miles away, at the edge of the town. About sundown Brother Pratt and I walked down to the public square where we had appointed to meet the priest. We felt as safe as if at

212

home in Salt Lake City.

On arriving, the priest and quite an audience were awaiting us, but there was no word from the officer, so we concluded to sit and chat.

A great many pertinent questions were asked and answered. The best of order prevailed and a good feeling was manifested. The priest said he would study our book and if he could not understand it he was willing for his people to study, and if they could see good in our doctrine, he wanted them to have the privilege of receiving it. He said that he was now getting old; that he had always worked for the good of the people, and that he did not want to keep any good thing away from them.

Next morning we started back to take up our road for home. We had turned off at Tejoloquechic. On reaching there the people had gathered a donation of corn and beans, for us and insisted on our receiving it. We took some but told them we could not haul much.

The next place where anything of interest occurred was at Namaquipe, a town on the Upper Santa Maria River. We arrived at this place on Sunday about ten o'clock, intending to spend the day of rest there. We camped in the shade of some cottonwoods near a large ranch house, across the river from the main town.

I went to the house to buy some dried meat. I met an old lady who sold me the meat giving quite a liberal quantity for twenty five cents. I made her a present of one of our books, and went back to camp.

Some time after noon this same lady with a very aged companion, came into camp. The old man looked over one hundred years old. We learned that he was a hundred and three years.

On being seated the old gentleman said, "You were up to my house this morning."

"Yes sir."

"You got some meat."

"Yes sir."

"You paid for it."

"Yes sir." I began to think of the *lot* I had gotten for my money.

"You left a little book."

"Yes sir."

"Did you get pay for it?"

"No sir. I did not want pay for the book. We do not sell these books."

"Yes, but you paid for the meat. That was not right."

Here the old man held the book up and said, "I have been reading

213

this book. I understand it and know who you are. You are apostles of Jesus Christ, just the same as Peter, James and John, and I know it. And I also know this book is true." He then turned to his wife and said: "Wife have I not been telling our neighbours for two years past that apostles having the true gospel would come to this land, and that I would live to see them?"

We were astonished to hear this testimony, so direct and positive.

Don Francisco Vasquez continued and asked us if we intended to return to the country soon. We told him we did not know but we hoped to. He said he would like to be baptised and receive the benefit of the gospel before he died.

Next morning when we passed his home he made us take four sacks of corn; all we could haul.

The old man lived to be one hundred and five years old, I visited his family ten years afterwards. The old lady was still alive. She told me that Don Francisco, on his death-bed, called his family around him and told them all to be baptised when the Mormons came. Some forty persons agreed to do so. His oldest son told me the same. They were still hopeful, but how long their hopes will hold out I cannot say. Possibly until the "Liberals" drive us out of this land into Mexico, where the greater number of the remnants live. Then and not till then will we feel the obligation of carrying the words of the *Book of Mormon* to the Lamanites.

Many times, when thinking of this old man and others of the district, I have cried like a child, never having seen, from that day to the present, any disposition manifested to continue a mission in that part of the country. Of late years I have concluded that the people are better as they are than they would be, unless those going among them go with the spirit of true friends and as colonizing missionaries.

CHAPTER 42

Soldiers on the Move

After leaving Namaquipe the next place of importance is El Valle. We arrived about noon and halted on the public square. We saw a large crowd collected at a corner store. I took a tin can and told the brethren that if we could not get the privilege of preaching here I would get some lard and we would move on. The crowd was watching us; as I approached them I could see that something special was up. I went into the store and inquired where I could find the *alcalde*. A man asked:

"What do you want with him?"

"I want to get permission to preach here."

"I can answer that you cannot; we have all the religion we want. We have held a mass meeting, and the citizens of this place have appointed me to meet you on your arrival and notify you that you can go on. We know who you are and want nothing to do with you."

I made no reply; but turned to the merchant and asked him if he had any lard. At this many of the crowd commenced to laugh and make pleasant remarks, saying that the stranger took it very coolly. The merchant said he was out of lard and did not know of anyone who had any but Don Pedro who had been talking to me. I asked him if he would sell me some.

"Yes, sir, but it is quite a distance from here to my house; if you wish to go so far with me I will let you have what you want."

"All right, I will go with you."

When we started most of the crowd followed. Don Pedro commenced talking in a very earnest manner, telling me that they had just received a letter from the Pope warning all Catholics against false prophets, etc., and that they were all fully prepared beforehand to reject our heresies. He kept up his talk until we arrived at his house.

215

He now got a pamphlet and commenced reading. This was the printed circular of the Pope. I listened patiently until my opponent finished. The house, a large one, was crowded, nearly a hundred persons present. I now asked permission to answer the Pope's letter and explain our side.

Don Pedro objected. My reply settled him. I told him I had been much in Mexico and mixed among the people a great deal and I had always found them mannerly and polite, especially to strangers and in their own house. That I was now under his roof and protection—a stranger—and appealed to him as a true Mexican gentleman to hear me. At this many of the crowd said, "Let the stranger speak."

Don Pedro now consented, but soon interrupted me. I reminded him that I had listened to him in perfect silence, and unless he did the same I should claim to be more of a gentleman than he was. This made quite a laugh, and the voice was for me to have the floor uninterruptedly.

In brief I will say that I fully satisfied myself; spoke with perfect freedom and handled the priests and Pope without gloves. When I got through Don Pedro said his whole opinion was now changed, asked for a book, saying he would read and study it whether the priests liked it or not. When we left all was friendly.

The district of country we had been passing through appeared to be the most desirable for colonizing. We made diligent enquiries about lands, titles, conflicting water interests and making notes, all of which were reported to Prest. Young on our arrival home.

As we neared the frontier settlements there was great excitement as the Apaches were out on the war path and had killed some men near Fort Bowie. They had had a fight with the soldiers and whipped them, and were now raiding the country in every direction.

Some of the officials at Galiana talked of stopping us from going any further. But we were very anxious to continue on so we told them we would be careful and not run into danger.

After leaving Casas Grandes our road was really lonesome and dangerous. It was some three days' travel to Cow Springs before we would see a ranch. However, we made the trip without accident, travelling the most dangerous parts in the night time.

One night we had our nerves sorely tried. My intention was, if we ever met the Apaches, to approach them alone, believing I could make peace with them the same as I had done before with other Indians.

While travelling along one night. Brother Ivins and my son riding ahead of the wagon, our little watch dog that had been of great service to us many times, gave notice that someone was approaching in the road.

I called to the boys to stop. I went and got on my son's horse, telling him to go back to the team. Brother Ivins and I rode on a short distance. The night was rather dark, but soon we saw a lot of what appeared to be savage-looking Indians coming. They were on foot and armed. They halted on seeing us.

I told Brother Ivins to go back to the wagon and I would go and meet them, and if they shot me, he and the others must jump into the brush and try and save their lives as best they could.

I got off from my horse and walked up to the Indians, who stood in a group, filling the road. As I approached alone they did not seem to make any move whatever. I spoke, saluting them in Spanish. They answered all right. I offered them my hand and they all shook hands with me. I asked them where they were going. They said down to their homes and asked where I was going.

I told them I was going to my home a long way off in the northern country. Thus we kept asking and answering questions till one asked why we were travelling by night. I told them that my companions were afraid of them, but that I was not for I was a friend to the Indians and did not believe they would ever kill me.

They began to laugh and asked me who I thought they were.

I asked, "Are you not Apaches?"

"No, *senor*, we are not Apaches," they answered, "but like you we are travelling in the night because we are afraid of them."

I now called to my companions who had been waiting in suspense. All my bravery and fortitude were wasted, further than to prove to myself that I was willing to stand the test.

We had a good long talk with these Indians who were of the Opitas, a people similar to the Pimas, and who live in the foothills of the Sierra Madre in Sonora.

As we neared the frontier ranches on the American side we found that the Apache war was a reality. We camped at Cow Springs. Much apprehension was felt at Burro Sienega. Here we met Mr. Connor whom we had met on the trip down. His father and brother were killed shortly after at this ranch.

We heard that soldiers were concentrating at Bowie with orders to capture and take all the Apaches to the San Carlos reservation. Apache signal fires could be seen in the mountains south of Bowie. Our route now led through the most perilous part of the country; hundreds of people having been killed along this road in past years, our feelings were to put our trust in God and go on. We arrived at San Simon where a lot of "hard cases" were camped. It was a question whether we were safer with them than alone; but they were afraid and felt better while we were with them. Next day was the "teller." If we could make Bowie all right, our chances would be better from there on as troops were *en route* to that post from Camps Verde, McDowell and Apache. Our day's travel from San Simon to Bowie was one of anxiety, but we made it in safety.

We decided to take a different route on our return from the one travelled going down. So, on leaving Bowie, instead of taking the main road back to Tucson, we decided to go by the way of Fort Grant, Camp Thomas, Camp Apache and on to the upper Little Colorado. The road from Camp Thomas to Camp Apache was reported to us as almost impassable for wagons, none having attempted the trip for some three years past. The troops moved across the mountains with pack animals. However, we concluded to try it.

From Bowie to Camp Grant there was a drive of nearly seventy-five miles without water. We made the most of the distance in the afternoon and night.

On turning out our teams just before day, they were too thirsty to eat the grass, it being somewhat dry. We only had about two gallons of water, which we had kept for drinking and cooking. On seeing the condition of our poor animals we took most of the water and wet up some bran we happened to have, giving a little to each animal. They ate it with a relish, then started for the grass, eating heartily for some time, when we hitched up and made the rest of the distance in good time.

Since this experience, when travelling through desert country I have made it a rule to carry a sack of bran. When water becomes scarce wet a feed of bran with one half gallon of water and it will do as much good on the last end of a hard drive as three times the water without bran.

Troops were being massed at Camp Grant. The orders were for all the Apaches to move to San Carlos, the greater portion being willing to do so. The Chiricahuis had not yet decided to come in. There were a number of scouts camped here. We laid over for a few days as we had a desire to learn something about these Indians and the condition of affairs before going on.

218

We managed to get acquainted with some of the leaders. They came to our camp and talked most of one night.

As I intend to devote a whole chapter to Apache history, I will then relate our conversation with these Indians, which was very interesting to all of us.

From Camp Grant to Camp Thomas we passed numbers of Indian camps. They would try to look savagely at us, but I could always get a friendly look before quitting them.

We had heard much about the Upper Gila Valley, the country settled now mostly by our people. Before arriving at the river crossing we fell in company with an intelligent Mexican who lived in Pueblo Viejo. He gave us such full and satisfactory information about the country that we concluded to make our report from it and not spend any time exploring.

While in camp on the Gila river, on our return home, we met an old-timer, who related to us some of his personal history. I was so much interested in the story that I have concluded to give it to the readers of this book.

Chapter 43

Further Hypocrisy

About noon, while we were in camp, a gentleman, apparently some forty-five years of age, came down the trail from the mountains. His outfit consisted of two fine looking mules, sleek and fat, with all his traps neatly packed. His riding rig and arms were all of the best; his blankets and clothing clean and neat. The owner himself was a large-sized, fine-looking man, and in every way presented the appearance of a gentleman. We were near the road and as from the direction he had come and the hour being noon, it was natural to suppose that he would make camp. We invited him to stop and share our shade tree with us. Politeness and hospitality can be, and often is, extended in the camp of the traveller as well as in the abode of a dweller.

As the stranger unsaddled we noticed his movements were graceful. His mules were perfectly gentle and seemed to understand their master's kindness to them. This captured me individually, for if there are more unpardonable sins allowed than are on the list, and it was my duty to furnish another, I believe I would hand in "cruelty to dumb brutes."

I have seen men who are considered both good and great by some people—themselves included—who would get angry with their animals and beat them in a cruel, senseless manner, even showing a murderous spirit. I have always believed that such persons would serve human beings the same way when in anger, only they are too cowardly to take the immediate consequences.

Our visitor accepted our invitation to dinner. We soon found that he was an "old-timer," having been in California and the west for many years. We insisted on his resting over Sunday with us and, finally, he consented.

Our conversation led on from one thing to another until our new acquaintance became quite communicative. His conversation was very interesting, as he had travelled a great deal in the west: He had visited Salt Lake City and knew many places and people that were familiar to us. Finally, he gave us his name and related the following story, as near as I can remember it:

He was a native of one of the Middle States. Was left an orphan with a small fortune, some thirty thousand dollars. His disposition was to make the best use possible of his time and money. After finishing at the common schools he attended an eastern college, studying medicine, etc.

While at college he was allowed a stipulated amount for pocket money. This was always used prudently, but not stingily, allowing himself all the pleasures he desired, such as would be proper in good society; but never spending a cent in vices of any kind.

At the same college there were a great many young men, sons of well-known capitalists. Many of these wealthy young men did not have occasion, seemingly, to spend any more money than did our friend; but many of them were addicted to habits that soon emptied their purses, and they would have to borrow, sometimes coming to the "Doctor" (as we will now call him).

Now, inasmuch as these rich young fellows were often "broke," whilst the Doctor always had money and to loan, and at the same time never showed any penuriousness, it became rumoured that he was immensely wealthy. This he knew nothing about, as he was rather retiring in his disposition and did not take part in the gossips of the day.

As time went on he found himself becoming very popular and sought after, being invited to parties, balls, receptions, etc. He thought nothing strange of this, as he met others whom he knew to be his inferiors, although much wealthier. Money influence never entered his mind, as he felt content with his little fortune, believing that, with a good profession and his start, he would be independent. His mind was at ease. He neither looked for a money-match or supposed that he was a "catch" for anyone.

Like all other places, this, where the Doctor was, had its *belle*—the handsomest, sweetest-dispositioned, most unselfish and kind-hearted divinity upon earth. All the young bloods were in love with her. This was before people got "mashed." Of course, she treated them all so nicely that each fool thought he was the favoured one. All divinities do this, I am told.

The Doctor, according to his own words, really fell in love with this she-angel. She returned his affection with compound interest—in her eye. The courtship was all that two fond hearts could wish, as the doctor's purse was, as before described, always equal to the occasion. All envied his success, yet respected his character and perseverance.

Everything looked bright. So the Doctor applied himself to his studies with double vigour, looking forward to the happy day when, with his diploma and his beautiful, intelligent, loving wife, he could go to his home and old friends and settle down to business, with as bright a future as ever man hoped for.

After graduating, the wedding soon followed. Everything went off in proper shape, no lack of means being in the way. The Doctor never asked or carded what the bride's fortune was; her heart and love were all the dowry he wanted. Having given his fullest and purest love, he fully believed that hers was as fully returned.

I do not recollect just where this occurred; but this much I do remember, that, after the wedding, the Doctor took his bride aboard a boat and started for home, supposing she understood his intentions, as he had talked of nothing else but their future home and happiness.

On arriving at a point where they took a conveyance, in a different direction to what the lady expected, she asked:

"Where are you going?"

The Doctor replied, "This is our way to—"

"Why, are you not going to Europe on a wedding tour?"

"Well, no; I had not thought of that. We are going home. We cannot well afford a trip across the ocean; besides, I am anxious to get home and attend to business."

This occurred in the presence of many persons.

The divinity(?) flew into a terrible rage, asked him who he was that business called him home, and that he could not afford a wedding tour.

In relating this the Doctor seemed to go through the whole scene in his feelings, the tears often showing in his eyes. He did not pretend to relate all that had been said.

Imagination can only picture his feelings when he learned that there was no love, that all was mercenary on her part, and as he never had in any way meant deception, it was a cruel blow. But like a true man he decided at once and took her back home; offered her a divorce which she refused. He gave her most of his fortune and started for California, probably as sad a man as ever crossed the plains.

While in California he was prospered and soon accumulated quite a fortune. After a time his wife seemed to repent of her cruelty to him. Wrote him kind and loving letters, asking forgiveness and excused herself for her unnatural conduct, by saying it was on account of her ill-health. The Doctor, with kind-hearted simplicity finally believed her and returned.

She had spent the most that had been given her. The Doctor now commenced anew, with all his former hopes and aspirations rebuilt as much as possible. All went well for awhile.

Two children were born and the Doctor really felt happy. But all was sham and hypocrisy with his wife. She was now acting so as to get hold of his money and property. At length another scene was enacted. The Doctor was told all that was wanted of him was his money. A divorce was again offered and urged. The lady refused, but declared it her intention to hunt him wherever he went, till the day of his death, and get all she could out of him, using the children as a means of working upon his honour and her rights as wife, to demand all she possibly could.

The Doctor again left for the west, leaving all his property. For many years his whole aim had been to keep track of the condition of his children, and send money for their education to a trusted agent; and keep himself hidden from the knowledge of his wife.

In doing this he had become a wanderer upon the earth, but he was still a gentleman.

I learned more about this man afterwards—of his private business. He was quite a successful prospector. But few if any ever heard this story from his lips, except ourselves. And as it was not given me for publication, I have given no names.

Like this man there are thousands in the far west who carry, in their bosoms, facts that would be far more interesting than the average fictitious romance.

CHAPTER 44

Arrival Home

We found the road from the Gila to Camp Apache to be most of the way about the roughest any of us had ever seen. It was all we could possibly do to get over some of the rough places, but finally made the trip without break or accident.

The country in and around Camp Apache is quite picturesque. Grass, timber, small streams and springs were quite plentiful from here to Cooley's ranch, and the country is pleasant to travel through.

At Cooley's we were hospitably entertained and given much useful information. From him we learned the condition of the new settlements being made on the Little Colorado, under the leadership of Lot Smith and Brothers Allen, Lake and Ballinger. We now felt somewhat satisfied with our trip, realising that we had been the most successful prospectors into the land of Arizona, our reports having been received and acted upon.

The greater portion of the settlements in Arizona, New Mexico and Old Mexico are on lands explored by our party on this trip. From Cooley's ranch we followed down the country to Stinson's farm, now Snowflake.

Mr. Stinson had also visited the Mormon camps and spoke highly of their labours. It was now June. As we neared the settlements we felt a feeling of joy at the thought of meeting friends from home.

On arriving at Allen's camp we met Prest. Wells, Apostles E. Snow and B. Young with several others, just from the settlements of Utah. Here we learned of the death of Bishop Roundy by drowning. I was glad to meet the brethren. Brothers Stewart, Pratt and Ivins had expressed a desire to return home. I had intended to go with my son Wiley to where we supposed Brothers Smith and Tenney were still labouring, but here learned that they had gone home.

Prest. Wells advised me to go home. I told him I hated to return just then, saying that I did not feel as though I had filled my mission. He addressed me a little sharply, speaking as though he did not believe me and telling me I had better go in with his company. Whether Brother Wells believed me or not I was willing to stay if left to follow my own feelings, but I did as he advised.

On the way I noticed a disposition to treat me rather coolly, many times being snubbed when offering some information about our trip. I could not understand this very well at the time.

On arriving at Lot Smith's camp I met my daughter, Mary, and her husband, J. Jordan. They had been called to assist in settling this country. My son, Wiley, remained a short time with them, then came on to Fairview, our home. The trip in from the Little Colorado was not very pleasant to me; the mode of travel was so different from what I had been accustomed to that I was continually out of humour. My mode of travelling was and still is to watch and take care of my stock, and give it all the advantages possible. I have always been able to go over country successfully with a common outfit, while I have heard of others, much better fitted up, failing.

We had made a trip of near four thousand miles and were now returning with the same animals we started with, some of them in better condition than when we left. Instead of getting credit for this, I learned, afterwards, that reports had been circulated to the effect that I was tyrannical and unjust, and these statements, doubtless, had their influence upon my friends. Nothing was said to me on the road about these reports, but I could see that something was "out of joint" from the treatment I received, which could not be particularly defined, but just such as would indicate indifference to me. Finally, it became so disagreeable that I concluded to travel alone; so I came on the last two days without a bite to eat, rather than be subject to the annoyances in the company with which I was then travelling. I got in thirty-six hours ahead of the rest.

The last day, crossing the Buckskin Mountain, I got quite hungry and thirsty. I had about a quart of corn that I intended to eat, but saved and fed it to my faithful little horse, "Tex," that had carried his rider, my son Wiley, already some three thousand five hundred miles.

"Tex" was in good condition and I had taken him to ride in from Little Colorado home. I would not do justice unless I mentioned this horse for he was the most reliable animal I ever knew. I gave him all the corn. I had a three pint canteen of water, when I was taking a drink

"Tex" came up and licked the canteen and looked at me as though he wanted a taste. I set my hat on the ground, sinking the crown so as to form a dish then poured a little water in, then the horse would sup it up. I gave him the last drop although I was then dry and had a big half day's ride yet to make before getting to Johnston's settlement.

After baiting I saddled up, arriving at Navajo Wells about one hour by sun. There was some squaws watering their horses. I got them to give "Tex" a little water, but it was too filthy for me to drink. There I again baited half an hour then got on my horse telling him how hungry and thirsty I was and that I had given him all the advantage and now it was but fair for him to take me in twelve miles in a hurry. This he did in fine style scarcely breaking the gallop all the way.

I met President Young at Kanab. He was glad to see me and hear the report from Mexico. Brother Young was a true friend to me and understood my disposition. He never allowed anyone to speak against me; he knew my faults, also some of my virtues. One that he always, appreciated was my stubbornness; when I started on a trip, I had always stuck to it. I said nothing to him about my annoyances.

Brother Brigham expressed himself well satisfied with the results of our trip; said it was an opening for a greater work. I reported all the brethren good and faithful, doing honour to those we represented. I never knew until coming to Salt Lake that there was any dissatisfaction. I knew we had differed in our opinions sometimes about standing guard, but as I always took my turn and sometimes more, I never dreamed of anyone holding ill-feelings for being required to stand guard.

I think that these reports, and what grew out of them, have affected that mission and do to this day. Time will bring all things right. Many strange things are permitted that we cannot see any use in at the time, that afterwards turn to be a blessing.

CHAPTER 45

Our Start from St. George

I arrived home about the 1st of July, 1876, found my family all well; I settled down to work at once making saddle-trees, as they were in good demand, and my family needed the help they would bring.

I had been at home about one month when I received a note from President Young requesting me to come to the city as he wished to talk to me about the Mexican missions.

On meeting President Young in the city he said, "I would like to have you pick a few families and take charge of them and go into the far south and start a settlement. Would you like to do it?" I answered, "Yes, I will go."

"Whom would you like to go with you? I want the settling to stick, and not fail."

I replied, "Give me men with large families and small means, so that when we get there they will be too poor to come back, and we will have to stay."

He laughed and said it was a good idea.

While in Salt Lake receiving instructions from President Young and preparing to go on the colonising mission, I heard for the first time of the hard stories told against me.

There is one thing I would like to say that I think should be considered by all Latter-day Saints, and that is, few men, possibly none, ever made an overland trip of four thousand miles over deserts and through the most dangerous country on the continent and got through without some little "family jars."

There had been attempts made to explore the southern country that had practically failed. President Young had expressed confidence in my ability to make the trip and so I felt determined to do my best.

I knew that our little mules and ponies were our dependence, for if we had lost them we might have perished, or at least suffered great hardships as well as losing time. And more still I realised the success or failure of our trip would have a great effect upon others who might follow after. All this made me extremely careful.

One fault I have always had, and with all my experience in life it still hangs to me, that is, anything that is clear to my understanding to be right I naturally think others ought to see the same. It was so on this trip. I naturally thought every man understood as well as I did the importance of taking care of our outfit.

I was so much discouraged at the effects of these reports that I felt as though I never wanted to take charge of another mission of any kind. I wrote a note to President Young, asking him to appoint someone else to take charge and I would go along as guide and interpreter.

President Young paid no attention to my suggestion. I went to Brother Woodruff and asked him to speak to Brother Brigham on the subject; instead of doing which he told me I was wrong to notice these reports, and that all men who were called to do a good work met opposition.

I told him that I really believed it would be a mistake to put me in charge of the colony; that I had been used to doing hard service so much that I had gotten in the habit of being arbitrary, and I was afraid I would not have patience to act as a presiding Elder should.

Brother Woodruff said he believed I was honest and sincere, and he would speak to Brother Brigham on the subject.

On visiting Brother Young, he said he wanted me to go ahead; that an angel could not please everybody. And added: "You know how to travel, how to take care of teams. You are better acquainted with the roads, the country, the natives and their language, and are better prepared to take charge of a company than anyone I know of. Go ahead and do the best you can. When you get things started we can send some 'good' man to take your place, and you can go on and open up more new country. This is your mission."

With this understanding I went to work with a will to get ready for the trip. I still felt quite sore about the stories circulated, for they were not just. But one thing I had to acknowledge that made me a little careful what I said to Brother Brigham. He had warned me against one of the company who had volunteered to go. He advised me not to take him, saying that he would try to take the mission away from me and would make me trouble. This I should have listened to; but the man seemed so earnest and desirous to go that I pled for him, and Brother Young finally consented. I was served just right. Brother Brigham spoke truly. Anyone doubting it can investigate for themselves; I have said all I wish to about the matter.

Brother Brigham said he wanted volunteers; that no one would be called unless he was perfectly willing, otherwise rather desired them not to go.

The following names, with their families, were soon enrolled for the mission: P. C. Merrills, Dudley J. Merrills, Thos. Merrills, Adelbert Merrills, Henry C. Rogers, George Steel, Thomas Biggs, Ross R. Rogers, Joseph McRae and Isaac Turley. Notice was given that we would meet at St. George about Christmas and there organise, President Young intending to winter there. I had to work hard and make many shifts and trades to get an outfit sufficient to move my family in comfort.

I was a little late in starting on the road. P. C. Merrills and his family overtook us at Sevier Bridge. We travelled together to St. George. On arriving there we found all the company in camp in a schoolhouse yard, with the privilege of using the house when needed in case of storm. It was now about the first of January and the weather was quite disagreeable. Here a Brother Williams joined us.

On looking over the outfit I soon found that many of the wagons were overloaded and that much of the loading being taken could be dispensed with. I advised the selling off of such as old stoves, sewing machines and many other heavy articles; but no one seemed to think but what they could pull their load.

My loading consisted of bedding, clothing, provisions, horse feed and such articles as were absolutely necessary. We had not ten pounds of anything that could be dispensed with. I considered it my duty to set the example, knowing that we had a hard trip before us and could not afford to haul anything but the actual necessities with the outfit on hand. I spoke to Brother Brigham about the situation.

He said, "Get your company in the best shape you can and as soon as possible move out. There is a nice little settlement, Santa Clara, on your road. There is a beautiful piece of sandy road from here to there, just such as will help you get the brethren to see the importance of lightening up. When you get there you can set up an auction store. The people are pretty well off and will be able to buy what you have to sell."

When all was ready we started out, and, as President Young said, when we got into the Santa Clara settlement many of the company were not only willing but anxious to lighten up.

The people of Santa Clara traded readily for the stuff, paying dried fruit, grain and some money. Sometimes the loading traded for was as heavy as that traded off. Brother Isaac Turley, who had travelled a portion of the road and who was an experienced traveller, was elected wagon-master. He advised the people not to be afraid to trade for corn, saying that he was willing to roll at a wheel to help get a sack of corn over a hard place, but did not like to strain his back to move an old stove along that was not worth hauling.

At this place we bade goodbye to President Young, who drove out to see us. He gave us his blessing and a few words of counsel. This was the last time I ever saw Brother Brigham—to me the best and greatest man I have ever known.

Our instructions were to go into the southern country and settle where we felt impressed to stop. The intention was to go on to Mexico eventually.

CHAPTER 46

My Associations with the Red Men

We passed down the Virgin River, crossed the Colorado at Stone's Ferry, then through Mineral Park, Walapai Valley, Cottonwood, Anvil Rock, Oaks and Willows and Walnut Creek, leaving Prescott to the left. We continued on the most direct route into Salt River Valley.

The trip was made without losing an animal or suffering in any way worth mentioning; in fact, to this day many of the company speak of the trip as one of pleasure rather than suffering. Everything was under strict discipline. No one can travel safely through a wild, dangerous country and be neglectful, no matter what those may say who are too lazy to stand guard without grumbling.

One incident of the trip I will relate that might be profitable in putting others on their guard.

One day, while travelling through a hilly, broken country, my son Wiley and Chas. Rogers, both young lads, took their guns for a hunt. It was cloudy; I warned them not to go far from the road. This they intended to obey, but soon after they left the train the road turned off to the right and changed the direction. It soon commenced to storm very hard, and we went into camp. We were now uneasy about the boys. The storm was the first of the season—cold and wet, and the boys were without their coats. I tried to keep from showing anxiety for their mothers' sake; but I felt about as much concerned as I ever did, for I knew there was great danger. About night I went on to a high hill, piled up several cords of dried cedars and set fire to them. About 9 o'clock we heard a loud hello. We knew they were coming. They were almost dead with fatigue.

After finding they were lost they had travelled round and round to keep from freezing to death. Their strength had almost failed when they saw the light. They had no matches, but were trying to strike fire

231

with their guns, when the light was visible from where they were. There was quite a mountain ridge between them and the fire. It was in a different direction from where they expected; it had barely shown a dim light in the mountain top.

Wiley said, "That's pa!" and started for the fire. This saved them.

On arriving at Salt River it became plain to see that we were not in a condition to go further, and, as everything seemed inviting to us to stop here, we took a vote on the question of continuing. All voted to locate on Salt River, except one man.

We made camp where Mr. Miller had directed me to the ditch site. Next morning we commenced work on the head of the ditch. Ross R. Rogers began surveying the ditch with a straight-edge and spirit-level.

We had been to work but a few hours, when a party came and claimed that we were on a ditch site already staked and owned. Mr. Miller had posted me on this.

The survey had been made and stakes set, but sufficient work had not been done to hold the right of way. So I told the gentleman in charge of the party that we would not interfere with his survey; that we had noticed his stakes and would not disturb them. He finally offered to sell us the right of way.

I told him we were not prepared to buy, but would try and be careful not to interfere with his rights. The party left and we heard no more from them.

We arranged affairs to the best advantage possible, according to the wisdom we had, and went to work on what was registered and is known as the Utah ditch.

On reporting to President Young, the following letter was received:

Salt Lake City, U. T.
Elder D, W, Jones, Camp Utah, Arizona,
Dear Brother:—On my return from Ogden, last evening, I found your note awaiting me. The brethren who have been called to go to Arizona reside in various parts of this territory. They will start as they get ready and come dropping in upon you from time to time, without any special instructions from the Presidency of the Church, only to commence their labours at as early a date as they reasonably can. For this reason we cannot say anything about making arrangements beforehand for

their flour; but they will have to do as we have done before—
get it as best they may after their arrival.

We should be pleased to learn from you how far you consider
it from your camp to the settlements on the Little Colorado
River, and which road you deem the best thereto. We should
also like to know what your intentions are with regard to settling the region for which you originally started. We do not
deem it prudent for you to break up your present location, but
possibly next fall you will find it consistent to continue your
journey with a portion of those who are now with you, while
others will come and occupy the places vacated by you.

We do not, however, wish you to get the idea from the above
remarks that we desire to hurry you away from where you now
are, or to force a settlement in the district to which you refer,
until it is safe to do so and free from the dangers of Indian difficulties; but we regard it as one of the spots where the Saints
will, sooner or later, gather to build up Zion, and we feel the
sooner the better.

Last evening I returned from Cache Valley, where I had been
resting a few days. Tomorrow myself and party start for Juab
and Sanpete counties to organise a Stake of Zion there, while
Brothers Lorenzo Snow and Franklin D. Richards will go to
Morgan and Summit counties and organise there.

We have thus to divide or we should not get through with the
organisation of the Stakes in time to commence the quarterly
conferences in those that were first organised.

We have no special counsel to give you or your company at
present, only to live so as to retain within you the Spirit of the
Lord, that it may be to you a present helper in every time of
need, and a guide that can be called upon on all occasions. Be
prudent in all the measures you enter into; economical with
your time and supplies; be just one towards another, and kind
and friendly with all men; do your utmost by precept and example to win the hearts of the Lamanites, and ever use the influence you acquire over them for good, for their salvation and
education in the arts of peace and industry. In this course the
blessing of the Lord will be with you, and you shall be established in peace, and prosperity shall attend your efforts to build
up God's kingdom. That this may be so is the prayer of

Your brother in the Gospel,   Brigham Young.

We commenced on the ditch March 7th, 1877. All hands worked with a will. Part of the company moved down on to lands located for settlements. Most of the able-bodied men formed a working camp near the head of the ditch, where a deep cut had to be made.

We hired considerable help when we could procure it for such pay as we could command, as scrub ponies, "Hayden scrip," etc. Among those employed were a number of Indians, Pimas, Maricopas, Papagoes, Yumas. Yaquis and one or two Apaches Mojaves. The most of them were good workers.

Some of these Indians expressed a desire to come and settle with us; this was the most interesting part of the mission to me and I naturally supposed that all the company felt the same spirit, but I soon found my mistake, for on making this desire of the Indians known to the company many objected, some saying that they did not want their families brought into association with these dirty Indians. So little interest was manifested by the company that I made the mistake of jumping at the conclusion that I would have to go ahead whether I was backed up or not; I learned afterwards that if I had been more patient and faithful that I would have had more help, but at the time I acted according to the best light I had and determined to stick to the Indians.

This spirit manifested to the company showing a preference to the natives, naturally created a prejudice against me. Soon dissatisfaction commenced to show. The result was that most of the company left and went onto the San Pedro in southern Arizona, led by P. C. Merrill. After this move, there being but four families left, and one of these soon leaving, our little colony was quite weak.

The three families remaining with me professed to sustain my management for a little season. Then they turned more bitter against me than those who went away; no doubt but they felt justified in their own feelings, and, as I am writing my own history and not theirs, I will allow them the same privilege.

It was not long until it became manifest that I would have to either give up the Indians or lose my standing with the white brethren. I chose the natives, and will now give as truthful a history of my labours among them as my memory will serve.

In about six weeks from the time we commenced we had sufficient water out to plant some garden stuff and a few acres of corn. When this was done Brother Turley took a number of teams and went to freighting for Mr. Hayden to pay the debt we had now made—

some fifteen hundred dollars. This debt could soon have been paid if all hands had stayed together, but as the most left, the debt finally fell upon me to finish paying up.

This tied me up on Salt River for some time.

CHAPTER 47

The U. S. Agent Forbids My Interfering with the Indians

As often as opportunity offered I talked to the Indians. As yet I had not found an interpreter that suited me; several whom I had met the year before had not come to our camp yet, their homes being some distance away. The interpreter I used, Geo. Roberts, was something of an adventurer, as the sequel will show.

I was at work one day in a field, planting, after we had been settled for some six weeks, when my interpreter came to me and said there were several of the leading men of the Salt River Pimas who wished me to come down to my camp, where they were, and baptise them.

I told him I did not think the Indians understood enough to be baptised; that I had not had time to teach them sufficiently. He said I had talked a great deal to him; that he understood and believed all I said, and fully explained all my words to these *capitancillos* (little captains), who also believed and wished baptism.

I did not feel satisfied. I have always been slow to baptise natives; my policy has been to teach them first, so that they would fully realise what they were doing. I have endeavoured more to get them out of their degradation and savagery.

When I met these Indians I asked them (using the interpreter) what they desired. They said they wished to be baptised and be Mormons. I told the interpreter to say to them that I did not want them to be baptised until they fully understood what baptism was for. I continued talking, explaining what the requirements were, etc.

The interpreter insisted, after talking quite a while with the chiefs, that they fully understood me and were ready. I then told him to say to them: "Go back to your camp; talk with your head chief and your people, and explain these things. Take time to reconsider and do not be in a hurry to get baptised."

A few days after this my interpreter again came to me and said many hundred Indians had come to my camp (I was again at work away from home), all ready and wanting to be baptised.

I was now sorely puzzled, for there was nothing in reason to convince me that these ignorant natives were really subject to such sudden conversion. Still, I knew that our people looked forward to a time when a nation will be born in a day, but I did not believe that time had come; yet it looked a little that way, so I went down.

On arriving at camp there were Indians in every place and direction; there were between three and four hundred, all looking pleasant and smiling. The chiefs were grouped, sitting quietly and sedately.

I commenced to talk to and question them, repeating what I had formerly said and added more, and in every way endeavoured to fasten upon their minds the responsibility of being baptised. I really desired to deter them, if possible, for I had no faith in the reality of the situation. But my interpreter, who talked at length to them, professing to explain all my words, insisted that they fully understood and wanted to be baptised—the whole tribe included.

Several Elders were present, and I asked, "What shall I do? I have no faith in this. There is something wrong."

All said I had done my duty; if they insisted, all we could do was to baptise them, as we had no right to refuse.

I told the Indians all right—we would go to the river. At this all hands started pell-mell, the young ones laughing and playing, the older ones more sedate.

As I started to the river I observed a strange Indian looking intently at me. He was dressed differently from the rest. I asked him if he understood Spanish.

He answered, "Yes, perfectly."

"Have you heard and understood the talk with the Pimas?"

"Yes, sir; and the Indians are deceived. Your interpreter is either dishonest or does not understand you; I hardly know which, but I think it is a little of both. He talks considerable Spanish, but he has not fully understood you. I fully understand and want to help you."

"Will you go with me now?—and I will again talk to them."

"Yes."

On the way to the river my new friend informed me that the main inducement offered for baptism by my interpreter was, that to

237

all who would be baptised I would give a new shirt; and to the men of families who had no land I would give lands. So it was no wonder at the number of converts.

When we got to the river bank I called the principal men together and taught them for a long time, fully explaining the true situation and requirements. The old chief, Chiacum, said he thought I must have lots of shirts and had looked around wondering where all my land was. My interpreter looked rather "sheepish."

When all was explained the old chief said he did not fully understand all I had said, but one thing he understood and was willing to try—that baptism required one to be a better man. Said he, "I am willing to be baptised and listen to your talk, for I believe it is good. I will seek to be a better man and try to learn more about God. Now here are three of us who are willing to do this; if this will do you can baptise us, we do not want any shirts; we will then try to learn and teach your words to our people, and when they are ready we will tell you and you can baptise them.

I now felt satisfied and baptised the old chief and the ones he named, feeling a real joy for I knew they were honest. This deception of my first interpreter had its effect that reaches far into the future. Believing on the start that he would be useful to me, I had given him a piece of land near by camp, where he had been doing a little work.

I now felt so disappointed in him that I wished to get rid of him. He said if he got his pay for the land he would leave. This he received in full, and I thought I would hear no more of him. In this, too, I was disappointed.

Often during the spring and summer natives visited our camp enquiring about our people and principles. I heard that the "shirt and land" story had reached quite a distance.

One party of Maricopas, fourteen in number, headed by an old chief, Malia, came to see us. They were very poor and destitute, but seemed more intelligent than the average. I was very busy, being obliged to go away from camp. The old chief said they were willing to help me, and insisted that I would show them some work to do, saying they would remain and work until I had time to talk to them. This old fellow talked good Spanish.

I showed them a piece of land that we desired to plant in corn. They went to work and cleared the brush from it. I afterwards gave this same land to these Indians.

When Brother Merrills left, our ditch was not nearly finished. In fact it was simply commenced, and we who were left were almost destitute and heavily in debt.

Some of the same Indians we had employed offered to take hold and help us finish up the ditch if we would let them have some land lying along the river bottom. The land was sandy and broken with hills and hollows, and there was considerable brush on it. It was a kind of land the whites did not desire but the very kind the Indians preferred. I agreed to let them have this privilege.

The first who came were the same party under Malia (Maricopas), who worked clearing off land. I gave them the eastern portion of the land. Francisco Chico Ochoa, a Pima, came well recommended as a good, honest man. He agreed to keep me posted in regard to the character of those applying for lands. The Pimas were to have the western portion of the lands.

The agreement was that no Indians would be allowed to remain on these lands except those who would observe good order, live honest, sober, etc., and work for their own living, and in no way molest the settlers.

I talked with Mr. Hayden and some others about my plans. They said the Indians were generally well-disposed, and that years before the whites had invited quite a colony of Pimas to leave the Gila and come and settle on Salt River, as a kind of outpost or guard against the Apaches. This had been a success. "But," said Mr. Hayden, "as the country builds up and these Indians are not needed, you will doubtless see some of these same men who invited them here join in to drive them away. You, no doubt, will have trouble with your Indians in time."

I was deeply interested in these natives, and felt determined to do all I could for them; in fact, it was Indian or nothing if we finished our ditch in time to do anything the following season. So I divided off the land between the Pimas and Maricopas, leaving the chiefs to divide the lands among their people.

They soon went to work enlarging the ditch. These natives were of the poorer class, having been living in settlements where the water had been shut off from them. They had been living for years in poverty and degradation. Their association with white men had only degraded them the more, and they were dwindling away and numbering less and less every year; so when they had the privilege of taking hold with us they were truly grateful.

When they commenced to move, some thirty odd miles, my son

Wiley took his team and hauled their stuff for them. The squaws appreciated this, as most everything would have been carried on their heads; many a time they would pack from seventy-five to a hundred pounds. Some may ask, "If these Indians were so destitute, what was there to move?" I will see if I can think what there was. I remember well there was an eight-mule load for the Maricopas.

Without giving the number and pounds, I will name some of the principal articles. There were earthen water jars and cooking utensils; baskets and more baskets; dogs—too poor to make it afoot; Mosquite beans; old rawhides, metats, primitive hand-mills; a few old shovels, hoes, axes, wooden plows, etc. These were about the average outfit of an Indian household. They were about destitute of provisions. I went and made arrangements with Mr. Hayden for their bread stuff.

The ditch was enlarged, during the fall and winter, so that there were several hundred acres of grain sowed by ourselves and Indians. I helped many of the Indians get their seed grain, and some of them borrowed from their more prosperous friends; they also got cattle to plow their fields from the Indians on the Gila.

As these people began to prosper, others came and wished to join in and continue to enlarge the ditch, and clear off and level down the broken lands. Sometimes the stock, belonging to the Indians living on their own lands on the opposite side of the river from our camp, would encroach on our fields. This was extremely annoying and many of the whites were sorely tried.

I was continually working to get a right understanding established.

The Indians claimed that no one had a right to occupy more country than they could fence or guard, and said that the people owning the fields were the ones to take care of them and watch the cattle.

Some of the settlers accepted the situation, and when the Indian stock would get onto their grain fields they would shoot them down. This rather got away with the Indians yet they would not get mad but would take the carcasses for food.

Owing to this trouble many of the white settlers became opposed to the Indians remaining longer on Salt River, so petitions were circulated and signed asking the government to remove them.

The agent visited me one day while I was working on the ditch, with some forty Indians helping. He accosted me in a very uncivil tone and manner and wanted to know what I was doing with his Indians. I said I was not aware that he owned these people. He said he was the U. S. agent from Sacaton; that he had heard that I was teaching these Indians Mormonism, and inducing them to leave the agency, and that he wanted the business stopped.

I told him it was none of his business what I was doing with the Indians; asked him if he knew what Mormonism was. He said he did not know anything about it.

"Then you had better wait until you do before commanding me to quit teaching it. I teach them to quit stealing, gambling, getting drunk and practicing other and worse vices; and to be cleanly and industrious; and advised them to earn their own living; and get ready to educate their young people; to quit killing witches; burning their dead, etc. How does that suit you?"

"O that is all right."

"Well, sir, that is a part of Mormonism."

He seemed a little "stumped," then said, "Well, if I hear of any trouble, I shall forbid you employing these Indians."

I here showed him a letter that I had received from him when we first came in, asking me to give employment to a party of Indians, saying that they were good men and willing to work, but had no means of support, and that anything I could do for them would be appreciated.

I called his attention to what I had done for this people, according to his request, and asked him if he would like a copy of the letter sent to Washington. I never heard any more complaint from the agent.

The Indians that I had taken in to help on the ditch had but little stock and had agreed to take care of it, which they generally did. But visitors would come to see them and would sometimes be careless.

But the greatest trouble we had was with some five hundred Pimas who were settled about five miles from us, that we had no particular control over, they having settled there before our arrival.

I, in common with others, was much annoyed by their cattle, but desiring peace I studied how to outgeneral these cattle. I had also studied very hard to get an insight into the Indian character and ways, and was on the watch for an opportunity.

The old chief whom I had baptised had some twenty head of work cattle belonging to his family and particular friends. They had come onto my fields several times. The old man always said it was his boy's fault, and seemed to regret it, sometimes paying a few sacks of wheat for damages. I told him that paying damages was a bad thing. It was loss to him and no gain to me, that I wanted the cattle kept off.

Finally an idea struck me. The cattle had damaged my crops a number of times. One day when I found them in my field I sent them to the chief with word that if they got on my field three times more that they would be mine, and that I would put my brand on them.

Soon the old man came over to see me, bringing a good interpreter. Said he:

"I do not understand what you say about branding my cattle."

Here I took a memorandum book from my pocket and commenced figuring. I explained to him that the cattle had been on my field and damaged me to an amount almost as much as the cattle were worth, and that three times more damaging would pay for the cattle when I would have a right to put my brand on them, having paid their full value. I talked pleasantly and kindly, admitting that he was a good man and wanted to do right, but his boys were bad and careless. I said I would loan them the cattle for a while as I did not need them, but would let him know when I wanted them.

The old man was puzzled, he did not know what to say or do. At length, after sitting and studying a while, he said: "Suppose the cattle never get onto your land again; how will it be then?"

I then showed him my book and explained to him that some accounts were in pencil and some in pen and ink; that his was still in pencil and if left that way would wear out after a time, but sometimes it lasted two or three years, and that if he would keep his cattle away for a long time I would not write with ink and maybe the pencil marks would all wear out. He seemed pleased at this, saying that the cattle should not get back any more, and the account would be sure to wear out before they came back.

I now gave the old man a piece of ground on our side near the crossing of the river. He said he would live there and watch the cattle himself and not let them cross. This was the land I had formerly given to my first interpreter who had deceived me so. This same fellow came afterwards and claimed the land. He was a Maricopa. This was on the end of the land I had given to the Pimas. I explained this to him. Although I considered there was nothing due to the man, I offered him land up among his own people. This he declined, but claimed the first piece.

I told him I had paid him for the land. He said I had not paid him for the land but for the work done on it; that the land was his. I finally told him to leave and bother me no more; that he was dishonest and I did not want to see him till he was a better man.

CHAPTER 48

My Arrest

More white people were coming into the valley all the time to settle, and a deep prejudice against the Indians was soon developed. I was accused of being in collusion with them in running off the settlers' stock so as to get a reward for returning it.

This charge was presented to the agent at the Gila Agency and from him it was sent to the military commander at Camp McDowell.

There had been many accusations against the Indians and myself before this, but nothing in a formal way. This time notice had to be taken, so Capt. Summerhays with a posse of soldiers came to my ranch. I had often been to the camp and had talked to the officers about my affairs with the Indians. There was, from the first, a disposition of honour manifested by the military toward my labours.

The posse arrived about sundown. The captain came in, opened some papers and said his orders were to arrest me for being in with the Indians in stealing stock, and asked if I could prove myself clear.

I told him I did not intend to try to prove my innocence, but would help him to prove my guilt if possible, for if guilty I wanted to find it out and quit it.

This rather pleased the captain who laughingly said: "Well you are a prisoner, but I will trust you not to run away."

Next morning we went out to see what evidence could be found. We first visited the Indians and heard their story. They said that the whites who were coming into the country were careless about their stock and it often strayed off a long ways. Some of the owners had offered to pay them for hunting it up. When they brought the stock some paid them, while others who were bad men would abuse them and tell them they had driven the stock away on purpose to receive a reward for finding it. They said Captain Jones always told them to be honest with everybody and had forbidden any Indians to come to his place unless they would do right.

The Indians were very earnest in their talk, saying they had been friends to the people that had come in, and that it was bad to be accused so unjustly, and said they would not hunt any more stock.

The captain told them that would be wrong as the people were poor and did not know the range.

One Indian, Valensuela, spoke up and said: "Well, I will teach these people better. I will go and get their stock and give it to them, and I won't take a cent if they offer it to me."

The spirit and manner of the Indians convinced the captain that they had been wrongfully accused. From the Indian camp we went to where the greater portion of my accusers were at work on a ditch.

The captain called the attention of the crowd and made known his business by saying, "Mr. Jones has been accused of causing the Indians to run off your stock. Do any of you know anything about the charge?"

No one answered against me. Some said they did not think I had done anything of the kind. We were now some three miles from my ranch. The captain drove back to the road and offered to take me home, saying he had got through.

I asked him what he was going to do with his prisoner. He offered to give me a letter to publish clearing me from all the charges. I told him I had become so used to such things that I cared but little about them. He replied that it was a good thing for a man in my situation not to be too "thin skinned."

Through this affair I got on record at the Post as reliable, and ever afterwards my word was taken in preference to any reports against me.

I was kept tolerably busy watching and defending the rights of the Indians; also in trying to correct evils existing among the natives. One thing that taxed all my ability was to break up witchcraft, their main superstition.

Both Maricopas and Pimas fully believed that all sickness and calamities of any kind were caused by witches. Their witch doctors claim the power to divine who the witches are. When this is done all hands turn out with clubs and stones and kill the poor wretch pointed out. Whenever there is much sickness among them someone has to die as a witch. This I had endeavoured to check by teaching them better, but I soon learned that my teaching had not reached the desire, as witches were killed among those settling with us of the Maricopas.

I went to their camp and told old Malia, who was quite intelligent in many respects, that if such an act occurred again that I would deliver them to the law to be dealt with as murderers. At the same time explaining to his people the general laws of health, showing them that the violation of natural laws produced sickness.

Some time after this a Maricopa woman came and told my wife that the Maricopas had decided to kill me; that the witches were killing their children and that I would not allow them to kill the witches. So the only way to protect the lives of their children would be to kill me, as I was a friend of the witches.

When I came home my wife told me of this threat. She seemed a little concerned for my welfare, but her faith was always with mine; so we decided that it would be best for me to go at once and put a stop to this feeling.

I got on my horse and went alone some three miles to their camp. Most of the Indians were gathered together. As I approached none spoke; all were sullen. This confirmed to me the truth of the squaw's report, as the Indians generally met me in a friendly manner.

I went directly to the subject; told them what I had heard, saying to them that I had no fears of their killing me and that there was no use for them to entertain any such feeling towards me, for I was their friend and teaching them the truth, and that God would protect me. I again talked to them a long time and finally seemed to gain some influence.

The Pimas had also been guilty of the same practice. When I heard of this I took a good interpreter and went to their camp, which was across the river among the old settlers not of our colonizers.

I had to labour long and hard before getting any satisfactory results. The old chief acknowledged that they had killed one witch and had almost killed another, who had recovered, and that they were then doctoring him to cure him, so that all hands could turn out and "kill him better."

I asked how they knew these men were witches. The answer was that the "doctor" had pointed them out.

I asked to see this "doctor" This was declined. I insisted, telling the chief that I would neither befriend him nor his people, nor talk to them about anything more until this "doctor" was shown me.

This the old fellow did not like; for I had done them much good already, and was continually watching and protecting their interests.

They all knew this and appreciated the same.

Numbers of the old men gathered around, chatting together. I continued to repeat my request to see the "doctor." Finally, he was brought out. I managed, after talking a long time, to really convince these Indians that it was wrong to believe in witches or, at least, to kill them. They agreed to quit the practice and I had reason to believe that they were partially converted, at least, for the poor fellow, who had been almost killed, came to my ranch a few weeks after this. He was terribly banged up; but, as soon as he could possibly travel, he came to let me know that I had saved him; that his people had agreed not to kill him, and that he would always call himself my boy, as I had saved his life.

Many persons were jealous of my influence with the natives and wondered how I managed to obtain so much power over them. I simply acted as a friend; and the Indians knew this.

One circumstance I will relate that will explain a little of this power. There was one of our white settlers who had lost his only cow. She was running on the river bottom, near the Indian camp. At the time this occurred the commander at McDowell was Captain Norval, a rather impetuous officer.

A letter was sent to this officer, stating that the Indians had stolen and killed the only cow that a poor man had and calling on him to come and redress the wrong. Accordingly, Captain Norval soon appeared, at the head of some dragoons, went to Mesa City and wrote an order, to be delivered to the Indians through me, that the cow had to be produced or paid for within six hours, or he would kill the last Indian to be found.

The Indians accused lived across the river, which was now very high. I immediately sent a courier for the old chief to come to my ranch, also informing him of the charge.

The old man came as soon as possible, having to swim the river. He was quite old and feeble, but managed to get over with the help of some younger men.

Captain Norval soon made his appearance and, with something of a flourish, reiterated his threat. The old chief looked at him in a dazed manner, then asked if the captain wanted them to pay for the cow when they knew nothing about her.

"No; but you have stolen the cow and killed and eaten her, and you have got to pay for her or I will turn my soldiers loose on you."

"Who says we killed this man's cow?"

"This letter says so."

"That letter lies; we know nothing about the cow. It would be better for us if we had killed her, for we could then confess and pay for her; but how can we confess and pay for what we know nothing about?"

The captain then asked what had become of the cow. The old chief said he did not know, positively, but thought perhaps he could tell. He said the day the cow was lost there had been a sudden rise in the river; the water coming down so suddenly that the cow, being on an island, was probably washed way and drowned. The old man was so simple and straightforward in all his talk that Captain Norval became convinced that he was truthful, and that the charge was more malicious than reasonable.

There was scarcely a week passed but what there were miserable, petty charges brought against the Indians, often on the slightest grounds, that had to be met.

CHAPTER 49

Peaceful Settlement

Soon after the events just narrated occurred, Major Chaffee took command at Camp McDowell. He soon "took in" the situation and took an interest in the welfare and rights of the Indians. To him, more than any one else, is owing the preservation of the Indian's rights and the final allowing of the lands to these people. I will give one more especial account and then go on. I could write a book on the doings of Salt River labours, but have not room in this for more than a few items.

Once the spirit ran so high against the Indians, that it was determined to drive them away unless they came to such terms as the whites should dictate. A mass meeting was called to meet at Tempe, for both whites and natives. At the time it was hardly safe for me to appear, as my life had been threatened. I had even been told to my face by a Captain Sharp, that he was ready to help put the rope around my neck any day.

However, I went to the meeting. Many demands were made of the Indians, all of which they acceded to that was possible for them to do. The whites were about satisfied with the disposition of the Indians, when one man got up and said he had a saddle stolen from him some two years previous, and that he would not consent for the Indians to remain longer where they were, unless they paid for the saddle. At this, several others commenced telling what they had lost and demanded the same.

I had kept perfectly silent during the whole parley. Now when this was explained to the Indians, they seemed at a loss what to say. Finally the chief said they were not able to pay for these things; that it was asking more than they could do. The spirit of the whites was really devilish; they seemed determined to drive the Indians to the wall, not one had spoken a word in their behalf.

I now felt impelled to speak. When I asked to be heard there were many hard looks given me. The chairman gave consent. As soon as I commenced someone interrupted me. I sat down. The chairman called for order. I then said, "If you gentlemen will hear me through without interruption, allowing me free speech, I will talk. When I get through my life is in your hands, do with me as you please, but I will not talk unless you agree to let me say just what I please." They took a vote to hear me through.

My defence of the Indians was to the point. I told the whites that they demanded of the natives, what none of them could do; that if they were required to make all their wrongs right that they had committed for the last two years, it would bankrupt them morally and financially. There were other thieves in the country beside Indian thieves, that may have stolen the articles. I referred to the virtue and honesty of the Pimas when the whites first came among them, showing that all their vile degradation and dishonesty was copied from the white man. Also, that many now present were corrupt and immoral, much more so than the average Indian.

Congressman Stephens was present. I never heard what he thought of my speech, but I conquered the most present, and they agreed to let the Indians have another trial. All of these men finally became my friends.

This meeting, just described, was with the Indians, the old settlers on the north side of the river. Those settling on the Utah ditch were not called in question at this time by the persons seeking to drive the others away.

To make it more easy for the reader to understand, I will speak of the Indians as north side and south side. The north side being those who were settled there by invitation of the whites before our colony settled on Salt River. All the control or influence I had over them was simply as their friend. The south side settlers were those who had colonised on lands watered by the Utah ditch. They were commonly known as "Jones' Indians."

The enemies that the latter had to meet, were many of the settlers, their immediate neighbours. Many and various attempts were made to have them driven back to the agency. Parties who bought shares in the Utah ditch as well as some of the original owners, disputed the right of the Indians to water, although they had done a large portion of the original work, and were always the most ready workers in making repairs.

These efforts to rob the Indians of their just rights, had a tendency to discourage the poor people from making improvements that they otherwise would have done. The question of the Indians' rights to water, finally became so hardly contested, that I applied to Major Chaffee, to cause an investigation to be made and protect the Indians in their rights. I had kept sufficient account of their work to show conclusively that they were entitled to water.

A commissioner was sent to make some preliminary enquiries. Most of the share holders claimed that the Indians had no legal right in the ditch, which was a fact, technically speaking, as no transfers had been made to them, simply verbally promised that by doing their share of work from year to year, that they could have water.

Every season someone would try to break this arrangement, and I determined to put a stop to it. A meeting of the share holders was called, to take testimony to send to this commissioner for the decision to be based upon. At this meeting I was threatened with the penitentiary if I established a claim for the Indians. The party who made the threat, said he thought he had bought unencumbered shares in the ditch from me; others claimed the same. Now the facts were, that each and every one who bought shares in the Utah ditch or lands from me, agreed to honour and assist in every way to help carry out the work of helping the Indians. Some betrayed their trust in a most dishonourable and unreasonable way.

My answer was that the Indians should be protected, prison or no prison. It was finally agreed by all the shareholders that, if I would cease to press the matter farther and sign the paper with the rest, reporting that the Indians had no legal right, all hands would agree to set apart a certain portion of water, measured through a head-gate, and sign an agreement, allowing the Indians perpetual use of that share on certain conditions.

After these conditions were agreed upon and a committee appointed, that I had confidence in, to see to the dividing of the water, I signed the report with the rest.

This I thought best to do at the timer reserving the right, however, that if the whites ever broke faith with the Indians I would seek to protect them at all hazards.

This contract has been measurably kept with more or less grumbling from some of the shareholders. The lands the Indians occupied I had secured to them the best I could by having my sons claim some of it in their names. One quarter-section was secured by purchase from a Mexican, who settled on a forty, allowing the Indians the balance. I bought the Mexican out and sold the forty to a supposed friend, with the understanding that he was to use the forty and let the Indians have the balance, as formerly agreed upon.

This agreement was broken. The party told the Indians that I had sold the whole quarter-section to him and agreed to drive them off. The poor Indians believed him and gave up the land, when the good friend (?) sold the whole to a third party, who knew nothing of the facts. The Indians felt very badly towards me about this. I knew nothing of the transaction until too late to remedy the wrong. This same man gave testimony against me afterwards, stating that I had sold the whole quarter-section, and I had to pay the Indians for dispossessing them.

It now became the popular idea to try to jump the Indians lands. The Indians on the north side were threatened with land jumpers from Phoenix and Tempe.

One party moved on their lands taking tools, surveying outfit, provisions, etc., and went to work just as though no Indians were around. There were quite a number of them.

They had sent their teams back home. The Indians gathered around them, and in a good-natured manner loaded all their stuff into their wagons, then by main force of numbers picked up the whites, loaded them on top of the loading, then seized the wagons by hand and hauled the whole outfit off from their lands laughing and joking all the time. The whites dared not make any resistance. This raised a big excitement, and armed companies commenced to gather both at Tempe and Phoenix.

It looked now as though blood would be shed. I went to McDowell and reported to Major Chaffee, he said he would be ready at five minutes' notice to come to the protection of the Indians; for me to go back and keep watch of the moves and let him know the minute any violence was offered. This whole business was broken up by the cunning of an Indian who lived at Tempe.

The Tempe company was headed by a captain who said the Indians had broken into his house and robbed him. He had raised a great excitement and quite a company, and was getting ready to join the company from Phoenix to make war on the Indians who had ran them off from their lands.

This Tempe Indian was standing looking at Captain J——'s company, when someone asked him if the Indians had really broken into Captain J——'s house.

Juan said: "Yes."

"What made them do it?"

Juan said "the captain owed an Indian for his squaw and would not pay him, and the Indian had got into the captain's house and stole his breeches to pay himself."

At this the company turned on their captain, gave him a good cursing, broke ranks and went about their business.

This soon reached the Phoenix company, who became disgusted and broke, whether Juan told the truth or not it answered the purpose, and had a lasting effect, for most everyone believed him.

Chapter 50

My Own Troubles

Major Chaffee had been watching the efforts of the whites to rob the natives of their rights. He had reported to the proper department the condition of affairs. He did all he could to protect the rights of the Indians. I kept him continually posted and I am satisfied that without his oversight of affairs the Indians would have been driven away and the work among them on Salt River broken up.

One piece of land that the whites had attempted to take from the Indians known as "Gironimo's farm," on a school section, had passed from one claimant to another, each one threatening that they would hold it.

One party went to work on this land. I warned him off and got a good cursing, a few days after this he in an exulting manner said to me "I have now sold this land to and got my pay. I would like to see you face *him*, I guess you dare not do it. He intends to put his teams to ploughing and I guess you will have to give up this time."

As soon as the teams started to plough I notified the young men to stop and to tell their father that he could not occupy the land. This, considering who the individual was, was considered not worth noticing and the ploughing continued. I went to camp and reported to Captain Chaffee. He sent a note saying they must get off or he would send a file of soldiers to put them off. *They went off considerably.*

Captain Chaffee had recommended the setting apart the lands occupied by the Indians as reservations, after much labour and investigation, this was finally done.

President Hayes declared the whole of Salt River Valley Indian reservation, including Phoenix, Tempe, Mesa City and the whole country occupied by the whites. When this proclamation came out there was a rattling among the "dry bones." All were astounded, the "flop" was so sudden, and complete. From daily expecting orders to come to send the Indians away, the towns, fine ranches and all were given to the Indians.

Many were puzzled over this proclamation, not knowing but what it was intended in earnest, but the majority knew it was a mistake as we had only asked for the lands occupied by the Indians. There was now a complete revulsion of feeling toward me by the old settlers. They acknowledged I had won. I was looked upon as a person who would never give up. All knew I had made the fight alone during the whole time. I was assisted by my family only and it stands on the record in the books of the settlement that my labours were not sustained by my associates. So for this reason I claim the right to speak singly. I would rather it had been different for I knew good works had been done by others but as they have placed their names on record as never having sustained me I will have to let them take their choice. As "bungling" as I may have been I got the Indians their lands.

It was nearly a year before things were straightened up and put to rights. Finally President Hayes modified the grant giving the Indians only the lands they occupied. During the whole of this time the Indians were steadily improving their farms, helping to enlarge the ditch, and generally advancing in good behaviour; and with a few exceptions becoming moral and industrious; raising good crops, selling large quantities of wheat and sustaining themselves without help from anyone.

Once our place was visited by an Indian inspector who reported the Indians in a better condition than any on the government reservations. Many had been baptised.

I had by this time become quite unpopular among those who, I thought, ought to be my friends. I had gotten into the habit of resisting every one who opposed my labours with the natives. Such seemed like an enemy. When I saw the Indians firmly established on their lands I desired to sell out and go on to Mexico.

Persons were appointed from time to time to take my place with the Pimas. But little progress was made until my eldest son, Daniel P. was placed in charge of them. A school house was built, and some few now took an interest in helping along the work.

Sisters Susanna Brady, Susan Savage and a Sister Harmon, formerly of the Sixteenth Ward, Salt Lake City, commenced teaching the children who made rapid progress. Many of them at this time can read in the third and fourth readers, calculate figures and write a very good hand. Sister Harmon has taught them music. Many of the young people are good singers, one having learned to play the organ.

Many of the older natives are intelligent and often speak in meeting with much force and understanding.

An effort was made by a company to buy me out but not being able to agree among themselves it failed.

My farm was quite valuable. From the products of it I had paid most of the old debts.

I now concluded to make Salt River my home, improve my place and live in peace, as I had done all I could for the Indians. I gave up all pretence of having any control or management of any kind whatever over their affairs, farther than to be friendly and give them such advice as a friend could. I supposed this would be satisfactory and end all trouble, but in this I was mistaken.

One day while at work ploughing on a ranch some four miles from home, one of my sons brought me a note stating that the Indians had made complaint against some of the settlers and that the charge was being investigated and that I was wanted as a witness.

I had heard of no trouble lately and could not call to mind anything wherein the Indians had a right to complain. My supposition was that it was some difficulty that had taken place in my absence as I had been away from home several days.

I wrote a note to the Bishop who was to conduct the investigation saying that I had no knowledge of any unsettled difficulties between the Indians and whites, and that I was not at present paying any attention to Indian affairs and could not possibly call to mind anything that would make my evidence needed, but if there was, to please send me word by my son and I would come immediately. I went on with my ploughing thinking nothing more about the matter.

Soon my son Wesley came at full gallop, looking quite excited. I asked him what was the matter, he replied, "They are going to cut you off from the Church, I heard them say so."

I asked, "Did they send you to tell me?"

"No, but I heard what they said and came as fast as I could to tell you; but I don't know what they mean."

I jumped on the horse and got to the place as soon as possible where the trial was going on, but they had adjourned. I wrote a note to the Bishop immediately, stating that I wished to make satisfaction if I had offended, as I had not intended to. In answer I received the following:

Elder D. W. Jones:

Understanding that you desire to appear in the Bishop's Court and apologise for your disregard to our notice sent you to attend and give testimony, we will be in session tomorrow, at 4 p.m., at the schoolhouse, at which time you can avail yourself of the opportunity.

—— ——,

Bishop.

Before the time of meeting, next day, I learned, to my surprise, that the whole business was against myself; that I was being tried for robbing Indians of their lands. This, to me, was so unjust, so unreasonable and in every way malicious that I made up my mind that I would make no defence whatever, but let the prosecutors go on and submit to whatever decision they gave.

My reasons for this were that I knew there was a deep prejudice against me—not entirely without cause—and the only way for me to break it up would be to submit to the parties who were trying to drive me to the wall.

Next day I appeared and asked forgiveness for not coming at the first notice. A motion was made to forgive me. Before this was put to vote I asked to make a statement so that my feelings would be fully understood, that was, that I should not have testified if I had been at the former hearing; that I was now here according to their notice, but that I declined to make any defence whatever.

The tribunal seemed puzzled to know what to do with me, but finally decided that I must make some more confessions. This I agreed to do at a public meeting. When the time came I made my apology, which was all right for the time and place, but a still greater humiliation was wanted. This I also agreed to. During these exercises my robbery case was being taken under advisement. However, I guess it will be as well to get through the confession while about it. Now, I do not wish anyone to think that my apologies were not sincere, I fully realised that I had been disrespectful, for I really had no respect for the whole proceedings.

The last decision was that I was to apologize before the whole ward and make full and complete satisfaction to all present. At the appointed time I stood up and did the best I could, but was told that it was not satisfactory. I then asked that a paper be prepared, just what would satisfy, and I would endorse it. This was agreed to, and under instructions the clerk commenced to write. I was standing, but was asked to take a seat. I declined, as I had the floor and was determined to keep it until the business was finished.

Finally, after many failures, a satisfactory confession was written out and read. I signed the same with my own free will and consent. There was nothing in the requirement but what was reasonable under the circumstances.

I find by the date of the decision against me, that it was given before the last confession, as that could not possibly have taken place within three days from the appeal. This is a copy of the decision given:

April 3rd, 1883.

Brother D. W. Jones:
It is the decision of the Bishop's court that you pay the receivers . . . . . . the sum of three hundred dollars for dispossessing Indians of their lands; said sum to be paid on or before the 14th of April, 1883, and if not paid by that time you shall be cut off from the Church of Jesus Christ of Latter-day Saints.

I made up my mind to abide the decision without appealing it. A short time before this trouble Brother Snow had visited Salt River and had, so I understood, caused to be settled some feelings that had existed for some time past between myself and others. I had in good faith agreed to work in unison with the authorities of the stake and had been doing my best to prove my sincerity.

When this decision was given I went to the President of the Stake and showed it to him. He expressed himself surprised, saying that he had always thought me over-tenacious about the Indians' rights. He said I could appeal it. I told him it would take time and trouble, and I felt like paying the fine and letting the matter rest, but that I feared there was a disposition to crowd me. The time was so short—only ten days allowed—and that money was scarce and hard to get. He replied that all that could be expected was for me to consent and pay as soon as I could. I told him I feared not, as the whole proceeding showed malice.

I went back home and wrote the Bishop a letter, saying that I would abide the decision and that he could take charge of a lot of wagons and stock which myself and sons owned that were now at home on the ranch. I gave a list of the same, and they were worth over one thousand dollars. I told him he could take charge of the whole of it or that he could pick and receive sufficient to cover the fine, and I would hold myself in readiness to assist under his counsel to get the money out of the property. If my offer was not properly worded I would sign any agreement that might be required of me; but when the letter was read one party remarked, "Jones has followed his rule and gone contrary to what we expected."

CHAPTER 51

Death by Accident of My Wife and Child

My offer was unfavourably received, and I was told to have the cash ready to pay by the time named. I counselled with those who presided over me, and though the advice I received was contrary to my ideas of justice and right, I followed it, though it was at the complete sacrifice of my home acquired by years of toil and hardship. I was determined to retain my standing in the Church at any cost, and leave judgment with the Lord, who will eventually deal out strict justice to all men.

I was so much used up now that I felt like hiding up for the balance of my days. I settled up my affairs in Salt River and moved to Tonto Basin, where but few people could live, the place being small. I commenced to make me a farm and fix for a quiet life. My family were kind and good to me. My wife was one of the noblest and best women that ever lived, and was so acknowledged by all who knew her.

On settling in Tonto my nature was to improve. I soon got started an extension of the public ditch and a road to the lumber region. My wife assisted in organising a Relief Society, and everything seemed prosperous for future peace and happiness, but my misfortunes were only commenced. During the winter it rained almost incessantly. We were living in a large tent with a shed in front. One day, during a storm, this shed fell, killing my wife and babe two years old. She was the mother of fourteen children, but seemed just in the prime of life and vigour.

All I will say is, that for over a year I would have been glad to have died. I could not remain in the place after this, so I went back to Salt River, settled in Tempe, built a nice little house and furnished it up completely. Brother B. F. Johnson, a neighbour, asked me one day why I was so particular to finish my house so thoroughly.

I replied, "We are promised many fold for all we sacrifice for the gospel's sake. I have given up several half-finished houses for the gospel's sake, and if I have to take them all back multiplied I want one decent place to live in while I finish them up."

Speaking of Brother Johnson reminds me of a circumstance that he will remember:

One day he and I were together, when Brother Milton Rey, who had been some time labouring among the Indians at Jonesville, came riding up to us in a hurried, excited manner, he said that he had just learned something greatly to my advantage; that he had been talking to the Indians and they had told him that I had never wronged them in any way and that it was all a mistake.

He wanted me to go immediately with him and get a re-hearing on all charges brought against me. I was really amused at his earnestness, as was also Brother Johnson. Brother Rey could not understand why I did not take more interest in what he was telling me, until I explained to him that I was well aware that through prejudice and not through guilt had I been condemned.

There were a few unworthy Indians whom I had to correct from time to time, they might have said something against me when prompted to do so, but the Indians as a body always honoured me more than anyone else, and do so to this day.

After getting my house finished in Tempe and moving my children from Tonto, I concluded to go ahead and do the best I could to make myself useful. The school district, one of the oldest and richest in the country, had one of the poorest school houses, owing to the former trustees not being able to understand the laws alike.

As there were now many Mormons living in the district it was proposed that they should have a representative; I was chosen for this place. The other two agreed to sustain me in building a good school house. We soon made arrangements, and one of the best houses in the county was speedily erected and ready for use.

I was also appointed to take the school census of the district, and to be assistant assessor for the Mesa and Jonesville districts. These active services helped me somewhat to bear the grief for the loss of my wife.

During the summer of 1884 my mind often rested on Mexico, and the obligation I felt resting upon me not to give up my mission in that country. I tried to rid my mind of these reflections but could not.

I remembered that I had agreed with Brother Brigham and George A. Smith to stick to the mission so long as I lived; I remembered that Brother Smith talked to me about this mission, even after we had to shake him every few minutes to keep him awake, so that he would breathe by force of will. I was with him daily just before his death. Once he said to me that he would like to live to help in the Mexican mission.

Brother Brigham's letter directing me to go on to one of the spots where Israel would sooner or later gather, etc., would come to my mind. Again, I remembered that Brother Brigham had told me that during my mission there would be times when I would seemingly be surrounded with a high, strong stone wall, and in which there would appear no opening. "But," said he, "don't kick at it for you will only make your toes sore. Be faithful and in time it will be removed."

It now occurred to me that I had forgotten the counsel not to kick, for I had been kicking at this very wall, and had got my toes terribly broken. I made up my mind to try and quit.

Finally the spirit and desire became so strong to visit Mexico that I could not resist the feeling. My children needed what we had left for their support, so I made up my mind that I would go if I had to make the trip on foot. At this time the land committee was working in Mexico. I often met some of them, but all seemed to avoid receiving any information from me. This was not at all strange for I knew that I was looked upon as rebellious, as my side of the story had never been heard.

About the time that I was thinking of starting, there was an old miner from Utah came to my house with a good travelling outfit, and wished to go to Mexico. He offered to take me through if I would furnish a certain amount of horse feed and provisions and assist him as interpreter in getting through the custom house, and get him introduced to some of the mine owners in Mexico.

I had heard some little about this man and had met him many years past in Utah. He made me such fair offers that I concluded to go along with him. As the most that I cared for was to get to Mexico with my saddler's tools. With them I knew I would be safe for expenses at any rate. My main desire was to get to the district of country and see what shape the spot was in that Brother Brigham had approved.

While in Provo one time Brother Brigham, in presence of Brother Cannon and others, took a map and motioning his finger around over

261

the map settled onto this very place and said, "Here is a gathering place for the Saints."

I knew the place but had never pointed it out to Brother Brigham. I had never been on the land but had been within a few miles of it and had heard a full description of the place. Knowing the desire was to get land in Mexico I naturally supposed that now was the time to get this place secured provided it was for sale. So I determined to go and find out and at the same time put myself in the way of giving such information as I had formerly obtained while in Mexico.

I had heard that the committee were trying to get lands from the government or land companies which amounted to the same. This I fully believed would fail having faith in the report given us while on our mission to Mexico by the old governor and accepted by President Young. Also knowing that the re-surveying of the country would make but slight difference in the conditions, having all this before me I hoped to go down and be of some use.

The trip through was made without any accident occurring worth mentioning. My companion seemed wholly absorbed in mining speculations, something I had never taken any interest in nor wished to. When we arrived at Ascension, I found quite a number of our people camped there. Some of them had been on the ground for some time, waiting for the land purchase to be made.

While here, the miner with whom I was travelling, and who agreed to take me on to Guerero, some two hundred and fifty miles farther, heard of some new mines, purporting to be very rich, that had lately been discovered. They were not far out of our way, and he wished to go by and see them and agreed, if he wished to stay there, to let me have the team to go on and not detain me over three days. We went to the place—Sabinal. Quite an excitement was up, rich prospects being found daily.

We made camp and I commenced to get dinner. My companion went prospecting and soon returned with some small pieces of rock and a big grin, saying that he had "struck it rich." He could scarcely spend time to eat his dinner; he wanted me to go and see his find. I told him that I neither knew nor cared anything about mines, but that I would take care of camp and the team, and he could go and finish his prospecting.

We were about six miles from water and desired to go there for camp. Soon Mr. S. returned with more rock; he was an old prospector and really understood his business. He said he had found a regular lead, where it was exposed in a ravine, and that it showed very rich.

I had been told what the laws were in regard to recording discoveries. They are different from the United States laws; no monument or notice is of any use. As soon as a discovery is made the finder must go and put the same on record. The one first recording holds the claim, having four months to do a certain amount of work required.

I explained this to the miner and also told him that anyone getting to the recorder ahead of him could take his discovery. We were with travelling carriage and seventy-five miles from the recorder's office—at Casas Grandes. There was a horseback trail much nearer and prospectors out in every direction, and liable to run into this vein. Mr. S. became excited and we started for Casas Grandes in a hurry; no time was lost.

On arriving there I helped to get all the necessary papers made out, and found a person to see that all was straight. When the papers were all filed and settled Mr. S. showed me my name as half owner in the find, and said, "You are now a rich man; if you will stick to me a few days you will soon be able to go on and buy your land," provided the rock assayed as much as he believed it would—some three hundred dollars.

To find this out it would become necessary to go to El Paso, some two hundred miles, for an assay. Again I was persuaded, as I had not yet got to the district I desired to reach, Mr. S. reiterating his offer that, as soon as he could get settled to mining, I could have the use of his team as long as I wished to go on my land business. So we went back to the discovery, which was on our road to El Paso, and procured some three hundred pounds of ore from the vein. I helped to get the rock; the vein showed well. When we arrived in El Paso and got the assay it showed over six hundred dollars, which was very rich. We had no trouble in getting all the help we needed to work the mine.

It was not long before my partner showed his real character. As soon as the means were secured to work the mine and he needed me no further he showed a murderous spirit. I now made up my mind to stay with him the four months and get my rights on record, for it was through my individual influence that the means were obtained to work the mine. I had to watch my life continually during the four months, not daring to eat or sleep with my partner. I will not weary the reader with what occurred at this camp. It would be rather unpleasant to read, but it is no exaggeration as many who were there from time to time can testify to say that my life was in danger most of the time while in this camp.

When I got my rights on record I left the camp, appointed a representative to look after my interests according to the laws of Mexico.

The mine was quite rich turning out much rich ore and making a large dump of ore that would have paid to freight. My partner spent most all the proceeds in high living and spreeing.

I left the mine in disgust and have never made an enquiry about it since, I have passed in sight of the district twice since while on land business and never cared to make an enquiry concerning either the mine or partner.

Chapter 52

I go on an Exploring Trip

While doing the assessment work one of my sons and a son-in-law came from Salt River to help me. My son-in-law, John Brady, shot himself accidentally by dropping a pistol. He died of the wound and was buried near the camp of Saints at Ascension. Brother Jesse Steele was at the camp at the time and helped to nurse him. He lived eight days after being wounded. Death was caused by the bursting of an artery that had been slightly wounded. This occurred in the night time. We were watching as usual but no suspicion of the bleeding existed until he was too far gone to recruit when the bleeding was stopped. This was hard on me as I felt toward him as a real son he having always shown me much kindness.

During these four months I often visited the camp of the Saints at Ascension.

The first time I met one of the brethren of the committee he asked me what I thought of their proposed land purchase. I said that I believed that it would be a failure. When I was asked why, I related all about our first investigations and our report to Brother Brigham, saying that I believed we reported the truth, and that if the present efforts succeeded it would prove our reports false. This was looked on more as an insult than as information.

I was told that conditions had changed since the time of our visit to Mexico; that our reports might have been all right at the time, but would not apply to the present. My answer to this was that I recognised the face of the country as being just the same as formerly; that mountains and valleys were all in place; that I saw no signs of earthquakes having changed the conditions, therefore I could not see why our reports if true then were not true now. I soon learned that any information that I might offer would simply be looked on as worthless.

I was told that Mr. Campos, who was the agent now offering them lands, was one like Hiram of old raised up for the salvation of the people. I answered that he was a fraud raised up to swindle them out of their money. I was severely rebuked for this remark, and told that Mr. Campos had been introduced and vouched for in a letter of introduction, as the man who opened the first door to the Elders in Mexico, in the City of Chihuahua, and that anything I might think or say would avail nothing. This was at first a surprise to me, for I was in charge of Chihuahua at the time and never heard of Mr. Campos, but I learned afterwards that he was a police officer at the time and possibly was on duty the evening we held meeting in the public Cock Pit.

As soon as I was thoroughly convinced that I could do no good here I made up my mind to continue on my first effort to get to the country I had started for.

During the winter and spring of 1885, while attending to the mining business, I made several trips to El Paso. Once, while in El Paso, I met Brothers Erastus Snow and Samuel H. Hill who were on their way to the city of Mexico on business of importance. They not wishing to be delayed accepted my assistance in getting their luggage checked, their money changed and other services that helped them along, as I was acquainted with the officers and business. This occurred February 19th, 1885.

At that time I explained to Brother Snow my desire regarding this land. He said for me to go ahead, hoping I would succeed. I knew that it would take considerable money to visit and thoroughly explore the country I desired to visit.

The products of the mine although rich, as before stated, were wasted and probably would continue to be as I could not control my partner without going into law, and this would be ruinous under the laws of Mexico.

I happened to meet a gentleman who had money and was desirous of going on the same business, he agreeing to bear the expenses for my services as interpreter, etc. And that any lands found that might be wanted by the Mormons was to be entirely under my control.

I now went home to Salt River to visit my children and prepare for the trip to Mexico. We went direct to the city of Chihuahua. Soon we were visited by different land speculators offering lands.

We visited and examined various ranches, some as far down as the southern part of the state. We found some excellent properties at reasonable prices, but paid no attention to the worthless lands; simply examining titled properties of good reputation.

We were in the city of Chihuahua, after having done considerable exploring, when we were approached by a man who described a piece of property that he had bonded, I soon became convinced that from the description and locality that it was the land I desired to find. When we were alone I informed my friend of this and we agreed to go and see the place.

We visited the parties holding the lands and agreed to go with them, it being some two hundred and fifty miles from Chihuahua, and in the district approved of by President Young for a gathering place.

On arriving at this spot I felt sure that I had now found the place wanted. Without further description I will say that it is the most beautiful valley that I ever saw; fertile soil, water plentiful, and timber more than would ever be used; the whole face of the country covered with the best of grass. Climate mild; crops are raised in the vicinity without irrigation. The land held by the parties was for sixty days only. The question now was for me to try and get this secured before the bond ran out as there were others wanting to buy this piece in connection with a large tract adjoining it from another party.

The owner of this piece I wanted was a friend to the owner of the large tract and had agreed that in case the present bond ran out that he should have the property to join onto his larger tract. The owner of the large tract had already entered into negotiations with a third party to sell the whole provided he got the small property.

I had not as yet learned all these particulars, but I had learned enough to convince me that if the property was not secured within the sixty days that the price would be raised at least. From what I had learned I expected that Brother Snow would be at the new Colony station at Piedras Verdes, as the purchase had been made from Mr. Campos, and the people were now moving on lands they supposed belonged to the purchase, but afterwards proved to be a portion of an old and well-known ranch known as Sandiago.

The question was how to get to Brother Snow's place the quickest way. It was at least two hundred miles distant across a country not much travelled, and some of the way considered dangerous because of Apaches.

The fear that the Mexicans entertain for the Apaches puts me in mind of something that I saw when I was a small boy. Some rude boys had tied a tin can to a dog's tail and he ran by yelping, soon the can came off. I could see the dog running with all his might for a long ways. I wondered what made him keep running when nothing now was to his tail. I was too small at the time to understand that he was still scared at his first experience.

The Mexicans are somewhat the same; to this day they are slow to forget past experiences, and seem to think the Apaches are still after them even in the localities where none have been seen for years.

After thoroughly examining the land we went to the county seat and my friend procured a bond for the sixty days. We then started back east toward the city of Chihuahua. My desired route lay north and would turn off at Temosechic, about twenty miles from where we were.

On arriving at Temosechic about noon I got out of our travelling carriage with my blankets and saddle bags, and without having made any arrangements whatever for the trip bade goodbye to my travelling companion.

This was the same place where we had been so well treated ten years before while on our mission. I had perfect faith in the goodness of the people. For I wished to take the same route that we had come out on before and remembered many friends formerly met, and I believed they would remember me.

I went directly to the house of Tomas Triboso, in whose house we had held meeting. I had his autograph in my old memorandum book. On showing him this he grasped my hand and called his wife saying: "Here is our old friend the Mormon who preached in our house ten years ago."

The old lady came in smiling, shook hands and embraced me, saying that all the women in town remembered my preaching. A good dinner was ordered at once.

Don Tomas asked how he could serve me. I explained my desire to reach the Mormon settlements as quick as possible, giving him my reasons. He replied:

"All right; I have two good saddle horses. I would like to have you stay and visit us; all the people would be delighted to see and hear you talk. We often speak about your people and are glad to hear that they are coming into Mexico. We hope that they will get here into our district in time."

After dinner my kind host saddled up and took me to Providencia; there introduced me to the manager, who next morning sent me to Namaquipe, where I met the family of the good old patriarch, Francisco Vasques, formerly spoken of.

In this way I was forwarded from place to place with dispatch, making through in good time with little expense.

I met Brother Snow at Coralitos, and showed him the following letter:

Messrs. Snow, Burton, Preston and others:
Dear Sirs:—At the request of Mr. Jones I write this letter. I have bonded the ranch, W——, for the period of sixty days, for $30,000 in good and lawful money of the United States. I have agreed with Mr. Jones to sell the same to his people if he can take up the bond within the time I have given him. Mr. Jones and I have been travelling together, looking at lands——Mr. Jones in the interest of his people and I for myself, looking for grazing. Mr. Jones has been of great benefit to me as an interpreter, and is well posted in Mexican lands, and I do this in appreciation of his friendship and services. This land is mostly farming, with plenty of good timber. After the payment of $15,000 the property can be delivered to purchasers. This property cannot be held long without much expense, which I cannot conveniently do at present; besides, delays are dangerous. I have given Mr. Jones my price on the land, which contains 31,000 acres, all told.
This is good country, which Mr. Jones is thoroughly competent to detail to you.
Hoping to hear from some of you gentlemen soon, I am
    Very respectfully yours,
                                                    F. G. South.
Temosachic, Mexico,
May 25th, 1886.

This was written on the back of the letter:

I have considered the foregoing and can say that, while I regard the tract favourably located along the Sierra Madre, some eighty to one hundred miles south of Corralis Basin, and, according to Mr. Jones' representation, is a desirable place, I am not in any condition, at present, to entertain the proposition; but hope in the future to see our people stretching out in that direction.
                                                    E. Snow.

Brother Snow said, in substance, that the money that had been appropriated, for the purchase of lands in Mexico, was about all exhaust-

269

ed and no very good results obtained; that there had been so much time and means wasted that he doubted if the authorities would pay any more attention to land purchases in Mexico, and if anything more was done that he believed it would be through private enterprise; also said that, if he had the money, he would help me out in the matter, but hoped that I could go and enlist help from some of the brethren who were able to buy on their own responsibility.

On receiving this word, I started immediately for Utah, came direct to Salt Lake City and offered this land. The first answer I received was that my land was too dear; that I should not expect such a price when good lands could be obtained for one-fourth this amount.

I was surprised at this ignorance of land matters in Mexico, for I knew all the lands offered for such low figures were almost worthless, and I supposed this was now understood. The land I was offering would have been cheap at ten times the price, in comparison to any yet procured—even as a gift. Poor land means poor people, and expensive water added to cheap land means dear homes.

I have often been puzzled to see how eager some people are to purchase acreage because the land was cheap, when the preparing of this land for homes would cost much more than good lands that could be obtained, where homes could be made easily and cheaply, and much better when made.

I worked hard to get this land secured. Finally, I met with a party, at Ogden, who agreed to meet me in Chihuahua within the time and, if the land was as represented, secure it. A day was set to meet. I hurried back to Chihuahua and got an outfit all ready for the trip, feeling safe, for I knew that the land would show for itself.

This party never came. I received a letter, giving some excuse, but saying they would come in a few days. Before the time proposed the bond was up, and the persons wanting the chance bought the land the day it was on the market.

I then telegraphed to the parties that they need not come, as it was too late.

CHAPTER 53

My Return to Salt Lake City

I now made up my mind to get the best understanding of various tracts of lands, then for sale. I succeeded to my satisfaction. I wished, before leaving Mexico, to get some of our people to go with me and see the tract of land that I had been recommending, for many persons supposed that I had exaggerated its merits.

I again visited Brother Snow's headquarters, hoping that I could get someone sent to see this land. I knew the parties who had purchased it, and had reason to believe that it could be bought of them still at a reasonable figure, considering its qualities.

I succeeded in getting the brethren interested enough to let two of the Elders—Brother Spencer and Bishop Williams, two of the most reliable pioneers in camp—to go with me. We were gone fourteen days. On their return they reported that I had shown to them the best country they had ever seen—Illinois and Kentucky not excepted; also, the most hospitable and well-disposed people they had ever met.

I now felt satisfied, as far as duty was concerned. This land was acknowledged to be much better than I reported it to be.

I now left Mexico, with the feeling that I had done all I could at that time. I came to Salt Lake again and offered some other good lands that I had listed for sale; but all faith in Mexican land matters seemed at an end. A great many persons, having visited and seen the country purchased, left in disgust, supposing there was none better.

The only way to account for this good land being passed by is simply to use the old hackneyed expression, "Wait; the time hasn't come yet."

After stopping in Salt Lake City for a short time, I started for home, in Arizona; on my way home I called upon the gentleman who had bought the land. He knew all about my efforts to secure the property, and pledged himself to me that I should have the handling of the property, should it ever be wanted.

When I arrived at home I found my son Wiley very sick. From over-work and exposure he had become consumptive. I was advised to move him to a cooler climate. We fitted up to go. His desire was to move to Mexico. I felt like doing anything to please him, for he was good and faithful to me and in every respect a true man.

He had been with me on some of my hardest missions and was always faithful. He tried hard to get me to load him into a wagon and start, but I could see that he was fast failing. After being confined but a few days to the house he gave up, saying, "Well, pa, I can't pull through; I will have to give it up. What shall I tell ma?"

I never saw a more common-sense death than his was.

This was a hard loss to me, for he was like a father to the children in my absence.

Another son, 16 years of age, was now taken quite sick, seemingly almost the same. We were about fitted up for a move. I now determined to start for Utah. Death seemed to desire the lives of my family. Others were complaining.

My sick son seemed uneasy and wanted to move, so we started out. After being on the road but three days, he died and was buried at the Vulture mining camp. My three oldest sons remained in Arizona, and are there yet, (1890).

I would often find myself counting over my children to see how many I had left. Sometimes I felt almost bewildered. After leaving Vulture, five children, two grand children and myself travelled through alone, coming by the way of Scanlan's Ferry.

We had no further trouble. After this Death seemed satisfied for the time being. We met travellers at different times along the road, sometimes a single wagon, never more than two or three.

As grass and water are scarce in many places, large companies cannot travel as well as small parties. The country is now safe to travel on any of the routes through to Mexico. Ranches and settlements wherever it is possible to locate for water.

We arrived in Fairview, Sanpete county, where my daughter, Mary, lived. We bought a home for the family. My daughter, Ella, having lost her husband, took charge of the children when I came to Salt Lake City to start business at my old trade. This I found would be difficult to do, as the trade had somewhat changed, and it would take time and capital to get a start. So I concluded to start on a project I had had in my mind for a number of years. That was to invent a better side-saddle than any yet in use and make the same adjustable to different-sized riders. This I have finally accomplished, after hard work and much more delay than I expected when I commenced.

I will now give what I have formerly promised—a short account of something I have learned about some of the Indian tribes I have visited.

CHAPTER 54

Slaughter of the Apaches

This chapter will be devoted to what I have seen and learned about Apaches and other southern tribes. The common supposition is that the Apaches are by nature and desire a bloodthirsty people, and have always been so. This is a mistake, but it is a fact that we have to go back almost a century to find them a peaceable people.

Their own story is that they were once vegetarians. They were so opposed to killing that they would say to the bear, "God made you; go in peace, I will not kill you." And to the birds, "God made you with feathers to protect you in cold air, and wings to fly. How good God has been to you!" And even to the rattlesnake they would say, "You have rattles and tell us where you are so that we can get out of your way. We will not kill you."

I am giving this as the Apaches gave it to me. They believe in God the Father, and in a God Mother; and that God dwells in a place where He can see and understand what they do; that they once dwelt with Him, and that when they die if they have done good they will go back to dwell with their Father and Mother, but if unworthy they are sent away from them in sorrow. They pray in the evening that they may be protected from their enemies and have good dreams, desiring that their dead friends may visit and talk to them.

They believe that they once had more power with God than they now have, and acknowledged that they had done wrong in killing their own people; saying that for that reason their prayers were not heard and answered as formerly. They say that Americans do not honour God, but throw His name at their mules and cattle the same as they do clods or rocks, and that it is their duty to destroy the wicked blasphemers from off the earth; that none have a right to live unless they honour their Father's name.

They reckon that by killing white men at the ratio they have been that eventually they will exterminate the white race. This was their belief a few years since Possibly they are beginning to think differently by this time.

They say that the cause of their fighting with the Catholic Mexicans is that when Mexico was conquered by the priests, they wanted the natives of Mexico to cease to worship the real Father God, and worship gods made of wood and stone. Most of the natives submitted to this, but the Apaches refused and went into the mountains away from the priests; After a while the Indians that commenced to worship the wood and stone gods made war on them by order of the priests, and drove them to bloodshed. After a while they agreed to submit and made a treaty to listen to the priests, but they soon found they were bad men and had been enemies ever since.

Now for a little history, partly written and partly traditionary.

Some two hundred miles in a westerly direction from the city of Chihuahua, among the Sierra Madre mountains, there is a beautiful valley of about fifty thousand acres of land, well watered and surrounded with timbered mountains. The Mexicans call this Paradise, or Garden of Eden.

About eighty years ago the Jesuits planted a mission among the Apaches in this beautiful valley. Everything went on happily for a season. The head priest had considerable influence with the natives, using his power for his own convenience.

In connection with many other selfish customs, the priests required of the Indians one of their handsomest daughters to live at the mission, making them believe that there was some religious ceremony, essential to their welfare, that required the presence of this maiden. A daughter of the chief was selected.

The priests had told the Indians that they lived pure lives before God.

After a while the daughter of the chief was missing. When the Indians made inquiries for her, they were told that she had been taken to heaven in a miraculous manner and was made a saint. The chief did not believe the story and suspected treachery. There was an old woman who had had charge of the Indian girl. The Apaches seized and tortured her until she confessed the truth. The priest had lived with the daughter as a wife. And when her condition became such as to betray him he had her killed and buried. The Indians found her body and confirmed this treachery. They then raised and killed all connected with the mission and destroyed everything possible. They swore vengeance on the priests and their followers and vowed that no Catholic should ever inhabit this valley.

I have seen the ruins they made within the last few years, and heard this story from the Mexicans living within a day's travel from this valley. They all dread the Apaches to this day. No Mexican has ever dared to make a home there. From that time until the present the Apaches have been at war with the Mexicans.

When white men first went to the region where the Apaches roam, the Indians looked upon them as a different class of people and did not make war upon the few white traders they met on the road to the city of Chihuahua, but they would go in and trade with merchant trains owned by Americans, and in no way molest them.

This peaceful state of affairs was broken up in the year 1843. At that time the State of Chihuahua was having a hard time with the Apaches, and the government offered a large reward for their scalps, ranging from $100 to $150 per head.

This offer got to the ears of Colonel Kerker, of Texas. He raised a company of Texans and went to the city of Chihuahua, and contracted with the Governor for Apache scalps.

The Colt revolver had recently been brought into use. This company of rangers carried these weapons concealed under their coats and went to Galliana, a town on the Rio Santa Maria, in the northwestern part of Chihuahua, near the mountains where the Indians dwelt.

This Kerker arranged to have the Apaches come to a feast prepared for them, agreeing to meet them unarmed, as friends. The Indians, believing these white men real friends, came in without suspicion, and, while partaking of the hospitality, the rangers commenced with their revolvers and killed over a hundred of them. The Indians could make no resistance, but were literally slaughtered. Kerker got his money, but lost the respect of all decent men.

A few years after this I was in the Apache country. They were killing both whites and Mexicans at every opportunity. Thirty-five years after I was again in that country and it was still the same.

For many years when a white man was killed by an Apache, the whites would remark, "There is another of Kerker's victims."

I saw this same individual in 1849 in Santa Fe, when he was there for a few days. So indignant were the people at him that there was a strong talk of lynching him.

Individually, I succeeded in making friends with most of these Apaches. I have talked with them, but they have no confidence in the Mexican or white man.

The move made by Gen. Crook that at the time proved a success, namely, getting one band to fight another, finally ceased to work and the scouts enlisted for the last few years have done but little killing. By the whites these Apaches are considered the worst Indians on the continent.

I have never heard an apology or excuse for their conduct by any one, so, like the old miner who attended a Methodist revival, when the preacher called on all who were for God to rise to their feet, all got up but the old miner. When all for the Devil were called to stand up the old miner arose. The parson asked him why he voted for Satan. The reply was that he never liked to see any man without a friend.

THE NAVAJOES.

A short sketch of this tribe may be interesting. They inhabit the country west of the settled portion of New Mexico.

In 1847, when I first knew them, they were great thieves, but not much given to killing. Their philosophy was to spare the herders so that they could raise more stock. They were great sheep thieves, often taking whole herds, and sometimes taking the herders along. The Mexicans feared to follow them through the canyons, and when the Indians once reached the mountains they were generally let alone.

After the U. S. government was extended and New Mexico became a territory, the U. S. forces commenced to try to stop these raids and, after many years, partially succeeded, and troops were stationed in the Navajo country. There was a battalion of Mexican volunteers, cavalry, under Col. Chavez, stationed at one of the outposts.

The Indians were seemingly subdued. They were always considered smart and somewhat politic, as well as thrifty and industrious, so they soon accepted the situation. When they found the U. S. Government was determined to make them behave, they made a treaty and agreed to quit stealing and allow these troops to be stationed in their country and live in peace.

This Colonel Chavez was a great gambler and horse racer. The Navajoes were fond of racing also. The colonel had a fine horse that he considered a "world beater." A race was gotten up with the Indians, who were willing to bet anything on their horse.

So sure was Colonel Chavez of winning that he bet some five hundred head of government horses, against the same number of Indian ponies. The Indians looked upon the colonel as owner of these horses. When the race came off, the Indians won. The colonel was in a scrape. He refused to give up the horses, so the Indians took them.

I don't remember whether a fight ensued immediately, or not, but I believe there did. At any rate the report was circulated that the Indians had declared war, and had run off all the soldier's horses.

A war of extermination was declared against these Indians, and troops were sent into their country. Their ranches, farms, and stock were destroyed, and many of them were killed. The remainder were stripped of everything. They were taken prisoners and put upon a reservation in the eastern portion of New Mexico. Here they remained in poverty for some years.

I do not know whether the facts were ever known by the government or not, but I believe they were. After a time the Indians were allowed to go back to their old country, a reservation set apart for them and some stock was given them to make a start. Being industrious and thrifty, they soon began to pick up. They made blankets and traded them for ponies.

Many of them about the years 1874-75 came into the Mormon settlements, some few carrying enough blankets on their backs to buy a mare pony. An Indian that could load a little Mexican donkey with blankets was considered a good trader.

It was not many years until these Navajoes had large bands of horses and sheep. They are again quite rich and prosperous.

YAQUIS.

A few words about the Yaquis might be interesting also. They inhabit the Rio Yaqui in Sonoro. They are an agricultural people and were occupying this same country at the time of the Conquest and were peaceable and quite numerous.

After the government under Spain was well established they offered to make a grant of the Yaqui country to the inhabitants. The Indians declined the offer, saying the country was and always had been theirs and that they did not ask it to be granted to them.

This was rather an insult to the arrogant Spaniard. The offer has been repeated from time to time, but the Indians have always declined the grant on the same old grounds. So the Yaqui country stands on the maps of Mexico as government lands.

Efforts have been made several times to oust these Indians from their lands. Grants have been given from time to time as was the Brannan grant, but the Indians have never given up their idea of prior rights.

There are a great many of the best citizens of Mexico in sympathy with the Yaquis.

TARUMARIES.

This tribe inhabits the mountain country in the western part of the state of Chihuahua. There are many villages situated in the Sierra Madre mountains, accessible only by very difficult pack-trails.

At the time of the conquest these people occupied, not only these mountain villages, but many of the fertile valleys along the foothills.

Many of the present towns of western Chihuahua bear the old Indian names and are inhabited by people descended from the ancient inhabitants. With a little foreign mixture, the pure bloods greatly predominate.

In many of these towns there are bands of these people who keep up their old customs, name, and language, but are recognised as citizens. They submitted to Catholicism in form, but of late years have almost entirely lost respect for the *padres*; saying that they cared more for their coppers than they did for their souls.

These people, both natives and mixed are very hospitable and industrious, and are more honest and virtuous than are the average Mexican.

The villagers of the mountains are peculiar They seem to have a dread of mixing or associating much with anyone, even the Mexicans whose neighbours they are. It is their habit, when anyone approaches their village, for all the inhabitants to leave their houses and retire a short ways, leaving their doors open and everything exposed so that if anything is wanted by the travellers they can help themselves. But one thing must always be done. The pay for the article taken must be left in sight or without grace the party taking ever so small an article without pay, will be waylaid and will be very lucky if he escapes, with his life. So positive are these rules that no one dare take the risk, and the people have commanded the utmost respect for ages by all who pass through their country. Unless imposed upon and insulted they molest no one.

These mountain Indians are excellent hunters. Deer, turkey and bear are plentiful in the mountains. They often go into the city of Chihuahua to trade. They pack most of their trade on their backs, travelling in single file, paying no attention to anyone except to do their trading and go straight back home.

Some years since, at the town of Santa Rosa, these Indians, while on a trading trip, were insulted and abused by the inhabitants. The Indians went home, gathered some four hundred armed men, marched back through a number of settlements, attacked the place and almost exterminated the people, then went home satisfied. They were never called to account for the act.

An account of the affair has been given to me several times by different Mexicans, who invariably tell it in honour of the character of these Tarumaries.

CHAPTER 55

Characteristics of the People

This old letter, copied from the *Deseret News*, I think will help in describing Mexico:

El Paso, State of Chihuahua, February 10th, 1876.
Brother F. Nicholson:

I herewith send you an account of the country and people of this region.

DESCRIPTION OF EL PASO.

The town of El Paso is situated on the right bank of the Rio Grande del Norte, in the State of Chihuahua, on a low bottom, liable to much damage from high water; land sandy. The streets are simply old cattle tracks, running in every direction. If an idea can be given of them without mapping it will be by saying they followed the forks of the trails, giving the grounds somewhat the appearance or shape of irregular triangles.

The river-bed being quick-sand, it costs a great deal to keep a water-ditch in order. The houses are one story, made of adobe; solid block, mainly after the old Moorish style of small fortresses; hollow, square in centre; one door in front.

CLIMATE AND PRODUCTS.

The climate is warm and pleasant; ploughing and sowing can be done any time during the winter. This makes the farmer rather indolent, as he does not have to hurry as ours of the colder climates do.

The products are wheat, corn, barley, beans, peas, onions, pepper, sweet potatoes and some few other vegetables. Many things more might be profitably cultivated, if once understood; but the people are satisfied with what they have, and manifest but little interest in new introductions.

The fruits are grapes, in great abundance and of the best quality; pears, which the people dry in great abundance, price, ten cents per pound. They are excellent eating. Their apples are small seedlings, not worth eating. A few peaches of an excellent kind do well here. I have seen no other fruits. I have heard that strawberries and some other small fruits have been cultivated by foreigners, and they do extremely well.

Rude Agriculture.

The mode of cultivation is with an old wooden plough, working their cattle by the horns. They scratch up the ground very poorly, afterwards doing much work with the hoe; they regulate their ground for watering by making small embankments around small, irregular plats, from thirty to fifty feet across, and flooding the land. I think this a poor way, as it causes their land to bake very hard; but this is the manner in which their fathers did it, so they think it is all right. They cultivate all open crops with the hoe, using the large, old-fashioned 'nigger' hoe. They cut their hay with the same tool. In Arizona we saw hundreds of tons, at the government posts, cut in this same way. They harvest with reap hooks and thresh with goats or flails.

Mechanics, Doctors and Lawyers.

Mechanics are scarce. In this town of ten thousand inhabitants there is one blacksmith shop, three or four carpenter shops, two tailors, three or four shoe shops, one wheelwright and one silversmith. And this is, as far as I have been able to learn, about the whole number.

"To compensate for this lack of mechanics, there is but one doctor and one lawyer; and the latter is supposed to be *insane*, as he has quit the practice, walks quietly around the town, says but little to anyone, is polite, dresses neatly and seems to mind his own business. My opinion is that he is the most sensible lawyer I have ever seen.

Limited Commerce.

The commerce of the country is limited. The people sell their wines and dried fruits generally as soon as ready. They go to all the surrounding country; to Chihuahua as well as up the country to Santa Fe and Arizona. There are three Jew stores and one Mexican store. Their business is small.

There are many small dealers of various kinds, and there are many people who seem to live on occasional small amounts; but how they

282

get their money deponent saith not.

Non-Progressive.

The people are slow to adopt improvements. Things look about the same as they did when I was here about thirty years ago, in '47. The town looks about the same. A very little has been done about the square and church—hardly perceivable. They use wooden-wheeled carts, and everything seems as though it was but a short time since I was here and saw things just as they now are.

Hospitality.

This is natural to the people of this country. A kinder-hearted people, naturally, I do not believe can be found. They are polite and mannerly—even the lowest of them. Their children are quiet and obedient, there being no 'hoodlums' here. Parents are affectionate to their children. Husbands are polite and affectionate. They have great reverence for Deity, their religion and old age. Get them once directed right and they will be the best people on earth.

Health and Morals.

The people are generally healthy, there being but little disease among them. There are a few Americans living here.

As to their morals, I believe the people of this town stand above par, compared with more civilized communities. The Apaches are the only people said to be strictly virtuous that I have met on this journey as yet, though it is generally admitted that the aborigines are much more virtuous than the mixed race of this country.

"Here the people are a mixture of the Spanish and native—the naive blood predominating. Of the pure bloods there are only about two hundred remaining in this town. Catholicism prevails more here than in the interior, so I am informed by persons from the lower States of Mexico. There liberty of conscience is beginning to be more popular, and priestcraft is beginning to lose its power over many, but not enough for them to be popular as yet.

Stock.

The stock of the country is scarce and inferior. Horses, cattle and goats are tolerably plentiful. There are a few pigs and fowls. The circulating medium is corn, copper coin greenbacks and a little silver. Dogs are in great abundance, noisy but seldom bite.

283

Taxes are light, except on work on dam and water-ditch. The municipal regulations seem good. They have a police force, but it is seldom needed. The officer, the Jefe Politico, seems to control. There are some more officers, such as police magistrates, etc.; but the first seems to be manager of everything of a political nature. The present incumbent, Pablo Padio, is serving his second term, having been re-elected lately. He is very much of a gentleman.

The people are very obedient to official authority, and show great respect to the same.

VARIOUS.

With all the faults of the people—which faults are more blameable to the manner in which they have been ruled than to the people— there are good and noble principles among them. Their devotion to their religion I consider a virtue, for they have had no chance to have any better. Their reverence is unbounded, and, as I before stated, let them once be enlightened with the gospel and I believe they will receive the truth—and they will not fall away, but will stick to the right.

D. W. Jones

Mexico, although a sister republic, with railroad communications and much commercial intercourse with the United States, is not well understood by the average American. There has been for a long time, and still is, to quite an extent a prejudice against the Mexican people by the Americans. We look upon them as far behind the people of the United States, and often make unfair remarks about the "stupid" Mexicans, not stopping to consider who the people are or what their opportunities have been.

A great many accuse the Roman Catholic church of being responsible for the ignorance and degradation of the inhabitants.

In as few words as possible, I will offer an apology for the Mexican nation, and compare what we have done with the same element.

When this continent was first discovered there were millions of Indians inhabiting it, extending from the Atlantic to the Pacific, and from the north sea to the Gulf of Mexico. That portion of the continent lying west on a line from Texas to Oregon, fell under the control of Spain, a Catholic government; that east under Protestant Christianity.

Up to the treaty with Mexico, nearly two-thirds of this continent was under Spanish rule. Let us see what the conditions of the country were at that time. There were about six millions of the inhabitants of Mexico, enjoying all the rights of citizenship. A great portion of the rulers of the country being of the natives, no distinction was made, but the priests offered to the natives the inducement of equal rights with the invaders.

Mexico is simply a nation of converted semi-civilized aborigines, living and having a being, and still numbering as many as at first.

The power and influence of the priests were extended into Arizona, New Mexico and California and thousands of Indians were brought into peaceable relations. No wars of extermination were declared against the natives, but missions of peace were the main means of conquest. Up to the year 1 848 there were in this Mexican territory, tens of thousands living, and at least enjoying an existence.

Now let us see what has been done by Protestant Christianity for the natives who dwelt on their side of the line. I do not propose to quote hundreds of pages of history to show, but will simply refer to the fact. They have been killed off just as have been the bear, the wolf and the wild animals detrimental to the interests of the good, pious Puritans who wanted the country.

The real and true comparison is, How do the natives of Mexico compare with those of the United States? Let that power and influence which took hold of the natives of Mexico speak and say to those who took hold of the other side: "Here is our work. Mexico as it is today is peopled mainly by descendants of the races we found here. Now show us your work."

The question is which are the greater people, Americans or Mexicans? The question should be, which are the greatest the Mexican or American Indians?

If Mexico continues to improve and the people to advance in the future as they have for a few years past, the question may yet become, which people are the most advanced?

The Mexicans have many national characteristics that might be copied to advantage by Americans. Whether national contact will destroy some of these nobler qualities or not is a question.

They are hospitable, polite, faithful to a trust, true to their friends, respectful to their superiors and parents. When they have the means they are ambitious to make home and everything around pleasant; and of late years are ambitious to advance and educate the people. They are tolerant to all religious denominations.

Many suppose that priests still reign in Mexico. The Catholic priest who has helped to preserve the life of a nation has no more privileges in Mexico today than the Protestant minister who has helped to exterminate the natives on his domain.

In many respects Mexico is far behind other civilized countries. Their system of giving out their lands in large grants has left the country in many places comparatively unsettled. It is no uncommon thing for one man to own from a hundred thousand to a million acres of land. In fact, on the very start, all valuable lands not given as municipal grants were given to individual favourites. So there is no such conditions as in our country, where a poor man can go and locate a homestead.

Many persons have been deceived by the offers of government lands in Mexico, supposing they could get good lands at a nominal sum. The only way to get good lands is to purchase from the owners of undisputed tracts. To do this safely the buyer or agent must be perfectly familiar with the language, also the customs and character of the people he is dealing with. There are sharpers, speculators and deceivers in that country as well as in ours.

Many of the officers of the government are interested in speculations in lands and will vouch for persons when their recommend is interested.

In getting titles they must be thoroughly and correctly traced back to the original grant, and all adverse claims settled. From what I know of land troubles in Mexico, I would not spend much money on any land that had ever been in dispute.

There are so many chances for deception that it is risky. There are many tracts of land where the titles run smoothly back to the origin where there never has been dispute or litigation. These are the lands to look for if one wishes to live in peace and security. When the grants were first allowed many times the boundaries were indefinite, the boundaries having been defined by mountains or streams, or something subject to dispute, the country not being fully explored. Those taking possession would set their monuments so as to take in all the country that would be considered valuable without particularly consulting the exact lines of the recorded grant.

After ages of occupation these monuments come to be considered proper. Sometimes they were short, sometimes extended beyond the lawful lines. There was often a great deal of waste land adjoining these grants. As Mexico is a dry country, no lands are of value except where water can be procured.

As the country began to be prospected by foreigners desirous of stock ranches, etc., and also the more advanced condition of the government, it became apparent that these grants should be more perfectly defined, so that what land still remained to the government could be sold. As these old grants stood there was no certainty even to a government title, as the grant could not be broken or infringed upon.

The attempt to get these government lands and the failure to get titles has given rise to the idea that there are no good titles in Mexico. Whereas the titles of these grants are so good that they cannot be broken; and when there is any controversy between the government and land grants, the grants almost invariably win.

Under the conditions it became necessary to cause a re-survey of the whole country. To bring this about the country was cut up into districts, and contracts let to persons to do the surveying, their compensation to be in part or whole or percentage of the lands left after the titled grants were defined.

It now became a question between the old land owners and the surveyors which would get the most land. Where the surveyors could crowd in the lines they had the more land, while the grants sought at times to extend or reach the first allowance. This has given rise to much litigation, and even up to the present some few controversies are still going on.

There is not much risk in buying old original grants that run regularly, without adverse claimants. In some few places, there were small plats of good land secured to these, surveyors by cutting off from the old grants. This being adjoining to the waste land would be used as a bait to sell their worthless lands.

This surveying business was conducted by corporations composed of the most wealthy and influential men of the several districts. As the lands and lines became defined, they having the option from the government on all the land, took possession of these new portions, and commenced to advertise and offer millions of acres for sale at very low figures.

Sometimes this surveying company would become owners of certain ranches. Many of the incorporators being land owners would arrange with the surveying company to add acreage from the worthless lands and on the reputation of the old ranch sell the whole tract.

To explain this I will instance one case that came under my own observation and was offered here in Utah. Without naming the ranch I will call it C——. What is commonly known as the Rancho de C——. When enquiry is made regarding it the common answer from the people is that C—— is a fine place, good land with plenty of water—a splendid place.

This means five thousand acres of good bottom land along the Rio C——, and that is all the Mexican ranchers mean when he speaks of the ranch. The old grant probably embraces two hundred thousand acres extending out from the water about as far as stock would travel from water. There is but very little water except in the river. This ranch is bounded on three sides by dry deserts and one side by mountains with some timber.

One attempt has been made to put this ranch, with five hundred thousand acres of worthless land added, upon the market on the reputation of the little fertile valley of five thousand acres of fine agricultural lands.

These schemes are still gotten up from time to time, and the ignorant are imposed upon in Mexico just the same as in any other country; but when men get bitten in Mexico they try to excuse themselves by reporting that there is no safety in titles.

Now all the answer that can be made to this is. Do business in Mexico just the same as you would in any other country. That is, determine what you want and then apply where it is to be had. Find good land with good titles, then secure it by purchasing from the owner. There are as good titles arid protection in Mexico as in any country on earth, and men who have lived there for half a century will verify this.

The climate of Mexico varies from very warm to temperate. All along the Rio del Norte and for some distance out the climate is warm. There is a mountain range running clear through from the north almost to the south coast. Much of the lands cultivated are high above the sea level. They are from four to seven thousand feet. The mountain valleys and table lands are temperate. All who have visited the Republic of Mexico agree that the climate is among the best on earth.

Many persons are incredulous when told that Mexico is not a hot country, referring to other countries not so far south being intensely hot. Many think the further south we go the hotter it becomes. The temperature depends upon the altitude, and, as stated before, a great part of the habitable portion of Mexico being high the climate is simply delightful.

Thousands of people live and cultivate successfully many of the higher valleys without irrigation. Still it is safe to have flowing water so that it can be used for irrigation when wanted.

There are conflicting reports about Mexico and her people, the same as there are about Utah. How often are we of Utah annoyed by the scribbling of some wiseacre who has spent a whole day in Salt Lake City, rode around and been stuffed by a Liberal hack driver, obtaining all the information needed, being thoroughly posted he writes up the country, people, customs, facilities, and explains what is needed, and advises legislation, etc., with all the assurance of one thoroughly posted. Some of our Elders who have made a flying visit to Mexico appear to me about as presumptuous. What they don't see or know would make a book. What they do see is often through a glass dimly. If one fast traveller of note happens to make a mistake in describing something all the rest copy. Like some smart idiot wrote years ago that the flowers of Mexico had no perfume; the birds no song. This has often been copied when there is not a word of truth in the statement.

Neither is it true that the thorns of the Giant Cactus, Sahuara, are crooked like a fish hook. I simply mention these things to show that these hasty scribblers are not reliable on things of more importance.

A person to know and understand Mexico and her people, as the Latter-day Saints should know and understand them, will have to go into the interior away from the commercial towns and cities.

There are large districts of country inhabited by an almost pure race, descendants of Lehi. Any one conversant with the *Book of Mormon* will have no trouble in finding abundant proof that the greater portion of the inhabitants of Mexico are descendants of the Jews, and are the very, people, or a great portion of them, to which the gospel is to go to immediately, from the Gentile. That the work in Mexico seems a little slow is a fact, but no fault can be laid to the natives, according to my observation and experience in that country.

When those whose duty it is to teach them are ready, according to the revelations given, the natives will receive them gladly.

Now, as this country, Utah, is fast filling up with inhabitants that have and are coming to stay, there naturally will be an element that will push on from time to time. "Go west, young man," is now obsolete; there is no west to go to, so the pioneer must either turn to the northern plains of Canada or the mountain valleys of Mexico, or allow the heel of civilization to be placed upon his neck for all time.

The questions arise, are there no more pioneers? Have they ceased to be—have we all found the haven of rest so long looked for? Are the waste places all built up? I cannot think that all progress is at an end, notwithstanding Salt Lake City is a great place. Still, I do not believe all will end here. So, in case there should be an individual or two who have the spirit of pioneering yet lingering within them, I will ask and answer a few questions for their benefit. In answering these questions I may repeat some things already explained in the book; but for the convenience of many persons I have concluded to ask and answer just such questions as are put to me almost daily, doubtless, many times, by people who wish to gain information. While some ask questions merely to be sociable, my aim is to give those who are interested in the welfare of the people of Mexico and might wish to go to that country, such information as will be of use and protect them from being misled.

The most important consideration is good lands with perfect titles. So to begin:

Can good lands be procured in Mexico? Yes; as good as can be in Utah or any country I have ever seen.

Are the titles good? Yes; there are many large tracts of good land, suitable for colonisng upon, that the titles originated in Spanish grants. These grants are proven to be perfect, as they stand good under all tests.

How about government titles? It is the report that a Mexican title for land is not very reliable. How does this report come about? There is no reason why a title from the present government of Mexico is not good. The only thing necessary is to get your location right. People of this country often make mistakes in locating properties. No government will defend a person on lands belonging to another party simply because they would like to have it, and make a wrong location.

Can a person settle upon and procure lands in Mexico the same as in the United States? No; there are no such laws in Mexico. In fact, at the present time, that Republic has no lands to be considered. This I have fully shown heretofore; your question must apply to titled properties. It is a waste of time to ask questions about government lands in Mexico.

Then you say all desirable lands must be bought of private owners? Yes.

What price will have to be paid for these lands? About the same average as public lands in this country.

How is that? I have often heard that good lands could be bought in Mexico for twenty-five cents per acre, either from the government or from land companies, who have control of large tracts.

Well, my friend, if you depend upon any such prospects you will be left, as others have been who have undertaken to get cheap lands in that country.

How is the country you recommend for timber? Is there plenty, and of what kinds? Pine, of the best quality, is in great abundance, as well as considerable oak and some other hard woods of medium quality.

Is the timber in the mountains and canyons, the same as here in Utah? No; there are millions of acres of timber lands adjoining the tillable valleys that the timber grows upon, the low hills and upland plateaus, where teams can drive among the timber without any road making whatever.

Then there must be considerable rain fall in this timbered country? Yes; there are thousands of inhabitants living in the district who never pretend to irrigate their lands, and they raise good crops, generally.

Do they never fail of crops? Yes, sometimes; they reckon an average of every seven years for drouth.

Would it not be safer to get land where there is water for irrigation, in case it should be needed? Yes; I would not buy land at any price in Mexico unless there was a reasonable amount of water belonging to the land.

Then you do not like to depend upon the rains entirely? No; and for good reason. We have found, by experience here in Utah, that irrigation is handy and profitable. A great variety of products can be raised, as we can apply the water when needed. When we depend upon rain, many times the seasons are so divided that we have the extremes of wet and dry. This is common in the district of Mexico that I recommend for settling.

When is the rainy season in that country? June, July and August are the rainy months; during the winter season there is considerable rain and some snow.

Oh, I thought it was an awful hot country. How is it you have snow when it is so far south? Mr. Jones, you must be mistaken. I have been down in Arizona; it is very hot there—too hot for me—and this Mexican country is a long ways further south, and you say you have snow there. My friend, you must study the geography of Mexico a little. If you will look upon the map of Mexico and find the State of Chihuahua you will observe a district of country showing where several streams head and run off in different directions, some running for hundreds of miles north; so you see, on entering the State of Chihuahua on the north one travels up-hill for several days. The facts are that some of the finest and most fertile mountain valleys of that country are, as shown by measurement, two thousand feet higher than Salt Lake valley. So, if Zion is to be built up in the tops of the mountains, we lack two thousand feet of being there yet.

Then you mean to say the climate is temperate? Yes; the altitude preserves us from the heat. While being so far south, the winters are moderate; all who have ever lived in the district admit that it has a fine climate.

What are the products? Corn, beans, potatoes, melons, cabbage, onions and anything common to a temperate climate, and good, mellow soil is or can be raised.

How about fruits—is there much raised there? While it is one of the best fruit countries possible, judging from what I have seen, there is but little progress yet by the natives, as fruit raisers.

Why is this? Simply this like in most everything else—the people are a long way behind. They know nothing about grafting or budding fruits; they plant the seeds and let them grow often in clusters, and take what comes. I have seen some of the finest seedling apples that were ever produced, picked from trees grown in a thick clump, without any cultivation whatever. Also pears, apricots, plums and such hardy fruits common to a temperate climate.

How about grapes? It is too cold for any except the hardy varieties.

Is it a good wheat country? Yes; wheat does quite well, except when the season is wet. About harvest time, when, like all rainy countries, the harvest is attended with difficulties, sometimes the wheat is damaged by rust. This can be hindered, somewhat, by drilling the wheat, giving it a chance to ripen early, and not so apt to be effected by damp weather, as thickly sown wheat. Rye, oats and barley do well.

How is the range? Splendid; the whole country is thickly set with excellent grass.

Then if it is a thickly timbered county with plenty of grass there must be plenty of game? Yes; there are deer, bear and wild turkeys in great abundance. A person fond of hunting can have all the sport he wants. There are springs of pure water and beautiful mountain streams all through the country, so that game has a fine chance to live and grow fat. Then there must be fish in these mountain streams? No; for some cause these streams are not stocked with fish of much worth. Is the country thickly inhabited? Are there towns and settlements where business could be opened up? If the country was thickly settled there would be no room for colonizers. There are several towns numbering from one to five thousand inhabitants within a reasonable distance.

There are also some of the richest mining camps of Mexico in the district of country, that would furnish an excellent market for all products raised. What are the facilities for different kind of manufactures or industries? Stock raising, especially fine horses, as the high altitude and solid surface, healthy atmosphere and pure water would be adapted to breeding a superior class of thoroughbreds. Now I am astonished to hear you recommend the raising of fine horses in Mexico. That revolutionary country where they will take everything a man owns and give him nothing in return. What would you do to protect your fine stock?

Now to answer this I will make the statement as given to me by many of the old settlers of the district I am writing about. That is, no revolutions or wars of a national character have reached that district for over a hundred years except to defend themselves against the Apaches.

The district is known as the Warrior district, but their warriors are for their own defence and protection; they are noted for minding their own business, being peaceable when let alone, but very ugly when interfered with; perfectly honest and united in protecting themselves against thieves. It is naturally one of the best protected countries on this continent, and a reasonable sized colony could and would be as safe there as any place upon earth. Would cattle raising pay? That is one of the principal businesses of the country. Cattle are bought annually and driven from that country to the United States. Is it a good sheep country? Yes; naturally so, but if I could have my way the immediate district, if colonized, would be protected from sheep depredations. If there is a people on earth who deserve the name of pirates I think it is the average sheep owner of Utah. They know no law but to crowd their sheep upon any and every place where they can live regardless of the rights of others.

There are large districts of country in northern Mexico well adapted to sheep raising, not suitable for farming or inhabiting to any great extent. Sheep men should be satisfied with such countries and not crowd themselves upon the settlers as they do in this country eating off the range from the home stock, befouling the waters and filling the atmosphere with a sickly stench for the greater portion of the summer season.

The answer to this is that it is for revenue. Yes revenue, but at the cost of the comfort, health and lives of many people. The revenue is to the few while the nuisance is to the many.

Anyone wanting a sheep ranch in Mexico had better not apply to me for information. I would rather wear a coat made of Australian wool than have a healthy, happy country tramped down and made a sickly, stinking desert by herding sheep around a settlement. But if anyone should wish to start a woollen factory they would have no trouble in getting all the wool wanted, for it is already cheap and plentiful.

Would a tannery pay? Yes; hides and oak bark are plentiful, that really would be one of the most profitable industries and easiest to start. Lumber and all kinds of building materials being near at hand.

Is there a demand for mechanical labour? My supposition is that a thrifty colony would demand work among themselves. Again, the country being new as far as modern improvements are concerned would, when an example was set, naturally begin to build up and create a demand for many kinds of labour that are not now wanted among the natives. It is a country naturally rich in resources, and would soon prosper and build up a people provided they applied themselves intelligently and industriously to improve the natural privileges.

How is the government? Do you think a man can live there in peace any length of time? I think a man will have all the privilege and protection that could be reasonably desired.

Well, now, why won't they legislate against our religion in time there just the same as is being done here? That is too big a question to be answered in a sentence. You must read the *Book of Mormon* in true belief, realising that it is true and plain. If you will do this honestly you will have no fears about the future in Mexico.

Well, now, how can a person be protected in his rights? By going slow and learning how from someone who is capable of teaching you.

Can a person single-handed do anything in the country you recommend? No, sir; it will not amount to anything except a colony of sufficient strength and means to get a good tract of land and be for a season self-sustaining.

Would it not be very expensive to move into that country? Not under proper system and organisation. How long would it take to go from here with a family and get settled to work? About fifteen days, allowing nothing for delays.

How far is it from the railroad? About one hundred and fifty miles to the district.

Can the necessary stock be procured to commence with? Yes, and quite reasonable.

How about provisions? Such as corn, beans and meat are in abundance. Flour is scarce and of a poor quality and cannot be obtained until mills are built as the natives have no good mills, the flour is bad, but the corn is excellent and will make good meal, which will answer for a season.

Well, Mr. Jones, I have sold out to a Liberal here for fifty thousand, and I don't much like the idea of going without my cake and biscuit. Ain't there no way to get good flour? Oh yes, you can get it for about nine dollars per hundred.

That will do; if I go I will take a few sacks.

How about custom duties? No trouble for regular colonizers that go in order and conform to the laws and make their applications beforehand, so that when they arrive at the custom house they are known as colonizers, haphazard work in Mexico makes trouble the same as in any other country.

Do you think there will be much of a move from this country to Mexico? I did think so at one time; but I am now under the impression that there will be no great move to that land.

What has changed your opinion? Simply this—the people do not wish to go. The inhabitants of Utah have good homes and have made up their minds to accept the situation and stay, and enjoy their wealth and luxuries the same as other people.

Then you have given up the idea of ever seeing a prosperous colony of Mormons settle in Mexico, in some of the rich valleys that you have been recommending so long? No, sir; not at all. I still have faith in the move; those who have faith in the *Book of Mormon*, and have a greater desire to see the words of the *Book* fulfilled that to have to accumulate wealth, will go.

Then you think it will be at the sacrifice of worldly wealth and comforts that people will take hold of the work? Seemingly so, but not in reality. There are many principles revealed to this people that we are slow to put in full practice. Among others United Order, a principle the Prophet Brigham declared would have to be practiced before further advancement would be made by this people. While the majority of the people called Latter-day Saints are inclined to look with suspicion on any move in that direction, the natives of Mexico favour and, in a good degree, practice the principle. A short description of their mode of farming will illustrate this.

In the spring, when planting time comes, all join together and go into the field of one party and plow and put in the seed; the poor man who has no cattle shares the same as the wealthy. This they continue until all the fields of the village are planted. If any lack seed it is loaned to them. If there is a scarcity of provisions the first field products fit for use, instead of being sold at an exorbitant price, become common property, and all the hungry partake of the blessing. When the crops are gathered in the owner of the early field receives such as his neighbours feel free to give him, which is always liberal in quantity.

Now, I would not advocate the doing just as these natives do; but will say this, their customs show that they have a principle of union and good fellowship among them that could easily be trained into more successful principles of union. They are true Israelites, descendants of the Jews, and, having left Jerusalem before the crucifixion of the Saviour, have not that curse resting upon them, but, on the contrary, have the merit of having descended from a people who received the Saviour and the gospel and lived for hundreds of years in a condition of peace, union and intelligence far beyond the Church at Jerusalem. They are entitled to the gospel, according to the *Book of Mormon*, immediately following the work among the Gentiles. The day of their deliverance cannot be far away, for if the fullness of the Gentiles is not close at hand, the Saints must have a hard experience before them.

Now, to finish up this work, I wish to give a few of my own observations and reflections. The sketches of history I have given as they occurred to me. My descriptions of country and inhabitants, according to the best of my judgment, after years of study and acquaintance. No person can describe a country from a single visit sufficiently well to predicate a reliable report upon, unless receiving information from a most trust-worthy and intelligent source. For this reason I have always made it a rule to visit country, where convenient, at different times and seasons; also to inquire from different disinterested parties, watching closely the general reports. The judge on his bench allows a person's general reputation to be a proper question for proof, but will not allow direct individual testimony, neither good nor bad. This rule should largely apply in determining the quality and conditions of a country. If the reputation is generally good, then we may look favourably on the subject; but if bad, like the person with a bad reputation, we should be careful in dealing with them.

Sometimes, when speaking of certain tracts of land in Mexico, persons will ask me if the titles are good. When I tell them yes, they will ask, "How do you know? I hear people are often deceived about titles; how do you know they are good?" There was an old lady told me the title is good. Now this might seem a light answer; but, in reality, is not the "old lady's" answers on general reputation, and many times more reliable than an interested party?

Of course, this information is preliminary; but it will, many times, enable a person to form an opinion as to whether it will pay to make further investigation. I would rather take the friendly report of a neighbour about the titles of a Mexican ranch than I would the information of an officer of state, that might have an ax to grind. People, who visit President Diaz and cabinet when on land business in Mexico, are likely to be kindly treated and receive such information as his Excellency and associates have to give, but, individually, I have always found it best to get posted from the neighbours or owners.

I came from Mexico to Utah nearly forty years ago. I have been interested in that country and people from that time until the present. I have often met Elders whose faith and testimony seemed strong, yet seemed to have but little faith or interest in the work among the remnants spoken of in the *Book of Mormon*. To me this has always seemed strange. We are all looking forward to the time soon coming when the gospel will be withdrawn from the Gentiles and go to the "Jews, of which the remnants are descendants," so says the *Book of Doctrine and Covenants*.

There can be no question but the turning of the gospel from the Gentile to the Jew means first to the remnants. Anyone studying the *Book of Mormon* carefully cannot help but see that the Word is to be carried to the remnants. It might be easier and more convenient to make a tour to Jerusalem, but it won't fill the bill. The remnants must be preached to, then they will believe and come to a knowledge of Jesus.

We who have been gathered from the Gentile world have the promise of coming in and being numbered with the remnants and helping them to build up the New Jerusalem, provided we harden not our hearts. Now what does this hardening of hearts mean? I will suppose a character and see if it will apply.

A person hears the gospel, his heart is pricked and naturally soft-ened. The love of God and the testimony of Jesus comes upon him, he goes forth after receiving the blessings of the ordinances and preaches the gospel to his friends and countrymen and baptises many, teaches them their duty, and finally gathers to Zion.

Then he settles down to the duties of home and life among the Saints. He is prospered and blessed, his heart is warm and soft. He en-ters into all the duties common to a faithful Elder, his family increases, he is persecuted for his belief and practice, all this he stands and feels good in doing his duty and maintaining his to principles.

Now this man has been gathered out from the Gentiles and will have the privilege of being numbered with the remnants, if he hardens not his heart. Now why should such an individual harden his heart? What motive or cause could there possibly be for the hardening of the heart? It may come in this way, the Lamanites are a poor, and to the rich and refined looked upon as a dirty, degraded people, still the Lord has promised that those of the Gentile world who receive the words of the Book should carry them to the remnants. Now will we do this, or will our riches hinder us when the time comes?

Doubtless there will be some who will say, "I am not interested in these dirty Indians." Possibly this is what hardening of the heart means. Some would apply this to the whole world who reject the gospel. I think it more consistent to apply it to the Elder who has received the gospel and had his heart softened to his duty and then allows it to be-come hardened through prosperity. To those who suppose the Laman-ites all low and degraded, I will add this to what I have already said in their favour. There are thousands of the finest artisans upon earth among the remnants. Also many of them are educated and refined, and as for natural intellect, who ever saw an Indian who was a dunce?

Without the aid of the remnants this people never would amount to much. We have increased and built up beyond any other people, yet our numbers are small considering the great work before us. Many will say wait, the time has not come to preach to the remnants. Pos-sibly this is so in a measure, still I never could believe but what many, of the people have been ready for some time past.

The mission to labour among the remnants has never been a pop-ular work. There are too many sacrifices to make. There is not an Elder who has laboured faithfully for the welfare of the Indians but what has been brought under trying ordeals, many times suffering worse than death. It is no wonder that but few have stuck to the work.

There will, doubtless, be a change when a more general spirit of preaching to the remnants come over the Elders. Missions will be conducted in a more systematic manner. More wisdom will be given and support extended.

I have seen this Church and people pass through many trials. They have always been able to stand and gain strength through their various experiences. The gospel teaches us that we should be ready to make any sacrifice for our religion; but I have never been convinced that we have a right to sacrifice, in the least, any portion of our religion, either individually or as a people, for the sake of convenience. Our enemies, the wicked of the world, have been crowding upon us from the beginning, seeking to make us abandon the principles God has revealed, until now we are virtually denied the rights of citizenship unless we abandon our religion. The concessions we have lately made—whether it has done us any good or not—has fully proven to God and man that there is no honesty in the propositions made; no concession will satisfy our enemies short of down right apostasy. If this people would really become wicked and fully practice the abominations common to the present generation, then we could vote, hold office and be "good citizens."

To say that the practices of this people cannot be tolerated in the nation, as a religion, is to say that the teachings of the Bible cannot be allowed as religion—for there is not a principle taught or practiced as religion by this people except Bible doctrines and precepts. This the world knows and have acknowledged as often as our principles have been put to the test. Many look forward to some move of importance taking place within a year or two. Sometimes I am asked if I have an idea. Yes. "Well, what is it?" I believe it will not be long before the Saints will acknowledge that the wisdom of man will not do to depend upon, and turn unto the Lord and ask Him, in sincerity, to direct them through His servants, whom He has commissioned to lead Israel. Politics will not do. There are powers that will beat us when we depend on our smartness. It may be a little humiliating to acknowledge, but the world are smarter, in some things, than we are. Young Utah will never do to lead this people. Whenever we undertake to get ahead, in any way, of the wisdom of our Elders, then we will fail to put a man forward as our best man, because of any earthly success will never do.

History points to a time when our rulers in this nation were honest and wise. Laws were made for the good of the whole people. No speculative jobs were put up in those days; both brains and principles were in demand. As the nation advanced wealth became principal, until today there is but little said about the intelligence, honesty and capability of national leaders only as financiers, and telling of the luxury and extravagance of their wives and daughters.

This wave of luxurious desire has even reached to Salt Lake City, and made a little ripple here during our last grand campaign. If we will look back calmly we will remember that financial ability was the main cry. The Lord will not change His laws and commandments to suit the proud and wealthy. Wealth leads in the world, but principles will lead this people; wealth does not necessarily do away with principles, neither does wealth prove that principle exists. So the first great move before this people will be to fall into line and be governed fully and willingly by the principles of the gospel.

The questions are often asked, how long will it be before the power of the wicked is broken? How long will this people be annoyed and oppressed by their enemies? This I cannot answer; but I refer the reader to page 122 of the *Book of Mormon,* showing clearly that there is a certain work to be done before the wicked will be used up. Any one reflecting reasonably upon the great work will see that it will necessarily take time. Nothing can be done only in order; God has promised to hasten His work, but He has not promised to violate His laws for our convenience. It must, of necessity take a few years of diligent labour from many of the Elders of the Church.

For anyone to suppose that the wicked will be destroyed for our protection before the remnants are ministered to is not faith, but presumption.

Biographies generally end with death, romances with marriage. I am not expecting to *die* for many years to come, as I am still strong and healthy.

LEONAUR

ALSO FROM LEONAUR
AVAILABLE IN SOFTCOVER OR HARDCOVER WITH DUST JACKET

LIFE IN THE ARMY OF NORTHERN VIRGINIA *by Carlton McCarthy*—The Observations of a Confederate Artilleryman of Cutshaw's Battalion During the American Civil War 1861-1865.

HISTORY OF THE CAVALRY OF THE ARMY OF THE POTOMAC *by Charles D. Rhodes*—Including Pope's Army of Virginia and the Cavalry Operations in West Virginia During the American Civil War.

CAMP-FIRE AND COTTON-FIELD *by Thomas W. Knox*—A New York Herald Correspondent's View of the American Civil War.

SERGEANT STILLWELL *by Leander Stillwell* —The Experiences of a Union Army Soldier of the 61st Illinois Infantry During the American Civil War.

STONEWALL'S CANNONEER *by Edward A. Moore*—Experiences with the Rockbridge Artillery, Confederate Army of Northern Virginia, During the American Civil War.

THE SIXTH CORPS *by George Stevens*—The Army of the Potomac, Union Army, During the American Civil War.

THE RAILROAD RAIDERS *by William Pittenger*—An Ohio Volunteers Recollections of the Andrews Raid to Disrupt the Confederate Railroad in Georgia During the American Civil War.

CITIZEN SOLDIER *by John Beatty*—An Account of the American Civil War by a Union Infantry Officer of Ohio Volunteers Who Became a Brigadier General.

COX: PERSONAL RECOLLECTIONS OF THE CIVIL WAR--VOLUME 1 *by Jacob Dolson Cox*—West Virginia, Kanawha Valley, Gauley Bridge, Cotton Mountain, South Mountain, Antietam, the Morgan Raid & the East Tennessee Campaign.

COX: PERSONAL RECOLLECTIONS OF THE CIVIL WAR--VOLUME 2 *by Jacob Dolson Cox*—Siege of Knoxville, East Tennessee, Atlanta Campaign, the Nashville Campaign & the North Carolina Campaign.

KERSHAW'S BRIGADE VOLUME 1 *by D. Augustus Dickert*—Manassas, Seven Pines, Sharpsburg (Antietam), Fredericksburg, Chancellorsville, Gettysburg, Chickamauga, Chattanooga, Fort Sanders & Bean Station.

KERSHAW'S BRIGADE VOLUME 2 *by D. Augustus Dickert*—At the wilderness, Cold Harbour, Petersburg, The Shenandoah Valley and Cedar Creek..

LEONAUR

ALSO FROM LEONAUR
AVAILABLE IN SOFTCOVER OR HARDCOVER WITH DUST JACKET

THE RELUCTANT REBEL *by William G. Stevenson*—A young Kentuckian's experiences in the Confederate Infantry & Cavalry during the American Civil War..

BOOTS AND SADDLES *by Elizabeth B. Custer*—The experiences of General Custer's Wife on the Western Plains.

FANNIE BEERS' CIVIL WAR *by Fannie A. Beers*—A Confederate Lady's Experiences of Nursing During the Campaigns & Battles of the American Civil War.

LADY SALE'S AFGHANISTAN *by Florentia Sale*—An Indomitable Victorian Lady's Account of the Retreat from Kabul During the First Afghan War.

THE TWO WARS OF MRS DUBERLY *by Frances Isabella Duberly*—An Intrepid Victorian Lady's Experience of the Crimea and Indian Mutiny.

THE REBELLIOUS DUCHESS *by Paul F. S. Dermoncourt*—The Adventures of the Duchess of Berri and Her Attempt to Overthrow French Monarchy.

LADIES OF WATERLOO *by Charlotte A. Eaton, Magdalene de Lancey & Juana Smith*—The Experiences of Three Women During the Campaign of 1815: Waterloo Days by Charlotte A. Eaton, A Week at Waterloo by Magdalene de Lancey & Juana's Story by Juana Smith.

TWO YEARS BEFORE THE MAST *by Richard Henry Dana. Jr.*—The account of one young man's experiences serving on board a sailing brig—the Penelope—bound for California, between the years 1834-36.

A SAILOR OF KING GEORGE *by Frederick Hoffman*—From Midshipman to Captain—Recollections of War at Sea in the Napoleonic Age 1793-1815.

LORDS OF THE SEA *by A. T. Mahan*—Great Captains of the Royal Navy During the Age of Sail.

COGGESHALL'S VOYAGES: VOLUME 1 *by George Coggeshall*—The Recollections of an American Schooner Captain.

COGGESHALL'S VOYAGES: VOLUME 2 *by George Coggeshall*—The Recollections of an American Schooner Captain.

TWILIGHT OF EMPIRE *by Sir Thomas Ussher & Sir George Cockburn*—Two accounts of Napoleon's Journeys in Exile to Elba and St. Helena: Narrative of Events by Sir Thomas Ussher & Napoleon's Last Voyage: Extract of a diary by Sir George Cockburn.

CPSIA information can be obtained
at www.ICGtesting.com
Printed in the USA
LVOW11*1251040318
568596LV00012B/278/P